PARADISE

OF THE

PACIFIC

PARADISE
OF THE
PACIFIC

Approaching Hawai'i

Susanna Moore

Farrar, Straus and Giroux   *New York*

Farrar, Straus and Giroux
18 West 18th Street, New York 10011

Grateful acknowledgment is made for permission to reprint the following material:
Portions of "The Echo of Our Song"; used with permission of Kamehameha Schools.
Material from Samuel Kamakau, *Ruling Chiefs of Hawaii*; used with permission of
Kamehameha Schools. Paul Rockwood, drawing of *luakini heiau*; used with permission
of Bernice Pauahi Bishop Museum. Taunay watercolor of Puʻukoholā *heiau*; used with
permission of Mark and Carolyn Blackburn.

Library of Congress Cataloging-in-Publication Data
Moore, Susanna.
    Paradise of the Pacific : approaching Hawaii / Susanna Moore. — First edition.
       pages   cm
    Includes bibliographical references and index.
    ISBN 978-0-374-29877-7 (hardback) — ISBN 978-1-4299-4496-0 (e-book)
    1. Hawaii—History—18th century.   2. Hawaii—Emigration and immigration—
History—18th century.   3. Hawaii—Social conditions—18th century.   4. Social
change—Hawaii—History—18th century.   5. Culture conflict—Hawaii—History—
18th century.   6. Acculturation—Hawaii—History—18th century.   7. Hawaii—
Social life and customs—18th century.   8. Legends—Hawaii.   I. Title.

    DU627 .M66 2015
    996.9—dc23

                                                              2015002967

Designed by Jonathan D. Lippincott

Farrar, Straus and Giroux books may be purchased for educational, business, or
promotional use. For information on bulk purchases, please contact the Macmillan
Corporate and Premium Sales Department at 1-800-221-7945, extension 5442,
or write to specialmarkets@macmillan.com.

www.fsgbooks.com
www.twitter.com/fsgbooks • www.facebook.com/fsgbooks

10 9 8 7 6 5 4 3

Frontispiece: Kealakekua Bay with Captain James Cook's ships HMS *Discovery* and HMS
Resolution, and Hikiau *heiau* on the right. Engraving after pen, ink wash, and watercolor
by John Webber, 1779, State Library of New South Wales, Sydney

To W. S. C.

Contents

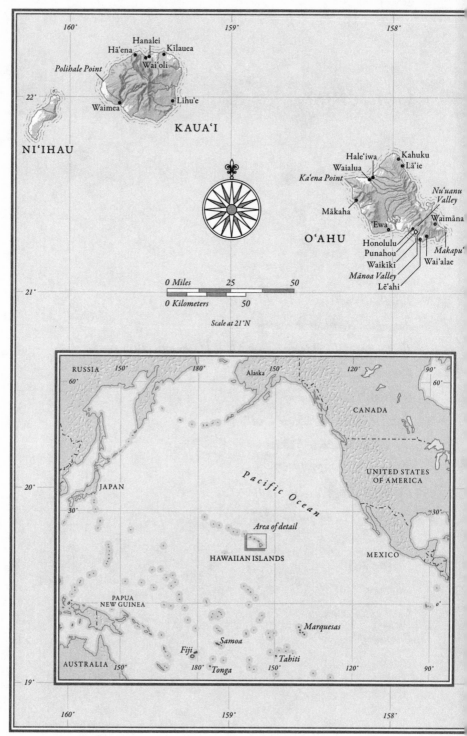

160°   159°   158°

22°

Hanalei
Hāʻena   Kīlauea
Polihale Point   Waiʻoli
Waimea   Līhuʻe
            KAUAʻI

NIʻIHAU

            Haleʻiwa   Kahuku
                Lāʻie
            Waialua
        Kaʻena Point   Nuʻuanu
                        Valley
                Mākaha   Waimāna
                    ʻEwa
                OʻAHU   Honolulu   Makapuʻ
                    Punahou   Waiʻalae
                    Waikīkī
                Mānoa Valley
                    Lēʻahi

21°

0 Miles   25   50

0 Kilometers   50

Scale at 21°N

RUSSIA   150°   180°   Alaska   150°   120°   90°
60°   60°
                                CANADA

                                UNITED STATES
                                OF AMERICA
JAPAN
20°
30°   30°
                        Pacific Ocean

                        Area of detail

            HAWAIIAN ISLANDS

                                MEXICO

PAPUA
NEW GUINEA   0°

                            Marquesas

                Samoa
            Fiji
AUSTRALIA   150°   180°   Tonga   150°   Tahiti   120°   90°

19°

160°   159°   158°

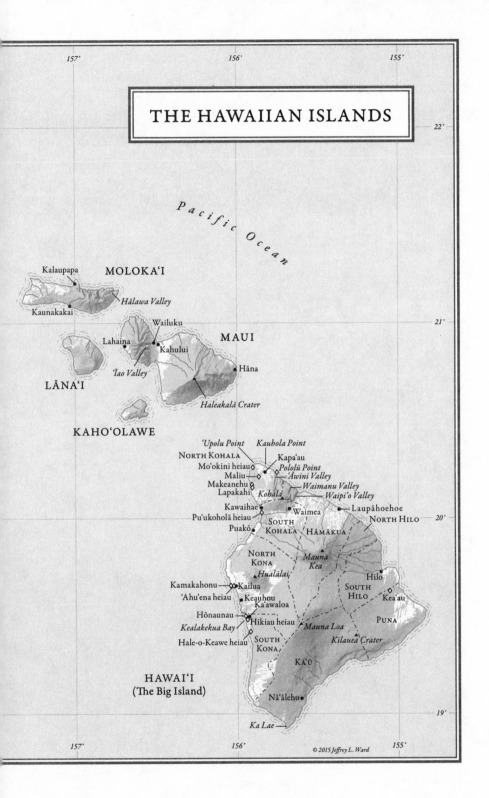

THE HAWAIIAN ISLANDS

Pacific Ocean

Kalaupapa

MOLOKA'I

Kaunakakai

Hālawa Valley

Wailuku

Lahaina

MAUI

Kahului

'Iao Valley

Hāna

LĀNA'I

KAHO'OLAWE

Haleakalā Crater

'Upolu Point   Kauhola Point

NORTH KOHALA   Kapa'au

Mo'okini heiau   Pololū Point

Maliu   'Āwini Valley

Makeanehu   Waimanu Valley

Lapakahi   Kohala   Waipi'o Valley

Kawaihae   Waimea   Laupāhoehoe

Pu'ukoholā heiau   NORTH HILO

Puakō   SOUTH   HĀMĀKUA

KOHALA

NORTH   Mauna

KONA   Kea

Hualālai   Hilo

SOUTH

Kamakahonu   Kailua   HILO   Kea'au

'Ahu'ena heiau   Keauhou

Ka'awaloa   PUNA

Hōnaunau   Hikiau heiau

Kealakekua Bay   Mauna Loa

Hale-o-Keawe heiau   SOUTH   Kīlauea Crater

KONA

HAWAI'I   KA'Ū

(The Big Island)

Nā'ālehu

Ka Lae

© 2015 Jeffrey L. Ward

PARADISE

OF THE

PACIFIC

This Realm of Chaos
and Old Night

Five hundred thousand years ago, the great volcanoes of the easternmost island of Hawai'i, among them Mauna Loa, Mauna Kea, and Hualālai, rose eighteen thousand feet above the floor of the northern Pacific Ocean, breaking the surface in successive eruptions and outpourings of lava. Volcanoes still remain active on the Big Island, the last of the eight major Hawaiian Islands to rise from the bottom of the ocean (the islands of Kaua'i and O'ahu are thought to have been formed ten million years ago). Moving from west to east, we find Ni'ihau and Kaua'i; O'ahu, the capital island; Moloka'i; Lāna'i; Kaho'olawe; Maui; and Hawai'i, with a combined area of 6,424 square miles (including the numerous uninhabited Leeward Islands, submerged seamounts, and atolls stretching 1,600 miles to Kure Atoll in the northwest).

At first and for a very long time, there was nothing but lava. The following was told to the anthropologist Martha Beckwith in the early twentieth century by J. M. Poepoe, a lawyer, legislator, and editor of the Hawaiian-language newspaper *Ka Na'i Aupini*:

> This was the beginning of the earth ... It was an insect that made the coral and all things in the sea. This was the beginning of the period called the first interval of time. During this time grew the coral, the shellfish (such as the sea cucumber, the small sea urchin, the flat sea urchin, tiny mussels, the oysterlike mussel, the mussels of the sea, the clam, the barnacle, the dark sea snail, the cowry and so forth) ... The water was made to be a nest that gave birth and bore all things in the womb of the deep.

Over millennia, plants and seeds found their way to the Islands, washed ashore with the spring tide of a full moon, blown by trade winds, carried inside birds or in their feathers, in the trunks and branches of trees, and floating in the jetsam of sunken ships. The chance of a seed or sapling reaching an island as isolated as one of the Hawaiian chain (a combined area of 6,424 square miles, including the numerous uninhabited Leeward Islands, and atolls stretching 1,600 miles to the northwest) is infinitesimal. If it managed to survive its unlikely journey, there remained the still greater difficulty of finding what biologists call a niche. A prerequisite of its survival (and the same would be true for some of the first human settlers) would have been the ability to survive on hard, dry lava or in sand. With time, those species that managed to grow were able to provide shade and food to less vigorous species that followed them.

> Indeed it is hypothesized that such an event occurred nearly 300 times during the history of the archipelago. Dividing this number into the number of years available in which such natural introductions could have occurred ... leads to the conclusion that, on average, one successful introduction need have occurred once every 20,000–30,000 years ... If one takes 70 million years as the life of the entire archipelago ... such an event need not have occurred more than once every 250,000 years.

In other words, not very often.

The first stanza of a birth chant for Kauikeaouli, who would become King Kamehameha III in 1824, refers to the spreading of the powerful Kamehameha dynasty, but also serves as a description of the birth of the Islands:

> Born was the earth, rooted the earth.
> The root crept forth, rootlets of the earth.
> Royal rootlets spread their way through the earth to hold firm.
> Down too went the taproot, creaking
> like the mainpost of a house, and the earth moved.
> Cliffs rose upon the earth, the earth lay widespread:
> a standing earth, a sitting earth was the earth,
> a swaying earth, a solid earth was the earth.
> The earth lay below, from below the earth rose.

In the spring of 1823, after a journey from New Haven of 158 days, the Reverend Charles Stewart, his wife, and their companion, the black missionary Betsy Stockton (who had once been a servant in the household of the president of Princeton University), along with fellow Congregationalist missionaries in the Second Company from Boston, watched from the brig *Thames* as it tacked along the north coast of the island of Hawai'i. "The broad base . . . covered with Egyptian darkness, came peering through the gloom," wrote Stewart in his journal. "The reality was too certain to admit a moment's question; and was accompanied by sensations never known before . . . The first tumult . . . quickly succeeded by something that insensibly led to solemnity and silence."

Canoes of natives pulled alongside the brig, and the excited Stewart, who would become an astute and even sympathetic observer, had his first view of the men he and his brother ministers and lay teachers had come to baptize in the name of the Lord:

> Their naked figures, and wild expression of countenance, their black hair streaming in the wind as they hurried the canoe over the water with all the eager action and muscular power of savages, their rapid and unintelligible exclamations, and whole exhibition of uncivilized character, gave to them the appearance of being half-man and half-beast.

A boat was sent ashore, and, when it returned, a ship's officer sternly advised the missionaries to remain on board the *Thames*. "If I never before saw *brutes in the shape of men*, I have seen them this morning. You can never live among *such a people as this*, we shall be obliged to take you back with us!"

Stewart was alarmed. He wrote, "*Can they be men—can they be women?— do they not form a link in creation, connecting man with the brute?*" The missionaries did not heed the officer's warning—how could they, after the great distance they had traveled and the avowals they had made?—but instead disembarked, confused and alarmed. Stewart was to remain so for some time.

There is still dispute and controversy as to the identity and origin of the first human settlers in the Hawaiian Islands, although most scholars agree that the initial voyagers sailed from distant islands, known by Polynesians as

Kahiki, in the South Pacific, most likely the Marquesas. Around 1200 B.C., the farmers and fishermen who had migrated over centuries from Asia to Australia, Indonesia, and New Guinea began to move slowly across the Pacific, sailing to Fiji, Tonga, and Samoa, which lie only a few days' sail from one another, where they became the ancestors of present-day Polynesians. After almost two thousand years, the islanders began to venture farther, eventually reaching Hawai'i to the north, New Zealand to the southwest, and remote Easter Island to the east.

Historians once believed that many of the islands in the Pacific were discovered by fishermen who had been blown off course, although the fact that the first voyagers to Hawai'i carried with them crops, seeds, and animals, as well as women and children, suggests that some of the journeys were deliberate and well-prepared. Abraham Fornander, a historian who was a circuit judge on the island of Maui in the late nineteenth century, believed that the first settlers arrived in the sixth century A.D. in what would become the Hawaiian Islands, and lived secluded and isolated for twelve to fourteen generations until the beginning of the eleventh century, when Polynesian folklore, legends, and chants attest a second migration of voyagers who made the journey north from Tahiti, a distance of 2,626 miles.

The double-hulled canoes of the settlers were eighty to one hundred feet long, rigged with masts, and triangular sails woven of *lau hala* (the dried leaf of the *hala,* or pandanus tree). A raised platform, screened and roofed with mats, was lashed across the hulls for the women, children, animals, plants, and, not least of all, the images of the gods that the travelers carried with them. When there was no wind, men sitting two to a bench would paddle with the guidance of a master steersman, who, trained since childhood, used his deep knowledge of the sky, wind, clouds, ocean currents, temperatures, and the habits of sea creatures and birds to guide them across the ocean.

The small companies of perhaps fifty men, women, and children brought with them dogs, pigs, and chickens, as well as food and water. They had seedlings of hibiscus, sugarcane, bamboo, mountain apple, coconut, breadfruit, mulberry, and tubers of wild ginger, *kalo* (taro), yam, and sweet potato, and rhizomes of tumeric. They are thought to have first landed on the desolate southernmost tip of Hawai'i Island, where the land rises gently to the summit of Mauna Loa. The settlers named their new home Ka'ū, or "the breast that nursed them," although the leeward coast (facing the direction in which the wind is blowing) would have been dry and hot, with little fresh water. Although parts of Kaʻū are now covered with layer upon layer of lava from successive eruptions, at the time of the first settlers it would have been wood and brush land, interspersed with broad prairies of native grass (the now ubiquitous *kiawe* tree was introduced in 1828 by Father Bachelot, the head of the first Catholic mission; the sugi pine arrived in 1880; the Australian bluegrass gum in 1870; the bagras eucalyptus in 1929).

The settlers would have known at once that their new home would not give them all that they needed. There was no reef and few beaches and coves, which meant that there were insufficient amounts of shellfish and seaweed, foods essential to Polynesians, but they would have seen, too, that it was a safe place in which to live, where they would not be threatened by enemies, human or animal. "Only the sea was treacherous, but only occasionally, and Polynesians are accustomed to the moods of Kanaloa [the god of the sea]."

The environment of Hawaiʻi Island, owing to trade winds from the northeast, the height of the mountains, and the warmth of the surrounding ocean, can shift within a few miles from bog to rain forest to coastal shrub, all with widely different levels of wind and rainfall. In the north, on the windward (facing into the wind) side, the settlers would find streams and springs, grasses, and trees. Thanks to the lush inland forests, the island would have been less windy than it is now, and there would have been more rainfall (eighteenth-century travelers describe snow on Mauna Loa in July and August). The hills of Kohala in the north would have been rolling grassland, much as they are today, with an occasional grove of native *ʻōhiʻa* trees.

In time, the settlers ventured to other islands in the archipelago. Cultivation began in Waialua valley on Oʻahu, and Hālawa on Molokaʻi. On Hawaiʻi Island, fertile Waipiʻo Valley was settled, and the sloping *mauka* (inland) highlands of Kona, Kaʻū, and Kohala, as the settlers sought the verdant valleys where water could be found ("The man with the water gourd, that is a god" is a line in the Kumulipo, the Hawaiian creation chant), spreading across the hills and plains overlooking the ocean to settle on land where soil and rainfall were sufficient for their simple needs. In the beginning, they lived in caves, low rock shelters built on hillsides or near the ocean, and in lava tubes, which are formed when a river of hot lava forces a path under lava that has already cooled and hardened. They built houses of grass in small villages near rich fishing grounds, although bays and inlets amenable to fishing or the use of canoes were few in relation to the length of coastline. To bring their canoes safely ashore, ladders were built with wooden runners or steps to make easier the task of pulling canoes from the rough surf, and over sharp lava. Those living near the shore bartered fish, seaweed, shellfish, and salt for the produce grown by those living in the hills and gulches. The historian Mary Kawena Pukui (1895–1986) described the sharing of food during her childhood in the book *The Polynesian Family System in Kaʻū*:

> In the days of the horse-drawn vehicle, [people traveling between Hilo and Kaʻū] often stopped at my aunt's to pass the night—usually unexpected. There was no market . . . and whatever of fish and meat there was, was salted. The family gave the *poi* to the guests, and the best salted meat, even if it was the last . . . Cowboys came too, tired and hungry, to share the salted fish, or meat with *poi*. Sometimes, they came with a portion of a wild bullock or pig—then there was fresh meat. But only for that meal.

As the settlers began to clear the endemic vegetation to grow the subsistence plants they brought with them, many native plants disappeared from areas of cultivation. The forest was both altered and exploited as trees were used to make canoes, house posts, religious statues, weapons, and utensils. The bird population, with few if any predators before the arrival of the settlers, was reduced by hunting, both for food and later to make *kāhili* (royal standards) and *leis*, and the feather helmets and capes worn by the chiefs. More than six hundred species of fish were once found in Hawaiian waters, and fish were farmed in carefully tended ponds built along the shore with sluice gates to allow passage of both fish and clean tidal water. Sweet potato and arrowroot, gourd vines, *kī* (the small evergreen *Cordyline fruticosa*), sugarcane, breadfruit, and coconut were planted.

Kalo was tended with reverence, and the preparation and eating of it was an act complex in meaning. A square mile of *kalo* was capable of feeding fifteen thousand people; forty square feet could support one man for a year. Mary Kawena Pukui remembered that her grandmother would not allow any serious conversation at dinner once a calabash of *poi*, the paste made from *kalo*, was placed on the table, as it would offend Hāloa, the progenitor of the Hawaiian race, and a poetic name for both *kalo* and sweet potato. Should anyone disobey, her grandmother would call out in a surprised voice, *"Kāhāhā! ke hōʻole mai neʻi ka ʻumeke poi!"* "Oh! The *poi* bowl does not consent to this kind of talk!"

As there were no fireproof cooking utensils or vessels—no iron or clay with which to make them—food, usually eaten cold, was first cooked in lined pits in the ground, or in calabashes into which hot stones had been dropped. Unlike rice, which causes an acid reaction in the body, *kalo* is full of vitamins A and B. It was early remarked by Europeans that Polynesian chiefs were unusually well developed in contrast to the ethnic stock from which they most likely descended, and it has been suggested that the switch from an acidic starch (rice) to that of *poi* was responsible for the robust health and beauty of the *ali'i*, or ruling class. *Poi*, rich in mineral and organic salts, was largely responsible for the large jaw structure of Hawaiians and their exceptionally fine teeth. The uniformity and strength of their teeth were later to astonish foreign sailors (no difficult task given the teeth of eighteenth-century English- and Irishmen), as was the size of their bodies, particularly those of the *ali'i*, which in both men and women was frequently more than six feet in height.

Charles Stewart found the *ali'i*, who were not simply local nobility but thought to be avatars of the gods, superior to commoners in their physical appearance:

> They seem indeed in size and stature to be almost a distinct race. They are all large in their frame, and often excessively corpulent; while the common people are scarce of the ordinary heights of Europeans, and of a thin rather than full habit . . . although little more than twenty-five years old, [one chief] is so remarkably stout, as to be unequal to any exertion, and scarcely able to walk without difficulty. This immense bulk of person is supposed to arise from the care taken of them from their earliest infancy . . . Many of the common people . . . have a great beauty of person, though of a less noble scale.

The later migrations of the eleventh through the fourteenth centuries, originating in Tahiti, are known as the Long Voyages. Like the earlier journeys, they are now thought to have been forays of exploration, rather than a flight from internecine struggle, war, famine, or epidemic. The travelers brought seeds and animals with them, but they also carried new gods, powerful beings who demanded the enactment of a system of strict *kapu*, or taboo.

This second migration, a period of enterprise and innovation coming after a sleep of fifteen generations, was to alter profoundly the customs, beliefs, and polity of the earlier settlers. Judge Fornander noted that as late as 1830 it was easy to tell where a man lived based on his use of the letters *t* and *r*, which had been brought to the Islands by the second migration of settlers from Tahiti. Kaua'i and O'ahu people used the original *k* and *l*, while other Hawaiians used the later Tahitian style, substituting *t* and *r* for *k* and *l*. Foreigners such as Cook and Vancouver often replaced the older *k* with the then contemporary *t*, as in "Tamehameha." As there was no written language before 1822, foreigners transcribed Hawaiian words phonetically, which resulted in the varied spelling of Hawaiian words in the writings of early travelers. Captain Cook used the newer Tahitian style when he called the island of Kaua'i "Atooi," as did Charles Stewart when he wrote the name Kamāmalu as "Tameha-maru."

The physician and ethnographer Nathaniel Bright Emerson, son of the missionary John Emerson, and an early translator of Hawaiian myths and chants, described one of these later voyagers, a legendary priest of the eleventh century named Pa'ao, as a man of "strong and vengeful nature, shrewd and scheming . . . versed in the ceremonial and bloody rites of southern worship . . . a magician." Pa'ao is said to have returned to Tahiti after landing in North Kohala, only to sail back on one of the last voyages to Hawai'i before migration mysteriously ended, bringing with him the design for a temple, or *heiau*, and the ritual of human sacrifice. (Emerson added, "We have no proof that he was a cannibal. The times were perhaps not ripe for the development of this particular quintessence of paganism and heathenism.")

Heiau were most commonly stone platforms of different sizes, often a quadrangle or parallelogram, some of them terraced and contained within four walls, and frequently placed to overlook the ocean (it is said that in the courtyard of one *heiau* built by Pa'ao, there was a sacred grove with specimens of every tree growing in the Islands). Some *heiau* were used for human sacrifice, and others were for healing (*lapa'au*), or for agriculture and fishing, or to honor the *hula* or the making of cloth, *kapa*. Large wooden images of the gods, wrapped in white *kapa*, were sunk into the enclosure grounds, or stood without the walls. Smaller gods were kept inside a grass hut built on the platform. A structure made of bamboo, called an *'anu'u*, or oracle tower, twenty-four feet high and eighteen feet square, was also wrapped in white *kapa*. The tower was used by a priest or king who hid inside to issue a god's pronouncements.

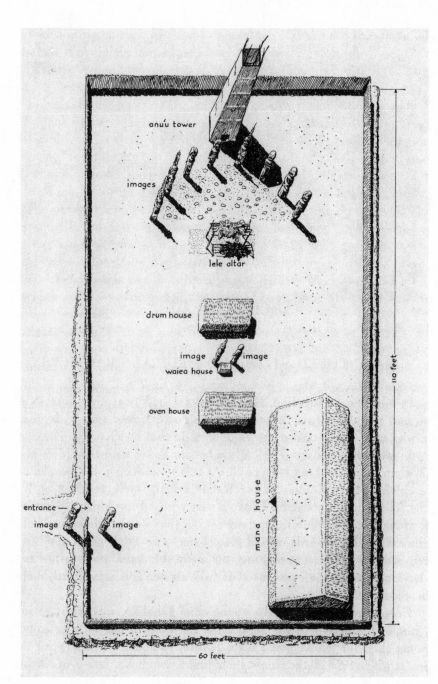

Drawing of a *luakini heiau* by Paul Rockwood, courtesy of the Bernice Pauahi Bishop Museum, Honolulu

View of the interior of a *heiau* on Kaua'i, the images shrouded in *kapa*. Engraving by Giulio Ferrario, 1827, after a pen, watercolor, and ink wash by John Webber, 1779

Commoners remained outside the stone walls, seated silent and motionless on the ground. Women were forbidden from entering *heiau*, except under special conditions, such as a period of mourning for a chief.

The Tahitians of the Long Voyages brought with them the god Kāne, lord of creation, the ancestor of both chiefs and commoners, and god of sunlight, fresh water, and forests; Lono, the god of clouds, winds, peace, agriculture, and fishing; and Kū, a male fertility symbol and the god of war, canoe-making, and the rising sun. There was Kanaloa, the Enemy, god of the sea, the Hot-Striking Octopus, but also god of healing. It was at this time, too, that the fire goddess Pele, capricious, cruel, jealous, and vengeful, appeared with her five compelling brothers and sister, to make her home in Kīlauea crater on the Big Island.

Those first Hawaiians became acquainted with two manifestations of divine power they could not have seen in the land of their birth. With a fine sense of relationships, and their realists' humor, they decided that these novel forces must be feminine. The blazing, impulsive, destructive, hot-tempered, and beautiful one who issued so unpredictably from her underground realm they called Pele. The haughty, pallid, silent, cold maiden who never deigned to descend from her lofty mountain citadels they named Poliʻahu . . . Pele as their Earth Goddess in her triple manifestations: as Mother, maker of mountains and of islands and humankind; as Lover-Pursuer-Virago, devourer of men who do not heed her power, no matter how handsome and accomplished they may think they are; and, finally, as Kuku Wahine, Grandmother, who receives in her wrinkled bosom the bodies of the dead, taking them into her care once more.

Hundreds of lesser gods represented temporal objects as well as abstractions and states of being—gods of fish, reptiles, birds, mountains, revenge, music, strange noises, trees, hills, rain, pigs, empty houses, the sick, peace and war, stones, the insane, the dance, canoes, and darkness and light. The very trees in the forests were spirits. The *ʻōhiʻa* tree was thought to have a human voice and to cry in pain when cut, and the wood used by a man to make an image of a god was thereafter *kapu* to him (in this usage, *kapu* does not mean forbidden, but special, unique, or exclusive). The enticing calls and songs of the woodland spirits filled the forests with incessant sound.

"The forty thousand little gods" . . . moved so easily in and out of the all-embracing spirit world. These lived in mountains and hills, in valleys, caves, and stones; in trees, herbs, ferns, and grasses; in fishes, birds, and beasts of every kind; in springs, streams, swamps, and drops of dew; in mists, clouds, thunder, lightning, winds; and in the wandering planets, the glittering far-off stars.

Like the original voyagers of the sixth century, the later settlers venerated the spirits, or *ʻaumakua*, who served as intermediaries between humankind and the great gods. An *ʻaumakua*, which was mortal as well as divine, could be, among other things, a shark, eel, hawk, limpet, a red-haired woman (symbolizing a volcano), lizard, wild goose, mouse, caterpillar, or owl. An *ʻaumakua*, which is particular to individuals and to families to this day, represented both fertility and a deified ancestor, the two becoming indistinguishable with time.

People were very frightened of a guardian, or *kahu*, of the shark, who smeared his skin with turmeric, kept his head covered, and spoke in a hushed voice. In *heiau* dedicated to shark gods, the priests rubbed themselves with salt to give an appearance of scales, and uttered piercing shrieks. *Kahu* of Pele, the fire goddess, coated their long hair with red dust, and made their eyes red. The fact that sharks happen to devour people, and volcanoes destroy entire villages, helped to underline the magical connection between the visible danger (the *kahu*) and the invisible danger (the god).

The nineteenth-century Hawaiian historian Samuel Kamakau (1815–1876), who converted to Christianity before writing his history of ruling chiefs, is careful, even impatient, to distinguish between the actual object or living creature, and a god:

> The owl itself is a worthless thing; it is eaten by the people of Kula, Maui, and Na'alehu in Ka'u, Hawaii, and thrown about on the road. The owl itself is not a god—it has no mana. The god is separate. Kukauakahi is the main god . . . who is consecrated in the body of the owl and who shows his mana in the worthless body of the owl . . .
>
> Is the owl a god? The writer of this history says that the owl is not a god—it is the form . . . taken by a god.

There were enough gods to keep a man busy, and very frightened should he fail to honor them in accord with the rigid and seemingly arbitrary, although in practice often efficient and purposeful rituals that each required.

For perhaps one hundred years after the arrival of the second group, there was sporadic warfare between the original settlers and the aggressive newcomers. The Tahitians prevailed, and those earlier settlers who did not become assimilated through marriage were transformed over generations into the elusive nocturnal elves known as Menehune. Whimsically and perhaps guiltily described as our memories of the past, the Menehune are said to have found refuge in the mountains, where some people still claim to hear their plaintive sighs and murmurs, although the ability to see them is denied to all but their own kind. They are thought to creep after dark from the caves and hollow trees where they live, summoned to build in one night a ditch, or a *heiau*, or a house constructed of the bones of birds.

As the number of new settlers from Polynesia grew, the original inhabitants slipped into servitude. Mary Kawena Pukui believed that the outcast slaves known as *kauwā*, kept for human sacrifice, may have been the descendants of the earliest people. *Kauwā*, who were regarded as foul-smelling things, were tattooed on their foreheads and made to hide their heads under pieces of *kapa*. Like the Untouchables of India, *kauwā* were scapegoats born into and imprisoned within an abhorred class. Confined to certain districts such as Makeanehu in Kohala, and Kalaemamo in Kona on the Big Island, they were forbidden to marry outside their caste, or even to enter the house or yard of a man who was not *kauwā*. If a child was born of a union between a commoner or chief and a *kauwā*, the child would be dashed to death against a rock, and the disgrace felt for generations. *Kauwā* were buried alive next to their dead masters, and often served as proxies for chiefs who had been sentenced to death for infractions of *kapu*, their heads held underwater until drowned. If it was discovered that a *kauwā* was among a man's ancestors, the man's eyes would be gouged from his head.

The small fishing and upland communities of Hawai'i, the property of certain hereditary high chiefs, were not important in a political sense. The primary unit was the scattered community known as *'ohana*, consisting of relatives by blood, marriage, or adoption, some living in the hills and some by the sea, but tied by descent, habit, and sentiment to a special area, which was the *'āina*, a word deriving from the verb *'ai*, to eat. The word *'ohana*, or extended family, originates with the planters of *kalo*, as *oha* means to sprout. The shoots of the *kalo* corm, the basis of the Hawaiian diet, are called *'ohā*. With the nominalizing suffix *na*, *'oha-na* literally means offshoots.

The small groups of chiefly families and priests were served by the makers of *kapa*, feather capes, helmets, and *kāhili*; canoe builders; singers and dancers; woodsmen; canoe men; genealogists; healers; and a large number of fishermen and farmers, known as commoners.

As sailors, they built their houses with tie and lash, rather than nails or pegs. A coarse wild grass (*pili*) that grew near the ocean was used, although a chief's house might be thatched in banana leaves, and the ends of the roof decorated with black grass to give it beauty and distinction. A house, often built on a platform of lava rock or smooth river stones, was dark inside, as there was only one small, low door, and no windows or chimney. The thatched roof sloped from a center ridgepole. The dirt floor was covered with dried potato vines and mats, and the corpses of family members were often buried beneath the floor. In cold mountain regions, like Waimea on the Big Island, houses had small fire pits for warmth, as cooking was done in a separate house or in the open. A well-built house would last from eight to ten years.

Kapa, cloth made from the bark of the *wauke*, or paper mulberry, a tree from East Asia, and the small native tree *māmaki*, was primarily the work of women. Samuel Kamakau, who collected *moʻolelo*, or stories and oral histories, wrote that men with an artistic leaning who were not inclined to pursue manly work were also allowed to make cloth, particularly the prized ribbed *kapa* used for men's loincloths, or *malo*, and the skirts worn by *aliʻi* women, called *pāʻū*. A *malo* was nine feet in length, and six or eight inches wide, although a king's *malo* might be twelve feet long, made of feathers, and weighted with dog and human teeth. A *pāʻū* was composed of five joined strips of cloth. Charles Stewart rightly found Hawaiian *kapa* to be exquisite in design and color:

> I have seen . . . mantles of it, as thin and transparent as Italian crape; which, at a short distance, it greatly resembled. That generally used for maros [loincloths] and paus (skirts), is more compact, like paper. The kiheis [short capes] of the men and covers for sleeping, are still firmer and thicker; and are composed of several sheets spread with a gelatinous wash made from the gum of a tree, and then beaten together. There is a kind still superior in texture and beauty, worn by the chiefs . . . made of the best (mulberry) bark, and is as thick as morocco . . . stamped with the brightest colours, and glazed with a composition having the effect of varnish . . . The cloth for sleeping, is the largest in size; each sheet, ten of which, fastened together at one end, form a bed-cover, being as large as an ordinary counterpane.

Female commoners wore skirts made with long ribbonlike strips of pounded hibiscus bark, leaves of the *kī* plant, or plaited reeds and grasses, attached to a drawstring encircling the waist The *kapa* skirts worn by both male and female dancers were so full that they resembled large balloons. *Aliʻi* women wore golden *palapalai* ferns on their heads, and another *lei* of ferns thrown over one bare shoulder and tied loosely at the waist beneath the opposite arm. Sandals woven of coconut fiber, *hau*, banana bark, or dried *kī* leaves were worn when walking over difficult terrain or lava, and always removed upon entering a house.

The compound of a chief would have contained at least six grass houses for his own use, including a small house in which the family gods were kept and honored, although the altar in the men's eating-house could also serve to shelter idols and the *'aumakua* particular to each family. There was a small house where *kapa* was beaten in bad weather, and a thatched canoe shed if the compound was near the ocean. During menstruation and after childbirth, women were confined to a special hut, called a *hale pe'a*, where they sat on discarded *kapa* stuffed with the root-stock fuzz of a large tree fern. Soiled *kapa* (only cloth that was worn around the hips could be used) was buried under the house when a woman's confinement of three to five days was complete, when she would be further purged by bathing in the ocean. The *hale noa* was the house where women lived, which was open only to a husband and young children (boys were taken into the men's house after circumcision at age seven). A man slept alongside his wife in her house, where no eating was allowed, as men avoided the utensils, dishes, and even fires needed to cook women's food.

Before the arrival of the carved beds brought from China by foreign traders, and the New England four-poster beds made for the most favored chiefs by the more handy of the American missionaries, the *ali'i* slept on platforms raised three feet from the ground and covered with thirty or more mats woven of either rush or the leaves of the *hala*, their heads resting on small rectangular blocks. (It was considered dangerous to sleep with your head next to the wall, as a spear thrust through the thatch could be fatal.) The quality of the mats varied greatly. The finest were woven with a small and delicate pattern, unlike anything else in Polynesia, often with a thick-fringed border. Floor mats, where a family and guests sat and talked, and children played, were of a wider mesh than the mats used for sleeping. A chief's favorite mat was carried over the arm of an attendant, to be used when needed for eating, sitting, or lounging.

As in most royal courts, *ali'i* life was profoundly different from that of commoners. When not at war, the chiefs spent their time in songwriting contests, gambling, surfing, games, mock warfare, religious rituals, and feasts. Two games that were very popular—there was one version for *ali'i*, and one for commoners—were versions of wife-swapping. Men and women sat on the ground in a circle and a leader touched one of the participants with a stick, indicating that he was free to leave with a chosen partner. A person could also be selected by spinning a coconut bowl until it stopped in front of one of the players. As long as the two lovers did not remain together past daybreak, there was no cause for jealousy.

The hunting of rats with bows (rats were descendants of the gods of Pō, the underworld) was much favored by the chiefs. The game of *kōnane*, similar to but more complicated than checkers, was a frequent pastime (King Kamehameha I was known to play by the hour with his chiefs). Boxing matches began as homage to the god Lono, who is said to have wandered through the Islands delirious with grief after he killed his wife, challenging every man he met to fight. Bouts, particularly during the Makahiki festival, which was held in honor of Lono, drew large crowds and were often injurious to the fighters. Another favorite sport, limited to the *ali'i*, was the racing of narrow wooden sleds (*hōlua*) down a steep slide cut into the side of a mountain and sometimes ending in the ocean. The course was often long (four thousand feet), and covered in dirt and wet grass to increase the speed of the racers, who lay on their stomachs on the sleds. The chief who covered the longest distance in a single run was the winner. In the display known as *'ōahi*, men hurled lighted firebrands from a cliff into the ocean below while people waited in canoes to retrieve the sputtering torches from the water. It was considered a sign of good fortune to brand yourself or a companion with sticks quickly retrieved from the ocean. Spectators and competitors bet on games, particularly sledding, boxing, and surfing.

Surfing was the passion of men, women, and children, commoner and *ali'i* alike. As with all things, it was a ritualized act. The right tree with which to make the board had to be found. The hewing and shaping of the wood was imbued with ceremony, in the hope that the gods would favor the board, its maker, and its owner. The first time that a board was put into the water had its own ritual, and its care (drying, oiling, wrapping in *kapa*) was accompanied by chants and prayers. People surfed naked, lying outstretched on thin boards made of either *koa* or breadfruit, five to seven feet long, and flat on both sides, although the most accomplished surfers would stand. The chiefs, who often put a *kapu* on the best surfing spots so as to have exclusive use of them, used glossy black boards made of *wiliwili* wood, which was lighter than *koa*, that could reach sixteen feet in length and one hundred and fifty pounds in weight. In a surfing contest, a buoy was anchored close to shore, and whoever reached it first was the winner. If more than one surfer reached the buoy, or no one reached it, a tie was conveniently declared.

Surfing at Lahaina, Maui. Watercolor by James Gay Sawkins, 1855, National Library of Australia, Canberra

A chief's household was established at his birth, when a *kahu* was assigned to the infant. *Ali'i* women frequently had little contact with their children, often living in a separate house, if not another district or island. As in the rest of Polynesia, children of both *ali'i* and commoners were often left in the care of grandparents, leaving the parents free to work, or to indulge in pleasure (such children were considered fortunate, as they would benefit from the family legends and cultural traditions taught them by the elders). A high chief kept between fifty and one hundred attendants, companions, counselors, and servants who lived with him, and whom he clothed and fed. The chief's intimate attendants each had a precise responsibility, often dependent on lineage—lighter of the chief's pipe; keeper of the loincloth; bearers of the feathered *kāhili*; court historian, who was a junior member of the family; executioner and his assistants; astronomers; dancers; orator; the "lap," who had taken care of the chief in childhood; night guards and day guards; chanters; treasurer; hereditary reader of signs (who could be put to death if his predictions were not thought to be accurate or even pleasing); person of the private parts, who cared for the chief when he was ill, and for a chiefess when she was menstruating; masseurs; and keeper of the household stores and goods. The guardian of the king's food was called an *ā'ī'pu'upu'u*, which means calloused shoulders. The man who watched over the king while he slept was called the keeper of the head. Men of lesser rank prepared and served food, and drew water, which was a long and tiring task, given its scarcity during the dry season.

Another valued member of a chief's household was the *punahele*, or favorite, who had been adopted or taken in by the chief, and who might be the son of a friend, or a foster son (the custom of *hānai* was common, in which a child, usually the firstborn son or daughter, was freely given to a grandparent or friend or relative to raise). Regarded as sacred to the chief, a favorite had the right to enter the *kapu* places. The favorite was not the same, however, as a *moe aikāne*, or a man's male sexual companion. A shocked John Ledyard, a marine from Connecticut who in 1777 accompanied Captain Cook on HMS *Discovery*, wrote that chiefs eagerly sought the most beautiful young men in the Islands, whom they brought to court and kept close to them. The chiefs, who were jealous of any unwelcome attention paid their favorites, appeared to Ledyard to be very fond of the boys, and to treat them with more kindness than they showed women. The Kohala high chief Kamehameha, later to be the greatest of Hawaiian kings, was twice described at age twenty-five as being extremely affectionate with a favorite. David Samwell, a surgeon also traveling with Cook, wrote in his journal that Kamehameha had a young male companion with him when he visited Cook's ships in 1778:

> Kamehameha, a chief of great consequence and a relation of Kario-poo [Kalaniōpu'u], but of a clownish and blackguard appearance, came on board of us in the afternoon dressed in an elegant feathered Cloak, which he brought to sell but would part with it for nothing but iron Daggers, which they of late preffered to Tois and everything else; and all the large Hogs they bring us now they want Daggers for and tell us that they must be made as long [as] their arms, and the armourers were employed in making them instead of small adzes. Kameha-meha got nine of them for his Cloak. He, with many of his attendants, took up his quarters on board the ship for the Night: among them is a Young Man of whom he seems very fond, which does not in the least surprize us as we have had opportunities before of being acquainted with a detestable part of his character which he is not in the least anxious to conceal.

Although commoners ate when they were hungry, one cooked meal was traditionally eaten just before dark, in the hope that ghosts would not be attracted to the food. Chiefs, however, ate four times a day, feasting amply on dog or pig, pickled or raw fish seasoned with salt water, and *poi*; the first time upon rising, followed by a second meal near noon, and then again in the afternoon and at night, with frequent snacks throughout the day of coconuts, bananas, and sugarcane. The chiefs, stretched across piles of mats, ate with one hand, while leaning upon an arm, although an attendant could scoop the food with his fingers to make a little ball, which he then dropped into his master's mouth, or he could first chew the food and transfer it directly from his mouth to that of the chief. Sharp splints of bamboo with which to cut meat, and calabashes of water in which to wash before and after eating, were held for the chiefs, and the hands dried with fresh ferns and leaves.

The English missionary William Ellis described a visit made by his fellow missionaries Asa Thurston, Artemas Bishop, and Joseph Goodrich to the house of Kuakini, governor of Hawai'i Island from 1812 to 1820:

Their baggage was removed from the vessel, and deposited in a small comfortable house, formerly belonging to Kamehameha, but which

Interior of a house of a chief at Kailua, Kona. An attendant holds a feather staff, or *kāhili*, over the chief's head. Watercolor, pen, and gouache by Louis Choris, ship's artist on board the *Rurick* under Otto von Kotzebue, 1816, Honolulu Museum of Art

the governor directed them to occupy so long as they should remain at Kairua. He also politely invited them to his table . . . The breakfast room presented a singular scene. They were seated around a small table with the governor and one or two of his friends, who, in addition to the coffee, fish, vegetables, &c., with which it was furnished, had a large wooden bowl of poe, a sort of thin paste made of baked taro, beat up and diluted with water, placed by the side of their plates, from which they frequently took very hearty draughts. Two favourite lap-dogs sat on the same sofa with the governor, one on his right hand and the other on his left, and occasionally received a bit from his hand, or the fragments on the plate from which he had eaten. A number of his punahele [favorite chiefs], and some occasional visitors, sat in circles on the floor, around large dishes of raw fish, baked hog, or dog, or goat, from which each helped himself without ceremony, while a huge calabash of poe passed rapidly round among them. They became exceedingly loquacious and cheerful during their meal; and several who had been silent before, now laughed loud, and joined with spirit in the mirth of their companions.

In 1828, a trader described a lunch that he gave on board his merchant vessel for Kamehameha III and his retinue:

My royal guest . . . knew the proper use of cutlery . . . although it appeared that he could more easily lift the food to his mouth with his fingers—especially a certain porridge called pooy, which he took from a bowl . . . held by one of his bodyguard sitting on his heels on the deck at the right side of the king in such a way that Kauikeaouli [King Kamehameha III] without looking could drop his hand in the porridge. He stirred it with two fingers, helped himself to about a spoonful of the stuff, and raised this to his wide-open mouth.

The name for a chief was the "shark that travels on land," and commoners believed that he could be denied nothing. All land was the unquestioned property of the king, or *ali'i nui*. Sections of land called *ahupua'a* (wedge-shaped divisions made at a high point on an island, running downhill to the ocean), were given to loyal chiefs and favorites as long as the high chief held power, and they in turn allowed smaller sections of land to be used by their retainers. The only restriction on the power of the *ali'i* was the land tenure system, which permitted a commoner to enter the service of another chief, should he wish to change masters. It was not unusual for people to protest the practices of a cruel or unjust chief, who was sometimes murdered for his crimes. Loyalty was not considered by the Hawaiians to be static—like commoners, a chief could change his allegiance at will. It was considered politic for *ali'i* of one island to marry into the royal families of other islands, which resulted in sometimes surprising alliances between rival clans.

Commoners were not compensated for their labor, although they did not pay rent for the right to farm their own small portions. Tenants were obliged to work on the chief's own land one day a week, when men, women, and children assisted each other in the *kalo* patches or sweet potato fields in the hope of finishing the work on time. Two-thirds of a commoner's crops, the animals he raised, and the *kapa* made by women (and after the arrival of foreign merchants, any small sums of money acquired through private trade) were owed to the chief, who did not hesitate to take all of a man's goods and land (and wife), should he decide he wanted them. If a tenant farmer refused to obey his chief, his parcel of land, his animals, and his modest goods were taken from him. In 1821, the English traveler Gilbert Mathison wrote that while he was in Waialua, on O'ahu, he observed a chief order hundreds of his people to the sandalwood forests to cut wood:

> The whole obeyed, except one man, who had the folly and hardihood to refuse. Upon this, his house was set fire to, and burnt to the ground on the very day: still he refused to go. The next process was to seize his possessions, and turn his wife and family off the estate; which would . . . have been done, if he had not . . . made a timely submission.

The levies of canoes, timber, pigs, dogs, dried and salted fish, chickens, vegetables, nets, mats, cloth, feathers, baskets, calabashes, and *kalo* collected by chiefs from the farmers and fishermen on their land were given in turn to the governor of the island. A commoner sometimes paid twenty pieces of *kapa* in tax. When Queen Ka'ahumanu, the widow of Kamehameha I, traveled with Captain George Byron to Hilo in 1825 to collect tribute, she was given two thousand pieces of *kapa*.

Before the unification of the islands of Hawai'i, Maui, Kaho'olawe, Lāna'i, O'ahu, and Moloka'i, each island was ruled by its own *ali'i nui*, whose rights were not guaranteed by simple linear succession but by genealogy and his proved ability to prevail among rivals. King Kamehameha's victory on O'ahu in 1795 was to end these long and bloody struggles, but for hundreds of years, local chieftains struggled ceaselessly, raiding each other in wars of gain, whim, revenge, or dynastic hegemony. As each chief had the right to apportion his land as he chose among his kin and followers, the constant shifts of power caused dissension and confusion, and rendered land ownership both unreliable and unstable. With the death of a king, or the defeat of a king in battle, land was again divided and distributed between chiefs, a practice which often led to a renewal of war. Samuel Kamakau attributed the constant battle for land to the value of the produce and goods of each district. On Hawai'i Island, different kinds of especially fine *kapa* were particular to the area controlled by the Kona chiefs, while the districts of Hilo and Hāmākua were known for their fast war canoes, and for the *mamo* and *'ō'ō* feathers required to make the cloaks, helmets and *kāhili* prized by the *ali'i*. The chiefs of Kohala in the north wanted land in the mild and dry districts of Kona to the southwest with their rich fishing grounds, while the Kona chiefs sought land in the mountainous districts for their fresh water, *kalo* terraces, and plentiful crops.

As much time was spent in war, fighting became the main occupation of the chiefs and their warriors. Except for the four months devoted to the great Makahiki festival beginning in October with the rising of the Pleiades, they studied warcraft, and staged mock battles. Archibald Menzies, a Scots surgeon and naturalist sailing with Captain George Vancouver in 1792, 1793, and 1794, witnessed a pretend battle in which Kamehameha I took part. Menzies was surprised when some of the men suffered serious injury, and even death (the corpses were used as sacrifices):

Finding what were supposed to be his party giving ground to the others very fast, he [Kamehameha] darted in to the middle of them without any weapon whatever, and placing himself at their head, a shower of spears was instantly aimed at him from the opposite side. He caught hold of the first that came near him in its course and putting himself in a position of defense, with his eyes fixed on the spears coming toward him, and by the spear in his hand he parried every one of them off with the greatest coolness and intrepidity, and watching at the same time with a vigilant eye every favorable opportunity of getting a good aim, when he would instantly dart back the spear in his hand and get hold of the next that was hove at him. In this manner they continued . . . with such apparent virulence that many of them received considerable hurts and bruises. At last they had resort of the pololus, which are spears of fifteen or eighteen feet long, pointed like daggers . . . They do not heave them like the other spears but charge with them in a close bodied phalanx to close action . . . They manage them with great dexterity, by resting them on the forearms of one hand to guide their direction, while the other hand pushes them on or gathers them in with great ease and alertness. They were not long engaged with these weapons when one of the warriors fell, and then a violent scramble ensued between the two parties for his body . . . as those who get the dead body were allowed to be victorious by being thus enabled to carry off the first sacrifice to the marae [Tahitian word for *heiau*].

The rules, etiquette, and ritual of both combat and mock battle were as formalized as those at any medieval European court. Competitions and entertainments, not unlike jousting, were used to further fighting skills, to win admiration and honor, and to encourage the sometimes vicious rivalries essential to upholding morale during battle. All fighting was done in daylight, and in a very methodical fashion, with the place, style of fighting, and time often determined before the battle (those chiefs who resorted to less predictable tactics, such as night raids, surprise attacks, and later, guns, had a clear advantage). The armies, arrayed in crescent formation, met on open ground, although one warrior could be chosen to fight from each side, while the two armies watched nearby.

Fighting, whether between an army or two chiefs, was limited to brutal hand-to-hand combat, using slings (which in Polynesia took the place of bows), spears, clubs, and javelins. Once joined, the grappling fighters were limited to choking, stabbing, and clubbing. Men wore as little clothing as possible, their long hair wrapped in *kapa*, although the chiefs wore their bright red, yellow, and black feather capes, made in designs of fins, rainbows,

Hawaiian warrior
in feather cape and
helmet. Engraving
by Nicolas-Eustache
Maurin, after a drawing
by Jacques Arago, 1819,
Honolulu Museum
of Art

sharks, and wings (the color yellow was associated with Oʻahu; black and red with the island of Hawaiʻi), flung over one bare shoulder to facilitate the use of weapons, and crested wickerwork helmets onto which hundreds of feathers had been sewn. Canoe men, often in squadrons of hundreds, wore forbidding gourd helmets decorated with ferns and fluttering strips of *kapa*. Captain Cook, who mistakenly believed the helmets were used in "mummery," described them in the journal of his third voyage (as recorded by one of his officers, Lieutenant James King): "It is a kind of mask, made of a large gourd, with holes cut in it for the eyes and nose. The top was stuck full of small green twigs, which, at a distance, had the appearance of an elegant waving plume: and from the lower part hung narrow stripes [*sic*] of cloth, resembling a beard."

No standing army was maintained, but each man kept his simple weapons ready in his house, constituting a reserve force that was always on alert. Chiefs sent men, most of them farmers and fishermen, in answer to an alarm, and if a man was discovered to have remained behind, his ear would be slit and he would be dragged to the battlefield in ropes. Women frequently went to war beside men, caring for their weapons, carrying food and water,

Warrior in a gourd helmet, trimmed with ferns and pieces of white *kapa*. Engraving by
Thomas Cook, after an ink wash drawing by John Webber, 1779

Mamo, the endemic Hawaiian honeycreeper (*Drepanis pacifica*), now extinct, whose tail feathers were used for capes and helmets. Watercolor by the naturalist William Ellis, made on Cook's third voyage

The *'i'iwi* (*Vestiaria coccinea*). The translation of the bird's Latin name, "scarlet clothing," refers to the capes and helmets made from its feathers. Print by F. W. Frohawk, 1898

The *'ō'ō* (*Moho nobilis*), once found only in the forests of the Big Island, was last seen in 1934. It was described by Captain Clerke of Cook's third voyage as "a bird with a long tail, whose colour is black . . . the vent and feathers under the wing are yellow." Engraving by John Gerrard Keulemans, 1893

The *'ō'ū* (*Psittirostra psittacea*), a large, plump forest bird of the honeycreeper family with yellow and green feathers, and pink legs. Particularly fond of the blossoms of the *'ōhi'a lehua* tree, it was last seen in 1989 on Kaua'i. Engraving by Jean-Gabriel Prêtre, 1838

Hale-o-Keawe *heiau* near the refuge of Hōnaunau on the Big Island. Engraving from a drawing by William Ellis, 1782

and tending to the wounded, but also joining them in combat. When a man was killed in battle or captured for ritual sacrifice, the woman accompanying him would be killed or enslaved. Those warriors who were not taken prisoner would attempt to flee to places of sanctuary like Hōnaunau, four miles south of Kona on the Big Island, and Lāʻie on Oʻahu, where a fighter's wives, children, and elderly relatives could also find shelter. If a defeated warrior, or likewise a criminal, could reach such a refuge, he would be granted mercy. Anyone who dared harm him would be considered to have broken sacred law and would himself be declared an outlaw. A person could leave the sanctuary after a lapse of time and return home without fear of retribution or punishment.

Awe of the Night Approaching

Any person, object, action, or place could be deemed *kapu* by a high chief or priest, which ensured that every aspect of existence, particularly for a commoner, was potentially imbued with danger. There were different categories of *kapu*—*kapu* of consecration, *kapu* of the kingdom, minor *kapu* (such as using a sleeping mat for anything but sleeping), the *kapu* applied to those persons who possessed the volcano as an *'aumakua*, and to those whose bodies had been entered into by the spirits of sharks. Some *kapu* were practical in origin, and used to protect diminishing supplies of fish or plants; others were commemorative of a special event in the family of a chief.

The extent to which *kapu* were enacted and enforced in Hawaiian society is thought to have been instituted locally in response to the fierce rivalry and competition among ruling families, and used to enforce the immense power of the secretive priestly clans. Both *ali'i* and priests had the right of life and death (only a high chief was given the awful *kapu wela*, which allowed him to burn alive anyone who offended him), enforced by a seemingly arbitrary system of strict rules and prohibitions, as well as a complex system of religious ritual.

The . . . tabu were strictly enforced, and every breach of them punished with death, unless the delinquents had some very powerful friends who were either priests or chiefs. They were generally offered in sacrifice, strangled, or despatched with a club or a stone within the precincts of the heiau, or they were burnt . . . The great mass of people were at no period in their existence exempt from its influence, and no circumstance in life could excuse their obedience to its demands.

Execution by clubbing. Drawing by Jacques Arago, from Louis de Freycinet's *Voyage Autour du Monde 1817–1820*, 1820

Throughout Polynesia, the idea of the cosmos was inseparable from the idea of society itself. The *aliʻi* were given the rights of gods in exchange for their protection, and their formalized enactment of sacred rites and ritual sacrifice ensured the well-being of the community and exemplified its spiritual and material endeavors. *Kapu* served to establish order, requiring men to respect the land, to honor the chiefs who were the literal representatives of the gods, and to serve the thousands of omnipresent big and little gods. In return, the gods endowed the land and sea with bountiful food, and protected people from danger (often the gods themselves).

The rigid taboos of the Hawaiians, particularly those that applied to women, served as reminders of the division between the mundane and the divine, emphasizing that humans were inferior to gods, and that women, who lived unlike men in a realm of darkness and death, were inferior to men (according to the historian Kepelino, a man born on the third night of the full moon would be fearless, brave, and kindhearted, while a woman born on that night was doomed to be an "ensnarer who ate filth"). The eating *kapu* was a fixed law for both chiefs and commoners, not because a person would die if he ate food that was forbidden, but to maintain the distinction between sustenance that was given to mankind and that which belonged to the gods.

The nineteenth-century historian John Papa ʻĪʻī in *Fragments of Hawaiian History*, a collection of essays written for the Hawaiian-language newspaper *Ka Nupepa Kuʻokoʻa* in the years 1866 to 1870, described in the third person the training he received as a child in preparation for becoming a hereditary attendant in the court of Kamehameha II:

> His mother placed on his back a bundle containing a wonderful malo made of feathers from mamo and apapane birds attached to a fine net, with rows of human teeth at the end . . . slipping his arms into the loops of the bundle, she taught him to cry, 'E noho e! Squat down!' . . . The proclamation of this kapu was an exceedingly common practice in the court, and one which flustered many a newcomer who did not know that he must squat quickly and slip off his tapa wrap or shoulder covering . . . If a person was wearing a lei on neck or head, he must remove it and throw it away when the cry to squat (noho) was heard, otherwise the penalty would be death.

When a chief and his male entourage, resplendent in long feather cloaks, helmets, and scented loincloths, ventured out of doors, they were accompanied by attendants whose responsibility it was to bear their spittoons, look after their cloaks, and carry their *kāhili*. If a chief possessed the prostrating *kapu*, which required any nearby person to throw himself facedown on the ground, executioners trailed after the chief the better to catch anyone who remained standing (a chief could choose to spare a person's life if he wished, placing his hand on the head of the offender and declaring him *kapu* to himself).

As it was believed that a person's shadow was his spirit made visible, a man could be put to death if his shadow fell upon a high chief, who was the possessor of the greatest possible *mana* (spirit power) and thus untouchable, which caused the chiefs to travel most often by night, using sedan chairs, as their very footsteps rendered *kapu* the earth on which they walked. If the shadow of a person fell upon the dwelling of a high chief, he could also be killed. Royal children were carried on the shoulders of a special attendant, chosen for his loyalty and strength, who walked with his arms crossed over his chest to make a resting place for the child's feet.

A *kapu* was announced by proclamation, or by the planting of sticks tied with bamboo or a piece of white *kapa*, used when a location or a house or even a fish was under proscription. Pigs that were *kapu* had a piece of civet drawn through a hole in one ear. During a time of *kapu*, priests would move through a village each evening shouting that all fires be extinguished, or that the trail to the ocean was open only to the king, or that a path on the hillside was for the gods' use alone. When a chief's feather staff, or the skirt of a chiefess, or the dirty bath water of an *ali'i* was carried through a village, an attendant warned commoners to fall to the ground lest they be dragged to a *heiau* and killed.

Those present when a chief and his men were eating knelt with knees tightly closed, forbidden to move until the meal was finished. If, in the presence of a high chief, a man's head was seen to be dirty with mud, he could be put to death. If a man mistakenly stepped on a chief's *kapa*, he could be put to death. If a man entered the house of an *ali'i* without first drying his loincloth, he could be put to death. Certain high chiefs and chiefesses were forbidden to hold a baby, lest the child soil their laps, a violation that would result in the child's death (because of this *kapu*, many high-ranking women did not tend their own children). If a man was to consort with a menstruating woman, he could be put to death, as to lie with a woman during menstruation was considered a greater offense than rape. A man could also be killed for sexual union with another woman during his wife's menses.

The following is from Chant Seven, known as "The Dog Child," in the Kumulipo. The "narrow trail" was the path to the *heiau*, forbidden to anyone but priests:

> Fear falls upon me on the mountain top
> Fear of the passing night
> Fear of the night approaching
> Fear of the pregnant night
> Fear of the breach of the law
> Dread of the place of offering and the narrow trail
> Dread of the food and the waste part remaining
> Dread of the receding night
> Awe of the night approaching.

Time itself could be placed under a *kapu*. Nine days of each month were *kapu* to certain gods (the third night of the full moon was favored for ritual sacrifice). The weeks preceding a religious ceremony and the period of a chief's illness were traditionally declared *kapu*. An entire island or a district could be made *kapu*, when no human or canoe would dare approach its shore or cross its border. During a season of *kapu*, all fires and stone oil lamps would be extinguished; people could not bathe or be seen outside their houses; dogs and chickens were muffled. It is said that during the time of 'Umi, *ali'i nui* in the fifteenth century, men had been forbidden to shave their beards for thirty years. Before the time of Kamehameha I (1782–1819), the average length of a *kapu* was forty days, although Kamehameha later shortened the time to five to ten days.

The rule that forbade men and women eating together was thought to protect men from female pollution, as food was a medium that could convey psychic influences. Women were allowed to eat with men only when they were in the field or at sea (but not out of the same bowl) and during the period of mourning that followed the death of a chief. A newborn girl could not be fed even a morsel of food from her father's calabash, or any food that had been cooked in his fire. Certain male attendants had the privilege of preparing food for a chiefess and were allowed to eat with her, but were then excluded from the company of other men while eating.

Women could not eat coconut, as the tree represented the body of the war god Kū. Pork was forbidden because it was food given to the gods (and to chiefs and priests), and was identified with the god Lono's avatar, the mischievous god Kamapua'a, who took the form of a pig. Bananas represented the body of Kanaloa. Jackfish (*ulua*) were sacrificed to Kū as a substitute when sufficient numbers of humans could not be found. Red goatfish were used as offerings in various rituals, including the consecration of the main post in a new sleeping house. Women were forbidden shark because it was the symbol of a high chief. In short, women were restricted primarily to *kalo*, breadfruit, fruit, some fish, seaweed, and the little hairless black dogs kept for food (described by Lieutenant James King, the most reliable observer of the officers in Captain Cook's retinue, as lazy, short-legged creatures with tiny ears). The Russian explorer Vasily Golovnin described a chiefess who visited his ship in 1818:

> Her long silk dress of an old-fashioned European style and an expensive looking white shawl were proof enough that she was "a lady of noble rank," but when we sat down to eat with the chiefs I could not persuade her even to stay in the cabin, let alone dine with us. All she answered was: "Tabu," which means forbidden, and she ate on the

quarterdeck with the wife of another chief. Their meal consisted of a dough made of taro root flour and raw fish, which they dipped in sea water instead of vinegar. They would not touch a morsel of our food except biscuits and cheese.

Historians do not tell us much about the willingness of the Hawaiians to comply with a system in which the constant threat of death was the means by which power was accrued and held by chiefs and priests. Nowhere in the numerous journals and memoirs of the period is there mention of any objection, except by Queen Kaʻahumanu, the favorite wife of Kamehameha I, who showed a glimmer of resistance when she was caught in adultery, and her young lover executed at Diamond Head by her husband. In her anger, she tried to incite chiefs loyal to her to kill Kamehameha, but his son would not agree to his murder, and Kaʻahumanu had to abandon her plan of revenge.

The nineteenth-century historian David Malo, who equated fear with conscience, believed that the assiduity with which people kept *kapu* was evidence of a strong moral sense:

The fidelity with which such obligations (kapu) were kept is proof enough that people had all the material of conscience in their make-up. It will be seen that the duties and faults that weighed most heavily on the conscience of the Hawaiian were mostly artificial matters, and such as in our eyes do not touch the essence of morality. But that is true to all consciences to a large extent. It should be remarked that the Hawaiian was a believer in the doctrine of the divine right of kings to the extremest degree. His duties to his alii . . . [were] . . . on the same footing with those due to the akua [gods].

Although commoners hid from the priests when they ranged through the villages hunting for victims, the punishments rendered when *kapu* were broken were obeyed in silence. More than that, Hawaiians believed in the necessity of *kapu*, and the sanctity of the system. Only once did John Papa ʻĪʻī question his mother as she prepared him for his responsibilities as young companion to Kamehameha II, asking why, if she held him dear, she wished him to go to court, especially as an older brother had already been put to death for breaking a minor *kapu*. Later, when he was serving the king, ʻĪʻī ac-

David Malo, journalist and historian. Lithograph from a drawing by Alfred T. Agate of the United States Exploring Expedition, 1838–1842

Samuel Kamakau, historian, journalist, and judge. He attended the Lahainaluna Seminary on Maui in 1833, where he was converted to Christianity by the Reverend Sheldon Dibble. This photograph was taken from a damaged daguerreotype, ca. 1917.

cepted without protest or even private complaint the punishment of death that would have befallen him had he been caught when he dropped the lid of the king's spittoon:

> Ii [*sic*], who was carrying the young chief's spittoon in front of him, had a brush with death when somehow the cover slipped off, struck his knee, and bounced up again. He was able to catch it and so was saved from death, for had it dropped to his feet, his fate would have been that of Maoloha [his brother]. As it was, he was criticized for forgetting the rule that the spittoon should be held at the back of his neck or shoulder, in which case the cover would not be stepped over if dropped. The boy became very nervous with chiefs watching him and talking about his narrow escape. When they reached home, the chiefs told some of the people there how he had passed the hill of death. Then they told him some of the other rules, and these were identical with those he had heard from his mother.

ʻĪʻī also described, again in the third person, a *kapu* of silence during which he could not keep from coughing. This second escape from death was during a *kapu* of a *heiau* built for the god Lono:

> On the night of Lono, the kahunas prayed continuously in unison from evening until the next morning, Mauli, when the great kapu was to be lifted by the koʻokoʻo prayer . . . The kapu was imposed with the words: "Kapu la, make la, a ʻapuʻe (It is kapu, it is death, a very strict kapu)." All talking and noises of every kind were silenced, under penalty of death.
>
> No sooner was the kapu imposed than the boy [ʻĪʻī] felt a tickling sensation in his throat that made him want to cough. He held his throat with his hands until his eyes and throat were red, but finally he could no longer bear it. He coughed two or three times, but, fortunately, was not heard by those who had imposed the kapu. Those who were in the house with him were distressed, and one person dug a hole for him to cough into while another supplied a basin of water. When the kapu-freeing prayer was uttered, and the need for discomfort [because of prostration] was over, he was greatly relieved. Had he been heard coughing, he would have been snatched from this world. Such were the many troubles that followed one about in the royal court.

Sacrificial ritual required from two to two hundred victims. Women were sacrificed less frequently than men as they, unlike men who were born of sky gods, were the lowly descendants of earth gods, which rendered them insufficiently divine to serve as blood offerings. (A sign of contempt, directed at someone whom a man wished to threaten or insult, was to make a fist and insert the thumb between the first and second fingers, which signified female genitalia.)

The dead victims, stripped of clothing, were laid facedown side by side on an altar, and dead pigs were placed on top of them. ʻĪʻī described the execution of three men who were caught eating coconuts with some chiefesses, and were killed because coconuts were forbidden to women, and because men were prohibited from eating with women:

> The chiefs assembled with the king and the three potential heirs to the kingdom, as well as the kahunas, the gods, and their keepers. The

kahunas offered the prayers with many words . . . the fires . . . [were] lighted and the pigs and the lawbreakers killed for sacrifices. These were to be laid together on the lele altar after the king had uttered the 'amama prayer . . . The skins of the men were scorched like those of the sacrificial pigs and laid together in a special place before the kahunas, the king, and all the others who had assembled there to worship.

In a ritual held in 1804 at Papa'ena'ena *heiau* at Diamond Head when Keōpūolani, the sacred wife of Kamehameha I, was ill, four hundred coconuts, four hundred bananas, four hundred pigs, and three humans were offered to the gods. (Fortunately for those humans next in line for sacrifice, Keōpūolani recovered.)

If sufficient numbers of the despised *kauwā*, prisoners taken in battle, or criminals were not on hand, the priest and his attendants went to sea for an *ulua*, using squid for bait. If an *ulua* was not caught, the priest and his men prowled through a village, shouting playfully to the people to come outside.

If any one did, they killed him and thrust a hook in his mouth . . . The kahuna shouted to wake up people . . . striking the doors with his paddle as he called out [that he had] a big catch of ulua or shark. Then the occupants of the house would, if green, run out to see the sight and thus give the murderous priest his opportunity. A dead man, not a woman, with a hook in his mouth answered very well as an ulua.

In his book, *Kepelino's Traditions of Hawaii*, Kepelino described the way in which a *kauwā* was taken for sacrifice. Kepelino (1830–1878) was a descendant of the legendary priest Pa'ao, and a convert to Catholicism.

The messenger came to them and said, "I am sent by the chief for one of you to be a man in the heiau," or for whatever else. The slaves heard, looked at each other and asked, "Which of us will go to die for our lords?" Then the crowd spoke in terms of pity, "You perhaps of us!" Then the person named looked at his children tenderly and rubbed noses with each saying, "Perhaps you are the one to die, but no! If you die you will not see the light. It is better therefore that of us two I die and you live. For if you die you are but a little shadow and I who live am a long shadow; between you and me, you and me, it shall be I!"

Then the father rubbed noses with his children and with the rest of the slaves and went with the messenger to the sea and was drowned.

After death, the soul was said to flee to certain bluffs along the coasts of each island, known as leaping places into the underworld, or Pō. It was believed that the soul was in peril during its journey to Pō—it could lose its way or fall victim to a vicious spirit unless protected by its family ʻaumakua, to whom it had obediently paid homage throughout its life. A barren isthmus between east and west Maui, and Kaʻena Point on Oʻahu, are said to be haunted by spirits who jumped from the cliffs.

Chiefs suffered from the possibility of disgrace occasioned by the loss of *mana*, caused by failure to obey an ʻaumakua, or by speaking ill of a relative, or failing to keep a promise, among other things, even if the offense was accidental. The following chant was made by a fallen chief, as quoted by the anthropologist E.S.C. Handy in a translation reflective of Handy's own Christian faith:

> What is my great offence, O God!
> I have eaten standing perhaps, or without giving thanks,
> Or these my people, have eaten wrongfully.
> Yes, that is the offense, O Kane-of-the-water-of-life.
> O spare; O let me live, thy devotee,
> Look not with indifference upon me.
> I call upon thee, O answer thou me,
> O thou god of my body who art in Heaven.
> O Kane, let the lightning flash, let the thunder roar,
> Let the earth shake.
> I am saved; my god has looked upon me,
> I am being washed, I have escaped the danger.

In some instances, an *aliʻi* caught disobeying a *kapu* could choose a surrogate to be killed or punished in his place. It was possible for a violator of a less important *kapu* (such as eating forbidden food) to escape death by paying a small fine of an armful of cloth, or several mats. A commoner found to have committed adultery with a chief's wife was punished, depending on the rank of the chief, by having his eyes put out, although the woman would not be harmed. Violators of *kapu* that did not warrant death were subject to kicking, or beating with a rope. Kamehameha I once discovered a group of women eating stolen bananas, but hearing their prayers for mercy, pardoned them with the stern promise that should they break the *kapu* again, he would ensure that they were killed. The high chiefess Kapi'olani confided to the missionary Lucia Holman that as a girl, she and another woman of high rank had been caught eating bananas: "They were tried for the ungodly deed," wrote Holman, "and condemned to suffer the penalty which was poverty, loss of rank, and to remain unmarried . . . unless suitable expiation could be made." As Kapi'olani lived to marry (she became a Christian convert), due recompense must have been given.

The Hawaiians' trust in magic, their dependence on similarities and analogies to reveal meaning, and their belief in the chance omens found in nature were stimulated by fear, superstition, and an empirical folk wisdom that had been strengthened and justified over many generations. The belief in beings who rule both the seen and unseen world and who determine the course of our lives presupposes that the forces of nature are variable, if not plastic, and that we should be able, if the right sacrifices are made and sufficient reverence paid, to influence these beings to our benefit.

As in many early cultures, phenomenological explanations are founded on proximity and similarity. Hawaiians buried the placenta of a child under a pandanus so that the child's eyelashes would grow as long as the thorns of the tree. Surfers struck the water with a vine of beach morning glory in the hope of good waves—the word *hū* refers both to the vine, *pohuehue*, and the verb "to rise up." It was bad luck for a fisherman to hear the song of the flycatcher, *'elepaio*, as its call, similar to the words *ono ka ai* (the fish tastes good), was thought to be a taunt. Sugarcane was forbidden to a chanter lest his performance be ruined, a precaution based on the double meaning (*kaona*) of the word *kō*, which means both sugarcane and achievement. For a people so poetical, so susceptible to allegory, metaphor, and imagery, such a nominalism would have had great appeal, while it is also true that the chewing of sugarcane renders one's voice hoarse and scratchy.

Given the distance in time and the lack of a written record, it is difficult to ascertain the origin or practical use of many superstitions held by the Hawaiians. For example, if anyone were to climb the ridgepole while the roof of a house was being thatched, or if a priest were to stick his head inside the house to check the progress of construction, it would cause the death of the owner. If the side posts of a house were crooked, it was a sign that the owner was stingy. A bulge in the *pili* grass thatch meant that someone would soon suffer from dropsy. Should a fisherman see a number of *uhu* (parrot fish) touching noses, it was a sure sign that his wife was unfaithful. If a spider dropped from its web onto the floor, a visitor might be expected, but if it scurried from the floor to the ceiling, it meant that the visitor was only coming to gossip (if there were knots in the spider's web, however, the visitor would arrive with a gift).

As there was a fear of alerting jealous gods by the praise and adulation of a child, one never said of a little girl that she was comely. In a gentle voice, one mumbled in passing that she was quite homely (if a harsh voice was used, it meant that the child was in truth ugly). Hawaiians were wary of answering a direct question about where they were going, as it might alert evil spirits. Should a man happen to be asked—usually by a *haole*, as no Hawaiian would be so careless—he would answer politely that he was going where he was going. It was in general considered extremely rude to ask too many questions, or to ask for something outright.

An eclipse of the moon was considered an especially harrowing omen. In his *History of the Sandwich Islands* (1831), the Reverend Ephraim Eveleth wrote:

> On the 16th of June, 1824, there happened an eclipse which was nearly total. It was a fine evening, and the missionaries having just retired to rest were disturbed by the hurried steps of the natives, running to and fro, and filling the air with loud lamentations and wailings. Inquiry was made as to the cause of this uncommon commotion, and it was answered, that "the people thought the king was dead, because the moon was dark." When the missionaries went out, they heard nothing but exclamations uttered in tones of deep agony—"the moon is sick, very sick,"—"an evil moon, evil in deed,"—"the gods are eating the moon."

Commoners were forbidden any contact with *ali'i*, or with their food, clothing, canoes, *heiau*, or sacred images, since anything possessed or even touched by an *ali'i*, including his nail parings, urine, excrement, and spittle, was considered invested with *mana* and could be used in sorcery. As a precaution, a high chief's intimate waste was daily carried away in the greatest secrecy by trusted attendants and taken out to sea, or buried, or hidden in a cave. Even the discarded clothing of commoners was buried so that it could not be used as *maunu* (the belongings or waste of an intended victim of an evil spell), and old-timers soaked their old clothes in water so they would disintegrate faster once the clothes were buried. One never gave a *lei* to anyone who was not a close relation, for if it fell into the hands of a sorcerer, it could be used to cause chronic scrofulous pustules to appear on the wearer's neck. Mary Kawena Pukui, who was born in 1895, wrote, "When I was a little girl, my grandmother used to take special care of my hair. She'd take any that came out during combing and roll it up and bury it in a hidden place . . . watching over every little thing because it could become maunu."

Most terrifying of all was a death spell, feared by chiefs and commoners alike. In order to conjure a spell, it was first necessary for a priest to collect the victim's *maunu*, which was then wrapped in *kapa* and ritually fed so as to nourish the volatile spirit matter imprisoned within the cloth. A flying god, *akua lele*, could be dispatched with the spell, taking the form of a ball of fire (like the comet that perhaps he was), racing across the sky to deliver illness, madness, and death. Certain deadly poison gods were used by a greatly feared sixteenth-century prophet and seer, Lanikāula, who lived on the east end of Moloka'i at Pu'u O Hoku. Kamehameha asked King Kahekili of Maui for one of these small wooden gods, about a foot high, which Kahekili gave to him. The god, named Kalaipahoa, after the tree of the same name found on Moloka'i, was considered so malign that Kamehameha kept it in a *heiau* with a special keeper. When Kamehameha died, the god was cut into pieces and distributed among his favorite chiefs.

If a man knew that he was the victim of a death spell, he would resignedly lie down on his sleeping mat to die. Even if he was blameless, or his supposed offense was not grave, the very thought that he was under a curse would cause him to fade away. F. A. Olmsted, a recent graduate of Yale who traveled to the Sandwich Islands for his health, wrote in *Incidents of a Whaling Voyage*

(1841) of a story told him by the pilot who guided his ship into Honolulu harbor:

> I was called upon to read prayers over the corpse of a foreign resident, and among the natives that thronged around, was a young chief, who had incurred the resentment of the deceased for some cause or other. As the burial service proceeded, he imagined that the prayers offered on the occasion were incantations offered to the god of the stranger for vengeance upon himself. So deeply was he impressed with this belief, that he was filled with terror and apprehension. It haunted him wherever he went, until he sank beneath the horrid images his fancy conjured up, and in about a week he was a corpse, a victim of his own superstitious fears.

The following is an *'anā'anā* prayer which was considered most effective when recited in a natural voice after eating the slimy part of an eyeball. Death was said to occur within five to fifteen days:

> This is a death I inflict (*ka'u make*): he is to go and lie in the roadway, and his back split open . . . a stench arise, and he be devoured by dogs. A death I inflict is to start in him while he is in his own place, and when he goes elsewhere he is to vomit blood, and die, and his grease . . . is to flow on the road, and he be eaten by dogs. This is a death I inflict: he is to go to the ocean, and when he returns to shore, his grease is to pour out of him as he goes. This is a death I inflict: he is to fall off a cliff and break his bones, and his grease pour out on the highway. This is a death I inflict: he is to be buried in the earth five *anana* deep, and be dug up by dogs. Such is the death I inflict.

The *pule kāholo*, or quick prayer, was considered so effective that if signs of death were apparent on the victim, you did not wail in grief for him, lest the curse be turned upon you and you yourself die:

> What is the food it is calling for?
> A man is the food it is calling for.
> Thunder cracks in the heavens,
> The earth quakes, the lightning flashes.

Your legs bend,
Your hands become paralyzed,
Your back hunches,
Your neck is twisted,
Your chin is crooked,
Your eyes are sunken;
Disease has broken into the brain,
Your liver rots,
Your intestines fall to pieces.

A great owl calls out,
Whistling as it calls.
What is the food it is calling for?
A man is the food it is calling for.
Thunder cracks in the heavens,
The earth quakes, the lightning flashes.

A sorcerer could also send a spell surreptitiously by shaking his clothing in a seemingly meaningless way, or by playing casually with four or five sticks held in his hand. If a man suspected that he had been prayed to death, help could be found, if done quickly enough, in a reverse spell, or through the severing of a spell by *'oki*, to cut, or by prayer (in modern times, the prayer could be Christian). Should word reach a victim that the ominous prayer to choke had been sent his way, he would eat the head of a live *manini* or *āholehole* fish (*hole* has the additional meaning of "to strip away"), both of which possess sharp bones in the dorsal fin that can cause strangulation should they be caught in the throat, as frequently happened. Another sorcerer, a *kahuna pale*, could pray to the fish for intercession, in the hope of saving the victim:

Choke and live; strangle and live.
Soften, O fish, cook through, O fish,
Fall to pieces, O fish, grow soft, O fish;
Let the bones decay, let the bones turn to ash.

You ate the *manini* fish,
You are strangled and choked; life draws out fine;

You are doubled up; life draws out fine;
You are doubled over, helpless; life draws out fine.
You ate the *aholehole* fish,
You are strangled and choked; life draws out fine;
You are doubled over, helpless; life draws out fine.

If the counter-spell or prayer was not in time, however, and the victim died, his family could perform a ritual in which the *maunu* of the dead victim was burned and the ashes strewn before the sorcerer, or in the water that he used for bathing, so as to bewitch him in turn.

The Christian convert Samuel Kamakau did not give much countenance to the presence of sorcerers, scornfully condemning witchcraft as the work of the devil:

> There were in old days few kahunas of the devil-worshipping . . . class who prayed men to death . . . These were a tabu class to whom did not properly belong the slant-eyed, the bold, those who went from house to house, the covetous of other men's wealth, extortioners, askers of favors. The true kahuna of this class was a person who lived quietly, was lowly, unassuming, humble of heart, not a gad-about, not a seeker of companions, not a pleasure seeker, a proud talker, or covetous, but one who suppressed his lusts. This was the kind of man who represented the true sorcerer. The one who began first to harm another by sorcery was generally the one who died first. These persons secured from the devil himself their knowledge . . . by burning fires . . . and by sending spirits on errands of evil . . . They were eaters of filth and of things defiled.

The missionary Harvey Rexford Hitchcock, stationed on Moloka'i from 1832 to 1855, gave sorcery sufficient credence to have stood over the coffin of a sorcerer who had threatened to pray Hitchcock to death, saying in Hawaiian, "*He 'io 'oe, he 'io au, he 'io na ānela o ke akua, ki 'i mai la no ia 'oe a lawe.*" "You are a hawk, I am a hawk, and the angels of God are hawks. They have come and taken you away."

An *'anā'anā* spell could also be used for good, such as inducing pregnancy and treating illness. Martha Beckwith recorded what she said was a true story, told to her by Mary Kawena Pukui:

In this family firstborn daughters for generations had been unable to bear children alive. A certain firstborn daughter . . . had eight stillborn infants. She consulted a kahuna and was told that only by the death of one male in the family could she have a child that would live. One of the uncles . . . consented to offer himself and in a short time he was . . . 'prayed to death that others might live.' The firstborn was a girl. She lived, and the five children born after her, but she never bore children. She died in 1933.

One could also seek a sorcerer's help in casting a love spell. The priest would pray on behalf of the person who had engaged his skill, who would then stand with his back to the wind, a flower in his hand, waiting in a spot where the object of the spell was sure to appear. He would then spit on the flower with the words, "Spit! You come to seek me of your own accord," and drop the flower to the ground. A person could also eat sugarcane and after dedicating it to Makanikeoe, the god of love, blow in the direction of the person he wished to enchant. The god, who was manifest in wind, carried the breath of air to the desired one, who instantly fell in love with the sender.

Less obviously severe than a death spell was the more commonly used curse. Although a curse was kept secret, it could be said directly, without the need of a sorcerer: "Be forever accursed for your wrongdoing." If the victim discovered the curse and considered himself guiltless, he could reject the curse and send it flying back to its original dispatcher: "What you have just given me, so return to you." This reversal was not said to work if the victim were indeed guilty, although one could have a curse removed by beseeching the sender's forgiveness, and amending the perceived wrongdoing.

If forgiveness was sought, pardon had to be granted and the curse removed. One who regretted making a curse could countermand it by declaring his wish to take the curse with him when he died, just as a victim could ask the corpse of one who had cursed him to free him from a spell. One who was dying could also assume all the outstanding curses in a family to take into the next world with him—a kind of curse debit account in which the balance would be erased.

The Source of the Darkness
That Made Darkness

In the winter of 1776, the English explorer and navigator Captain James Cook left London on his third journey to the Pacific as commander of HMS *Resolution*, accompanied by the ship HMS *Discovery*, under the command of Captain Charles Clerke, who had been Cook's second lieutenant on an earlier voyage to the Pacific (1772–1775). Cook's second lieutenant on the *Resolution* was a young officer named James King, who was responsible for astronomical observations, along with James Burney, who was second lieutenant on the *Discovery*. William Bligh, who later commanded HMS *Bounty*, was master's mate aboard the *Discovery*. Serving under Cook were George Vancouver (midshipman), Nathaniel Portlock (master's mate), and George Dixon (armourer), all three of whom became distinguished officers and explorers. Cook also had on board a Tahitian man named Omai, who had been a curiosity in London, and whom he was returning to his home island of Huahine, as well as a bull, two cows with their calves, and some sheep that he hoped to give to the Tahitians.

Born in 1728, Cook was the son of a Yorkshire day laborer. His quickness and intelligence were evident in childhood, and one of his father's employers arranged for him to go to school (his disappointed father had hoped that he would become a shopkeeper). He had a passion for the sea and was apprenticed on a coal ship, which was considered hard training for any man. He later volunteered in the Seven Years' War, and within a month's time, was promoted to master's mate, taking part in the survey of the St. Lawrence River and parts of the Newfoundland and Nova Scotia coasts, which earned him distinction as a skilled marine surveyor. In 1766, when he witnessed an eclipse of the sun, his notes were sent to London, where he became known at the Royal Society and the Admiralty as an astute observer.

His first voyage to the Pacific in 1768 had been to observe the Transit of Venus from Tahiti, and to verify the existence of the continent of Australia. Cook's confidential charge from the Admiralty had been to observe "with accuracy the Situation of such Islands as you may discover in the Course of your Voyage that have not hitherto been discover'd by any Europeans and take possession for His Majesty and make Surveys and Draughts of such of them as may appear to be of Consequence . . . You are likewise to observe the Genius, Temper, Disposition and Number of the Natives . . . the Beasts and Fowls that inhabit or frequent it, the fishes that are to be found in the Rivers or upon the coast and in what Plenty." The Admiralty particularly wished Cook to find a passage from the northwest coast of America to the Atlantic Ocean.

Sailing to Polynesia for the third time in 1776, Cook stopped at Van Diemen's Land (Tasmania) and New Zealand, storing supplies of wild celery and scurvy grass, before continuing to Tonga and Tahiti, where he was cured of a bad attack of rheumatism (he was in his early forties) by being punched and squeezed from head to foot by native healers. Before leaving Tahiti in September 1777, bound for North America, Cook inquired if the natives knew of any land or islands to the north or northwest, and they said that they knew of none.

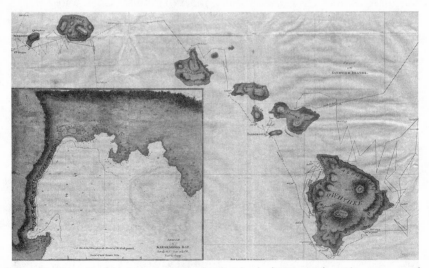

Captain James Cook's visit to the Sandwich Islands (1776–1779), with an insert of Kealakekua Bay, from the 1785 edition of Cook's and Lieutenant James King's book, *A Voyage to the Pacific Ocean . . . in the Years 1776, 1777, 1778, 1779, and 1780,* possibly drawn by Lieutenant William Bligh

Four months later, on January 18, 1778, Cook sighted the island of O'ahu, and shortly after, the island of Kaua'i. At sunrise the next day, O'ahu was several leagues to the east, and Cook bore north, discovering yet a third island, Ni'ihau (he gave to his discovery the name Sandwich Islands, after his patron, the Earl of Sandwich, First Lord of the Admiralty). Cook saw several villages on the larger island of Kaua'i, both along the beach and on the hillsides, but the wind prevented the ships from approaching the island, whose name Cook pronounced in the Tahitian style, "Atooi." The ships stood off and on during the night, tacking along the southeastern coast and nearing land the following day, when canoes of curious natives came to the ships. Cook wrote in his journal:

> It required but very little address to get them to come along side, but we could not prevail upon any one to come on board; they exchanged a few fish they had in the Canoes for any thing we offered them, but valued nails, or iron above every other thing; the only weapons they had were a few stones in some of the Canoes and these they threw overboard when they found they were not wanted. Seeing no signs of an anchoring place at this part of the island, I boar [*sic*] up for the lee side, and ranged the SE side at the distance of half a league from the shore. As soon as we made sail the Canoes left us, but others came off from the shore and brought with them roasting pigs and some very fine Potatoes . . . several small pigs were got for a sixpeny [*sic*] nail or two apiece, so that we again found our selves in the land of plenty . . .

Cook was still unable to anchor the following day, when natives again left the beach in canoes and paddled to the ships, which they approached with less fear than they had shown the previous day. "One asked another," wrote the historian David Malo, "'What are those branching things?' and the other answered, 'They are trees moving about on the sea.' . . . The excitement became more intense, and louder grew the shouting."

At the first sight of the mysterious ships, some of the chiefs had been eager to kill the strangers before running the ships ashore for plunder. Other chiefs, recalling the legend of Lono, the harvest god who had promised to return one day to the Islands, wished to humor them, and gave them gifts of pigs and bananas. The chiefs met in counsel, where after some dissension it was decided to send yet more gifts. John Rickman, second lieutenant on the

A view of the village of Waimea on "Atooi," Cook's rendering of the name of the island of Kauaʻi. Engraving after a drawing by John Webber, 1778

Discovery, wrote in his *Journal of Captain Cook's Last Voyage to the Pacific Ocean* (1781) that, "This diffused a joy among the mariners that is not easy to be expressed. Fresh provisions and kind females are the sailors sole delight; and when in possession of them, past hardships are instantly forgotten; even those whom the scurvy had attacked, and had rendered pale and lifeless as ghosts, brightened upon this occasion, and for the moment appeared alert."

Among the women taken to the ships was Lelemahoalani, the daughter of the high chiefess of Kauaʻi, who, it is claimed by David Malo, spent the night with Cook, who was more and more thought to be the avatar of the god Lono: "And Lono slept with that woman, and the Kauai women prostituted themselves to the foreigners for iron." If it is true, Cook, who was said to be abstemious regarding alcohol and women, consorted that first night in Waimea with a pagan princess. (Judge Fornander wrote in 1870 that the last generation of Hawaiians whom he interviewed openly claimed that Lelemahoalani slept with Lono—that is, with James Cook.)

Cook was at first, and perhaps always, unaware that the Hawaiians saw him as Lono. David Samwell, surgeon on board the *Discovery*, quickly perceived the difficulties inherent in deciphering and understanding the language of the Hawaiians, both symbolic and literal, as well as the behavior

Portrait of Captain James Cook. Oil painting by John Webber, 1782, National Portrait Gallery, Canberra

of a people so profoundly unknown to them, despite Cook's somewhat vainglorious belief that he understood the Indians, as he called them, very well. Samwell wrote that, "There is not much dependence to be placed upon these Constructions that we put upon Signs and Words which we understand but very little of, & at best can only give a probable Guess at their Meaning."

Certain similarities (not unlike the coincidences and seeming fulfillments of prophecies that marked the arrival of Hernán Cortés in Mexico in 1519) caused the Hawaiians to believe that Cook was the god's incarnation—Cook appeared at the time of Lono's Makahiki festival, and the god's traditional symbol, a white length of *kapa* wrapped around a wooden cross-bar, was very like the sails of Cook's ships. Some historians speculate that a mysterious voyager in the distant past had arrived in the Islands at the same time of year, carrying with him tributary offerings and new gods. The stranger introduced games, athletic competitions, and a system of annual taxation in which much wealth was acquired by the god during his counterclockwise circuit of the island before he departed for Kahiki, the inclusive name of all distant places from Easter Island to Malaysia, with the promise to return someday.

The understandably wary Hawaiians grew sufficiently reassured to approach Cook's ships in greater numbers. Cook wrote in his journal that, "Their eyes were continually flying from object to object, the wildness of their looks and actions fully express'd their surprise and astonishment, at the several new objects before them and evinced that they had never been on board of a ship before." The Hawaiians wondered where they might sit, and if they were allowed to spit. Others fell to the deck and prayed. They thought the white men were saying, *"A hikapalalē, hinolue o walwala ki pohā,"* untranslatable gibberish which has since become an expression meaning anything incomprehensible. When they saw the sailors eating melon, they thought that it was human flesh, and gave them the name *akua waha ʻulaʻula*, or red-mouthed gods. They believed the tricornered hats of the officers were part of their heads, and the sailors' clothing their skin, with holes in the sides from which they drew treasure.

The people seemed friendly to Cook, despite a troublesome propensity to steal. Once they realized that stealing would not be tolerated, they began to trade sweet potatoes as large as fourteen pounds for nails and other pieces of iron lowered to them on ropes by the sailors. Some scholars believe, as did Cook, that in the sixteenth century, Spanish ships en route to the Philippines and ports farther west introduced the Hawaiians to iron, while other historians insist that the natives' familiarity with metal came from scavenged wreckage. If a log with iron nails washed ashore, it was by tradition offered to the gods—that is, to the priests—who then presented it to the *aliʻi nui*. (Kamehameha I is said to have first uttered the proverb *"O luna, o lalo; o kai, o uka—o ka hao pae ko ke aliʻi ia."* "Above, below; seaward, inland—the iron that washes ashore belongs to the chief.") A small nail could get the British enough pigs to last them a day, and they soon had as many stores as they could carry, which was fortunate as the supply of iron that they could spare was fast diminishing.

On HMS *Discovery*, Captain Clerke was honored with a visit from a high chief, which caused the Hawaiian men already on board to leap into the ocean. The curious chief was polite, but his attendants, upset that Clerke had clapped him on the shoulder in greeting, kept their distance, refusing to allow the chief to step all the way on deck. The chief's large double canoe slid unconcernedly over the small canoes of commoners and lesser chiefs, many of whom quickly threw themselves onto the bottoms of their canoes, or jumped into the water to submerge their heads. Cook himself noted:

> Three things made them our fast friends, Their own good Natured and benevolent disposition, gentle treatment on our part, and the dread of our Fire arms; by our ceaseing [*sic*] to observe the Second the first would have worn of [off] of Course, and the too frequent use of the latter would have excited a spirit of revenge and perhaps have taught them that fire Arms were not such terrible things as they had imagined, they are very sencible [*sic*] of the superiority they have over us in numbers and no one knows what an enraged multitude might do.

When one of the Hawaiians could not resist the theft of a butcher's cleaver and jumped overboard with it, Cook did not hesitate to send boats after him, under the charge of an Irishman named Williamson. When Williamson fired at the man, the Hawaiians who were on board Cook's ship took fright and dove into the ocean, but the thief swam safely to shore and disappeared. Lieutenant Williamson had also been given the task of finding a watering place on the island, and as he approached land, natives rushed into the surf and jumped into the boats, grabbing the muskets and oars, causing Williamson again to shoot at them. This time, a Hawaiian was killed, and there was no further trouble.

As early as the second day of his landing, Cook took precautions to keep the venereal disease that was manifest among his men from spreading to the Hawaiians:

> As there were some venereal complaints on board both the Ships, in order to prevent its being communicated to these people, I gave orders that no Women, on any account whatever were to be admitted on board the Ships, I also forbid all manner of connection with them and ordered that none who had the venereal upon them should go out

of the ships. But whether these regulations had the desired effect or no time can only discover. It is no more than what I did when I first visited the Friendly Islands [Tonga] yet I afterwards found it did not succeed.

Cook gave orders that only one man accompany Lieutenant Williamson ashore to replenish the ships' supply of fresh water, "that I might do everything in my power to prevent the importation of a fatal disease into this island, which I knew some of our men now laboured under, and which, unfortunately, had been already communicated by us to other islands in these seas."

The village of Waimea had perhaps sixty houses near the beach, with another forty inland. Cook, who was mystified by the tall towers he saw on the hillside, unlike anything he had seen in the Pacific, walked inland with William Anderson, the ship's doctor, and the ship's artist, John Webber. The towers were built alongside a number of stone platforms, which the men recognized as similar to the *marae*, or temples, of Tahiti. Their native guide showed them the *kanaka kapu*, where the bodies of sacrificial victims were buried, and pointed out the skulls of dead chiefs lining the tops of the temple's stone walls.

A few days later, the *Resolution* was driven by strong winds across the channel to Ni'ihau, where salt, water, and yams were taken on board. Cook gave the islanders some goats, pigs, and seeds, but the anchor of his ship began to drag, and Cook soon left the Sandwich Islands, sailing northwest to the Aleutians, which were his original destination.

Cook considered his cruise that winter along the coast of North America to be a failure in that he did not find a passage from the Pacific to the Atlantic (the English navigator Sir Martin Frobisher had begun the search in 1576), although he did succeed in making for the first time a map of the coast. Cook's sailors liked to claim that even when a ship was far from land, Cook's intuition would wake him at night and he would come on deck to change course. Despite his reputation for abstinence (Lieutenant King wrote that Cook's temperance could hardly be considered a virtue, so great was his self-denial), according to David Samwell, Cook always kept a good table at sea. It is thought by some scholars, however, that at the end of this third voyage, Cook had begun to tire, and as a consequence suffered lapses in stamina, which caused him to decide not to spend the seven long months of winter in Kamchatka, as he had planned. Instead, he turned his ships once again to the Pacific, convinced that there were as yet more islands in the Hawaiian archipelago.

One month after leaving Alaska, he was gratified to see the coast of Maui and, later that day, the island of Moloka'i rising on the horizon. The canoes of the Hawaiians made for the ships as they neared Maui. When men came on board to barter, Cook was alarmed to see that some of them showed symptoms of venereal disease. Lieutenant King wrote that three of the Hawaiians asked for help "in their great distress: they had a Clap, their Penis was much swell'd, & inflamed." There was animated discussion among Cook and his officers whether it was possible that the disease could have spread so quickly in the ten months they had been in the Northwest, and whether Cook's men could be held responsible for it. At both Kaua'i and Ni'ihau, Cook's order that women be kept from the ships had proved impossible to enforce, especially as the sailors had taken to disguising the women as men to sneak them on board. Cook had little doubt that his men had infected the Hawaiians, and he was despondent that his measures to prevent the spread of the disease had failed. King wrote that "[t]he manner in which these innocent People complained to us, seem'd to me to shew that they consider'd us the Original authors." A dispirited Cook did not enforce his order to keep women from the ships.

"The god enters, man cannot enter in" . . . so sang poets, seated before the great temples, as they intoned the verses of the Kumulipo. But on that misfortunate day, when at last the ocean-moat had been crossed, not only the god entered in. Man, too, entered in—lustful, carnal, heedless, and diseased man rushed in, thrusting aside all the guardian deities of Heaven and Earth. "The source of the darkness that made darkness" had come.

That November, Kalaniōpu'u, king of Hawai'i Island, described by Lieutenant King as "a little old man, of an emaciated figure; his eyes exceedingly sore and red, and his body covered with a white leprous scurf," sailed in his double canoe from Maui, where he had been at war, to see the strange white men for himself. Among his warriors was the young Kohala chief, Kamehameha, who the British noticed was a particular favorite of the king. When Kalaniōpu'u, who was Kamehameha's uncle, left Cook's ship, Kamehameha

King Kalaniōpuʻu, with gifts of feather capes and idols, greeting James Cook at Kealakekua Bay. Detail from pen, ink wash, and watercolor by John Webber, ca. 1781–1783, State Library of New South Wales, Sydney remained on board with five other young chiefs. Kalaniōpuʻu sent a fast canoe to bring the chiefs to shore, but they refused to leave, and the canoe was towed astern through the night.

Kamehameha, who was seven feet tall, was a descendant of the old Polynesian stock, dynamic and dominant, whose traits are said to be particular to natives of the Big Island. The southern tip of Hawaiʻi Island was the landing place of the first voyagers of the sixth century, and the strength of its people is attributed to the rough grandeur and looming danger of the landscape. The future king was born around 1750 (Abraham Fornander and Samuel Kamakau believed that he was born in 1736; Don Francisco de Marín, a Spanish adventurer who lived in Honolulu, wrote in his diary that the king was sixty-six when he died, which would place his birth in 1753; the Hawaiian Historical Society concludes that Kamehameha was born sometime between 1752 and 1761; Kamehameha's friend and adviser, the English sailor John Young, claimed he was born in 1748) in Kōkoiki, near ʻUpolu Point in North Kohala. His father was the high chief Keōua of Kona, and his mother was Kekuʻiapoiwa II, a high-ranking chiefess of Maui. There is a legend that during Kekuʻiapoiwa's pregnancy, she wished to eat the eyeball of a chief (she was given the eye of a shark instead), an omen that the child she was carrying would one day become king. The night before his birth, a blazing streak passed across the sky, later thought to be Halley's Comet (which would make his birthdate the winter of 1758). It was taken as another omen, as were the rain, thunder, and lightning that marked his birth.

Because of these signs, certain *aliʻi* in the court of the child's great uncle, King Alapaʻinui of Hilo, conspired to kill the infant, saying the words, "*E ʻaki maka o ka lauhue.*" "Nip off the bud of the poison gourd."

A numerous guard had been set to await the time of birth. The chiefs kept awake with the guards (for a time), but due to the rain and the cold, the chiefs fell asleep, and near daybreak Ke-kuʻi-apo-iwa went into the house and, turning her face to the side of the house at the gable end, braced her feet against the wall. A certain stranger was outside the house listening, and when he heard the sound of the last bearing-down pain . . . he lifted the thatch at the side of the house, and made a hole above. As soon as the child was born, had slipped down upon the tapa spread out to receive it, and Ke-kuʻi-apo-iwa had stood up and let the afterbirth . . . come away, he covered the child in the tapa and carried it away. When the chiefs awoke they were puzzled at the disappearance of the child. Kohala was searched that day and houses burned.

The "certain stranger" was Naeʻole, a chief of Kohala loyal to the child's father. Naeʻole was pursued through the night and at last trapped, but he was allowed to keep the infant, and to become his *kahu*. The two lived alone in the isolated ʻĀwini gulch of North Kohala, earning the boy the nickname the Lonely One, until he was five years old, when he was taken to Hilo by Alapaʻinui to be raised at court, as befitted a chief.

At the death of Kamehameha's father, thought to have been poisoned by Alapaʻinui, his father's half brother Kalaniōpuʻu attempted to send a war canoe to bring him south to Kaʻū, but rival chiefs discovered the plan and Kamehameha remained in Hilo. When Alapaʻinui died, Kalaniōpuʻu, who inherited the title of *aliʻi nui*, at last brought Kamehameha to his court, where he continued his training in warcraft and religious ritual.

Tattooed Hawaiian chief. Lithograph by Antoine Maurin, after a drawing by Jacques Arago, 1819, Honolulu Museum of Art

Kamehameha was one of eight hundred chiefs renowned for their bravery and high martial skills who formed Kalaniōpuʻu's elite force known as the Chiefly Army of Keawe. Agile, swift, and cunning, he was said to be utterly without fear, not only in battle but, perhaps more important, in his acceptance of new and strange ideas and people. Along with his younger brother, Kealiʻimaikaʻi, he was considered one of the handsomest men of his time, and the two were given many gifts and favors by the chiefesses who sought them as lovers. Kamehameha seduced Kalaniōpuʻu's wife, or perhaps it was she who seduced him, and she had a child by the young prince.

Thus beautiful physiques and handsome features earned them a livelihood. This led to trouble with their uncle Kalaniopuʻu, for they were taken by Kaneikapolei, wife of Kalaniopuʻu. This happened twice . . . Their uncle was "peeved" and would not allow his nephews to see his face . . . [Keaweamauhili] told his half-brother Kalaniopuʻu to stop resenting his nephews because everyone knew that a woman was like an easily opened calabash, or a container with a removable lid. Upon these words, Kalaniopuʻu's anger ceased, and he sent for his nephews to come see him.

The historian Gavan Daws writes in his book, *Shoal of Time* (1968), that Kamehameha was tall and "physically fearless," and "moved in an aura of violence . . . Already he had a considerable notoriety, and he paraded it with an imperiousness that matched and even exceeded his rank as a high chief." According to Lieutenant King of the *Resolution*, Kamehameha's hair was "plaisted over with a brown dirty sort of paste or powder, & which added to as savage a looking face as I ever saw, it however by no means seemed an emblem of his disposition, which was good natur'd & humorous, although his manner shewd somewhat of an overbearing spirit."

Kamehameha and the chiefs left Cook's ship the morning following their first meeting and Cook crossed the channel from Maui, seeing for the first time the island of Hawaiʻi. The ships hove to off the Kohala coast, and for the month of December beat round the east side of the island, sailing close to shore when they needed to trade with the natives. Cook was dismayed, as a naval officer, by the lack of fortification and, to his eyes, the disorder of the villages along the coast.

Though they seem to have adopted the mode of living in villages, there is no appearance of defense, or fortification, near any of them; and the houses are scattered about, without any order; either with respect to their distances from each other, or their position in any particular direction. Neither is there any proportion as to their size; some being large and commodious, from forty to fifty feet long, and twenty or thirty broad, while others of them are mere hovels . . . The entrance is made indifferently in the end or side, and is an oblong hole, so low, that one must rather creep than walk in; and is often shut up by a board or planks, fastened together, which serves as a door; but having no hinges, must be removed occasionally. No light enters the house, but by this opening; and though such close habitations may afford a comfortable retreat in bad weather, they seem but ill-adapted to the warmth of the climate. They are, however, kept remarkably clean; and their floors are covered with a large quantity of dried grass, over which they spread mats to sit and sleep upon. At one end stands a kind of bench, about three feet high, on which their household utensils are placed. The catalogue is not long. It consists of gourd shells, which they convert into vessels that serve as bottles to hold water, and as baskets to contain their victuals, and other things, with covers of the same; and of a few wooden bowls and trenchers of different sizes.

At daybreak on January, 17, 1779, when a safe anchorage was at last spotted on the west coast of Hawai'i Island, the ships entered Kealakekua Bay, in the district of Kona. Cook and his men were astonished to find numbers of people awaiting them. Nowhere in the Pacific had Cook seen such a gathering of natives. Eight hundred canoes circled the ships, and the water was full of men, women, and children who had swum from shore. The officers estimated that there were at least twenty thousand people in the water, in canoes, and on the beach, where they held wooden images wrapped in sheets of white cloth, and gifts of bananas and squealing pigs.

Women came to the ships to offer themselves to the sailors in exchange for scissors, beads, iron, and mirrors. When they first saw their likenesses, the women were frightened, thinking the mirrors alive, and scraped away the quicksilver, only to regret their haste once their reflections disappeared. The British worried that so many nails would be extracted from the ships, both by the sailors to give to the women, and by Hawaiian men who used their

Kealakekua Bay with Cook's ships HMS *Discovery* and HMS *Resolution*, and Hikiau *heiau*, dedicated to the war god Kū. Engraving after pen, ink wash, and watercolor by John Webber, 1779

new gifts of adzes to pry loose the nails, that the ships would soon be pulled apart.

John Rickman wrote that the king's son, most probably Kiwalaʻo, came to the ships with a small cooked pig and some breadfruit, wearing a "curious mantle of red feathers." The pig was exchanged for several axes, mirrors, bracelets, and "other shewy articles which took his fancy." Rickman watched as King Kalaniōpuʻu sailed into Kealakekua Bay accompanied by more than 150 large war canoes, carrying four idols covered with cloaks of red, yellow, black, and green feathers, said to be war gods. John Ledyard wrote in his journal:

> On the 22nd of January some of the chiefs and other warriors, who had been at Mauwee [Maui] came into the bay and the next day several more hundred made their appearance but it was not until the 25th that Kireeaboo [Kalaniōpuʻu] came. He was attended by a number of double canoes, the largest we had ever seen, being between 60 and 70 feet in length, and a large retinue of stout, comely, bold looking hardy chiefs, besides other attendants and about 30 men with paddles. In the fore and hinder parts of his canoes were placed several ill-formed images of wicker work covered with a variety of feathers, of different colours, but chiefly red and black. These they carry to war with them. They took little notice of the ships as they entered the bay, but landed immediately on the beach near our encampment, which

Cook observing, and being anxious to salute Kireeaboo rowed in his penance [pinnace] directly to the tents from whence he went out to meet him . . . They seemed from that moment to conceive an uncommon attachment to each other. Kireeaboo was an old man and very feeble about 5 feet 8 inches high, and of a slender make, he had a countenance very expressive of conscious dignity and merit, and conducted himself at all times worthy a ruler of the people.

Kireeaboo made his dinner solely with bread-fruit and a drink of water; but his chiefs who were younger, used both pork and fowls— they made no use of knives or forks, and cramed [*sic*] their mouths as full as they possibly could, but the quantity they eat was very moderate, they also drank only water, refusing wine, porter, rum or any other kind of liquor. After dinner they were conducted upon deck, where they were again highly entertained with a new scene, and one much better adapted to their understanding than that they had lately been at on shore. Some of them were employed in measuring the ship's length, and others her breadth, which they did with a line, and then measured it into fathoms as we do, and some of them ventured as far aloft as the main and fore-tops . . . None of them would go higher or offer to venture out upon the yards. Others again were in the ship's hold at which they expressed the utmost admiration. Kireeaboo was on the quarter deck with Cook, and had every minute some of the chiefs running to him and relating what they had seen for his information. After this the penance was manned with the crew in black caps and white shirts, and rowing uniformly to the Discovery, the French horn playing. The evening was spent on board with Capt. Clerke. Kireeaboo was so much pleased with the attention that had been shewn him and his chiefs that he desired Cook and Clerke would spend the next day with him and his chiefs on shore, desiring also that they would bring their chiefs with them, which was readily agreed to, and the next morning both Captains and all the officers that could attend dressed in their uniforms, and went to Kiverua where Kireeaboo generally resided. They all dined together in Kireeaboo's house: The dinner consisted of a hog and potatoes baked after their manner spread on green plantain-leaves, round which they all seated themselves cross-legged, there was no ceremony, except that of washing the mouth and hands both before and after dinner with clean water, and the only utensils at the feast were pieces of bamboo, which were used as knives; the natives drank water, and our officers to conform as near as possible to the contour of the entertainment drank cocoanut-milk. After dinner they went out to take the air under an adjacent shade, where they were entertained with a dance by the women while they were voluptuously stretched along the grass or reclined against the trees. One of the gentlemen from the Discovery brought his violin with him, and one from the Resolution, a german-flute, and as the company seemed to want a variety, they played upon each in turn. The violin produced the most immoderate laughter among the natives, who seemed to relish it as many do the bagpipe, or much more indifferently, but when we accompanied it by a voluntary dance or cotillion they had a different opinion, the flute they much admired and examined very curiously. The drum and fife (though not present) is the music they most delight in. When the fun was upon the decline Kiree-aboo and his suite crossed the bay to Kirakakooa in order to compleat the entertainment of his guests by an exhibition of the gymnastic kind at which a large concourse of people of all denominations were present.

Captain Cook, Lieutenant King (who was thought by the Hawaiians to be Cook's son), and the ship's astronomer William Bayly went ashore to look at the temples. King wrote that they were met by an old priest named Koa, and four men who carried sticks tipped with dog hair, "pronouncing with a loud voice a short sentence, in which we could only distinguish the word Orono [Lono] . . . The crowd, which had been collected on the shore, retired at our approach; and not a person was to be seen, except a few lying prostrate on the ground." The priests led Cook and his men to a platform of stones with a wooden tower ('anu'u), similar to the structures the men had first seen on Kaua'i. The following is from the log of Captain Clerke:

We enterd the Area on one side near the houses, and the Captain was made to stop at two rude images of Wood, the faces only were Carved, & made to represent most distort'd mouths; with a long piece of Carved Wood on the head. These images had pieces of old Cloth wrap'd round them, & at the foot . . . a few old Coconut husks. After Koa and a tall grave young man with a long beard whose name was Keliikea repeated a few words, we were led to the Area where the

A ritual offering made in the presence of Captain Cook and his officers. Engraving after pen, ink wash, and watercolor by John Webber, 1778

Scaffold was; At the foot of this were 12 Images ranged in a semicircular form, fronting those opposite the Center figures was a corrupt'd hog, placed on a stand, supportd by posts 6 feet high, exactly resembling the haka of Tahiti, & at the foot were many pieces of Sugar Cane. Coconuts. Breadfruit &c. Koa led the Captain under this Stand, & after handling the hog and Repeating a prayer, he let it drop, & conducted him, to the Scaffolding which they ascended, not without great risk of tumbling, Koa kept hold of the Captain's hand . . . For some time Keliikea & Koa kept repeating sentences in concert & alternately, & many times appeared to be interrogating; at last . . . he and the Captain descended, & Koa led him to different images, said something to each but in a very ludicrous & Slighting tone, except to the Center image; which was the only one cover'd with Cloth, & was only three feet hight, whilst the rest were Six; to this he prostrated himself, & afterwards kiss'd, and desir'd the Captain to do the same, who was quite passive, & suffer'd Koa to do with him as he chose.

Heiau at Kealakekua, with skulls on the palings. From a drawing by William Ellis, 1782

The ceremony continued with a procession of men, and more chants and the chewing of ʻawa (*Piper methysticum*), while the word "Arono" was repeated without pause. "The Captain recollecting . . . the Putrid hog could not get a morsel down," wrote King, "not even when the old fellow [Koa] very Politely chew'd it for him."

During the month of January, the ships were refitted and the victuals they had received as gifts or in exchange for goods were preserved and stored. An observatory to study the night sky was set up in a sweet potato field made *kapu* by Kalaniōpuʻu to ensure that the foreigners were not disturbed in their work. Lieutenant King described Hikiau *heiau*, sacred to the god Kū, on the same beach where Cook would soon be killed:

> It was a square solid pile of stones, about forty yards long, twenty broad, and fourteen in height. The top was flat and well paved, and surrounded by a wooden rail, on which were fixed the skulls of the captives sacrificed on the death of their chiefs. In the centre of the area stood a ruinous old building of wood, connected with the rail on each side by a stone wall, which divided the whole space into two parts. On the side next the country were five poles, upward of twenty feet high,

supporting an irregular kind of scaffold; on the opposite side toward the sea, stood two small houses with a covered communication.

On January 26, Kalaniōpuʻu again visited the ships. Lieutenant King wrote that the chiefs were most magnificent:

In the first canoe was Terreeoboo [Kalaniopuʻu] and his chiefs, dressed in their rich feathered clokes [*sic*] and helmets, and armed with long spears and daggers; in the second, came the venerable Kaoo, the chief of the priests, and his brethren, with their idols displayed on red cloth. These idols were busts of a gigantic size, made of wicker-work, and curiously covered with small feathers of various colours, wrought in the same manner with their cloaks. Their eyes were made of large pearl oysters, with a black nut fixed in the centre; their mouths were set with a double row of the fangs of dogs . . . The third canoe was filled with hogs and various sorts of vegetables. As they went along, the priests in the centre canoe sung their hymns with great solemnity; and after paddling round the ships, instead of going on board, as was expected, they made toward the shore.

The British returned the generosity of the Hawaiians by arranging a show of fireworks on the beach, the occasion of the first of many misunderstand-ings. John Ledyard wrote in his journal:

As soon as it was well dark, Cook landed at the spot where the prepa-rations were, attended by Kireeaboo, and a great number of men and women in their canoes. The natives had been some of them all day waiting, and their expectations were wound up to the last extremity, some of them had begun to jeer us, and expressed contempt of our heiva as they called it. Cook expected some laughable circumstances, and was willing to improve it, he therefore took the necessary precau-tions, and when every thing was ready, and the people as silent as the night he ordered a sky-rocket off. I do think this part of the scene undescribable—Cook and the officers near him certainly could not do it they were so entirely overcome with laughter: They could hardly hold the old feeble Kireeaboo and some elderly ladies of quality that sat among them, and before they had any ways recovered themselves from this paroxysm nearly the whole host that a moment before surrounded them had fled, some towards the town, some to the hills, and some into the water, many they did not know where, and many had been trampled under foot and remained motionless there. It however happened luckily that the object which at first caused their fear did not long continue, and as that expired the terrors of those who fled as well as the few who remained behind subsided.

As the time neared for Cook's departure, the British discovered that there was a shortage of firewood on the ships. To the surprise of Lieutenant King, the priests agreed to give them the outer fence of the *heiau*, including some of the wooden images, asking the officers repeatedly when they thought they might sail from the bay, as their supply of food and firewood was growing short. Samuel Kamakau wrote that the Hawaiians were also beginning to wonder if Cook and his men were indeed gods: "One man said, 'The woman who was on the ship says that they groan when they are hurt. When the woman sticks her nails into them they say, You scratch like an owl; your nails are too long; you claw like a duck!'" The Hawaiians suggested to Lieutenant King, whom they admired, that he remain behind, offering to hide him until the British ships were out of sight.

The two ships at last left Kealakekua on the morning of February 6, having exhausted the Hawaiians' food reserves, as well as their good will. John Ledyard wrote in the log of the *Discovery*:

On the evening of the 5th we struck our tents, and every thing was taken on board, and it was very manifestly much to the satisfaction of the natives. A little after dark an old house that stood on a corner of the Morai [*heiau*] took fire and burnt down; this we supposed was occasioned by our people carelessly leaving their fire near it, but it was not the case, the natives burnt it themselves, to shew us the resentment they entertained toward us, on account of our using it without their consent, and indeed manifestly against it. We had made a sail loft of one part of it, and an hospital for our sick of the other, though it evidently was esteemed by the natives as holy as the rest of the Morai, and ought to have been considered so by us.

We had now been 19 days in the bay of Kireekakooa, in the Island of Owyhee, we had repaired our ships, had regaled and refreshed our people, and had lain in a supply of pork that would probably support us six months; the only article we wanted in particular was water, which was here very brackish and bad. In order therefore to procure a supply of this necessary article, we determined to visit the island of Mauwee, where we were informed by the natives we might get plenty of it, and that there was a good harbour.

On the 6th of Feb we unmoored and came to sail standing along the south side of Owyhee, intending to visit Mauwee and water our ships.

On the 7th we had a hard gale of wind, and being close in with the southern and western shore of Owyhee, which being high land had occasioned the wind that came partly off the land to come in irregular and most terrible gusts, such as we had never seen.

On the 8th the gale became not only more violent but more irregular and embarrassing, and before night was improved into a mere hurricane; we wrenched the head of our foremast, and sprung it about 9 feet below the hounds [top of the mainmast], and also made a great deal of water. During this severe night the Discovery had lost us.

On the 9th the violence of the gale or rather the tornado ceased, but the excessive mutability of the wind, and the irregular sea, was such as demanded our best skill and unremitted attention to keep the ship under any kind of command.

On the 10th the weather became tolerably settled, and hauling off the land we saw the Discovery in the S.E. quarter, and before night spoke her all well. We informed her of our situation, and that in consequence of the misfortune, it was determined to return again to our old harbor at Kireekakooa.

On the 11th of Feb we again entered Kireekakooa bay, and moored both ships in their old berths.

On the 12th we got the foremast out and sent it on shore with the carpenters, we also sent our two observatories on shore, and a markee for a guard of marines.

Our return to this bay was disagreeable to us as it was to the inhabitants, for we were reciprocally tired of each other. They had been oppressed and were weary of our prostituted alliance, and we were aggrieved by the consideration of wanting the provisions and refreshments of the country which we had every reason to suppose for their behavior antecedent to our departure would not be withheld from us or brought in such small quantities as to be worse than none. What we anticipated was true. When we entered the bay where before we had the shouts of thousands to welcome our arrival, we had the mortification not to see a single canoe, and hardly any inhabitants in the towns. Cook was chagrined and his people were soured. Towards night however the canoes came in, but the provisions both in quantity and quality plainly informed us that times were altered, and what was very remarkable was the exorbitant price they asked; and the particular fancy they all at once took to iron daggers or dirks, which was the only article that was any ways current, with the chiefs at least. It was also equally evident from the looks of the natives as well as every other appearance that our former friendship was at an end, and that we had nothing to do but to hasten our departure to some different island where our vices were not known, and where our extrinsic virtues might gain us another short space of being wondered at, and doing as we pleased, or as our tars expressed it, of being happy by the month.

Returning to Kealakekua Bay, Cook was surprised by the hostility of the Hawaiians. On the night of February 14, the *Discovery's* cutter was stolen. A landing party was sent ashore with orders to take Kalaniōpuʻu hostage until the boat was returned, and boats were sent to the north and south ends of the bay to keep any canoes from leaving. At eight o'clock the next morning, Cook left the ship with nine marines under the command of Lieutenant Molesworth Phillips, while Lieutenant King was stationed at the observatory in case there was trouble on shore. Cook found Kalaniōpuʻu in the village. While the king was not responsible for the theft of the cutter, he agreed to go with Cook, accompanied by his two young sons. As the party reached the beach, however, the king's wife and some of his men learned that a chief had been shot in the bay, and refused to let the king go with Cook. The number of Hawaiians on the beach began to grow, and Phillips lined up his marines on some nearby rocks. Cook, realizing that there might be violence, had abandoned his plan to take Kalaniōpu'u prisoner, when a messenger from one of the boats ran up with the news, already known to the queen and chiefs, that a canoe had tried to leave the bay and shots had been fired, killing an important chief.

At this news, the already agitated Hawaiians grew enraged, and began to throw stones at the sailors. As Cook and Phillips made for their boat, Cook was threatened by a man carrying a large iron spike, and he fired a round of small shot. The man was wearing a thick mat as armor and was not hurt, but one of the chiefs attempted to stab Phillips, who hit him with the butt of his musket. Cook fired again, killing a man. It is thought by some that Cook was waving to the boats to come to shore, rather than signaling to them to shoot, but the marines began to fire into the crowd from their position on the rocks. The Hawaiians rushed at them, killing four marines and wounding others, and Phillips was injured. Cook was struck from behind and fell face-down in the surf. The Hawaiians held his head under water as they thrust their spears and iron daggers into him. Unable to save Cook, Phillips and the marines dragged the wounded to the boats and rowed to the ships. Thirty Hawaiians had been killed, including eight chiefs.

Once on board, Clerke took command. The British were stunned. It was inconceivable that Cook was dead. King was sent to recover his body, but was told that it had already been cut into pieces in preparation for burning. The following night, a priest arrived in a canoe with some of Cook's bones, scraped of flesh and wrapped in a bundle of *kapa*. Cook's body, he said, had been treated with the reverence due a high chief. King wrote that the bones were covered with a cloak of black and white feathers:

> We found in it both the hands of Captain Cook entire, which were well known, from a remarkable scar on one of them, that divided the thumb from the forefinger, the whole length of the metacarpal bone; the skull, but with the scalp separated from it, and the bones that form the face wanting; the scalp, with the hair upon it cut short, and the ears adhering to it; the bones of both arms, with the skin of the fore arms hanging to them. The thigh and leg bones joined together,

The death of Captain James Cook, February 14, 1779. Oil painting by Johann Zoffany, 1794, National Maritime Museum, Greenwich

but without the feet. The ligaments of the joints were entire; and the whole bore evident marks of having been in the fire, except the hands, which had the flesh left upon them, and were cut in several places, and crammed with salt, apparently with an intention of preserving them. The lower jaw and feet, which were wanting, Eappo told us, had been seized by different chiefs, and that Terreeoboo was using every means to recover them.

At sunset the following day, the officers slipped Cook's bones into the bay. Clerke, to his honor and credit, did not seek vengeance. He understood that there had been no plot or even desire to kill Cook, and thought that the Hawaiians, surprised and frightened, regretted Cook's death. When the repaired foremast was in place and its rigging complete, the anchors were weighed and the ships left the Islands for the last time. As far as is known, no other foreign ship visited Hawai'i for the next seven years.

Kalaniōpu'u's son, Kiwala'ō, was on Maui when Cook was killed, but Kamehameha is thought to have been among the chiefs who tried to keep Cook

High chief Ka'iana, whom Fornander believed may have killed Cook. Engraving after a drawing by John Webber, 1790

from taking Kalaniōpu'u hostage. Parts of Cook's body were divided among the chiefs, the hair going to "Maia-maia," that is, to Kamehameha. John Rickman wrote that following the death of Cook, "a few guns were fired from the ships to disperse them [the natives], by which the king's second son, Mea-Mea was killed . . . ," which is an erroneous report of Kamehameha's death. Captain Nathaniel Portlock, who with Captain George Dixon (both of whom had been with Cook in 1778 and 1779) was later to start the lucrative fur trade between China and North America, wrote in his book, *Voyage Round the World* (1789), that "Kamehameha took an active part in the unfortunate affray which terminated in the much-lamented death of Captain Cook." Portlock believed that Kamehameha's refusal to visit his ship in 1786 was because he feared that Portlock had come to avenge Cook's death. Kamehameha later encouraged foreigners to believe the lie that he had poisoned his uncle, Kalaniōpu'u, in revenge for Cook's death. Judge Fornander wrote that Kamehameha once told Captain Douglas of the *Iphigenia*, who was in Hawai'i in 1787, that Kalaniōpu'u had been poisoned by himself and other high chiefs in retribution for killing Cook. William Ellis, surgeon's second mate on the *Discovery*, wrote in his journal that Kamehameha, who was thought to have been wounded in the gunfire during the attack on Cook, was in earnest in his sorrow, adding less convincingly that Kamehameha had kept the angry chiefs from killing all of Cook's officers.

At the time of Cook's visit, the Islands were divided into four kingdoms. Most of the island of Hawai'i, excluding Hilo, was ruled by Kalaniōpu'u, who had also conquered the district of Hanā in east Maui. Apart from Hanā, Maui was ruled by King Kahekili (said by some to be Kamehameha's natural father). Kaua'i and Ni'ihau were in possession of the chiefess Kamakahelei, and Kahahana was ali'i rui of O'ahu. On the island of Hawai'i, the primary figures at Kalaniōpu'u's court were his eldest son, Kiwala'ō; Kiwala'ō's sixteen-year-old half brother, Keoua; and their cousin Kamehameha, who was then about twenty-five years old. As Keoua's rank was lower than that of his brother and cousin, Kamehameha would one day succeed Kiwala'ō as *ali'i nui*.

After the departure of Cook's ships, Kalaniōpu'u returned to his habits of drinking *'awa*, and dancing the *hula*, in which he is said to have excelled despite his age. As the descendant of chiefs who had gained ascendancy over shark gods, Kalaniōpuʻu claimed the protection and services of sharks. The following shark *hula* written for him is thought to have been the terrifying noise at night later heard by horrified missionaries, although it is not thought to have been danced after 1830. It is performed in a sitting position:

> You are a white-finned shark riding the crest of the wave,
>   O Kalaniopuʻu:
> a tiger shark resting without fear
> a rain quenching the sun's eye-searing glare
> a grim oven glowing underground.

Sometime in the year 1780, a lack of food, thanks to the provisioning of the British ships, led Kalaniōpuʻu to move his court to Waipiʻo Valley in Hāmākua, where he called a council of chiefs. Limbs shaking from a lifetime of drinking *ʻawa*, Kalaniōpuʻu formally declared Kiwalaʻō heir to the kingdom, and named Kamehameha high chief of Kohala, giving him land that already belonged to Kamehameha. More important, he bequeathed to Kamehameha the guardianship of the feathered war god, Kūkāʻilimoku, whose name means Island Snatcher, and the attendant responsibility of conducting rites and tending the god's *heiau*. Kalaniōpuʻu's gift gave to Kamehameha a significant political and religious advantage over other high chiefs. The war god—a wickerwork head five feet tall, to which thousands of small red, yellow, and black feathers had been attached, its gaping mouth lined with dogs' teeth—was carried into battle by a special priest. The terrifying screams that poured from its mouth were said to be the cries of the god himself.

To sanctify the ceremony of succession, a rebel chief of Puna, on the east coast, was taken captive to serve as a sacrifice. As Kalaniōpuʻu's heir, Kiwalaʻō was required to conduct the death ritual, but when he hesitated (he was said to have been better suited to be a court historian or poet than a king), making instead an offering of a pig and some bananas, Kamehameha leapt forward to kill the Puna chief, earning the hatred of rival chiefs, who demanded that he in turn be killed. Kalaniōpuʻu, who was fond of his nephew, instead ordered Kamehameha to return to his land in the north of the island.

For the next several years, Kamehameha lived quietly in Kohala, at Kapaʻau, with his two wives and his attendants, cultivating his extensive lands and strengthening his alliances with neighboring chiefs, among them the tempestuous Keʻeaumoku of Kona. With the help of Kekuhaupiʻo, his tutor in war (he tasted all of Kamehameha's food before allowing him to eat), Kamehameha organized his retainers into four armies of sixteen hundred warriors, while cultivating numerous terraced plantations of sweet potato and taro to provision them.

With the death of Kalaniōpuʻu in 1782, Kiwalaʻō quickly fell under the influence of his father's half brother, the high chief Keawemauhili of Hilo, who saw a chance to increase his holdings in the redistribution of land that was customary with the death of a king. Four chiefs of Kona, among them Keʻeaumoku, asked Kamehameha's help in their fight to win a more favorable distribution of land for themselves. Kamehameha sailed to Kona to negotiate with his cousin Kiwalaʻō, and Kiwalaʻō's brother, Keoua, as well as the chiefs of Puna and Hilo. John Papa ʻĪʻī wrote:

> After the Kau chiefs had been at Honaunau a while, Kamehameha and his canoe paddlers arrived in his single canoe, named *Noiku* . . . No sooner had his foot touched land than those on shore were ready to hurl spears of hau wood at him, a custom observed upon the landing of a high chief . . . Those on land watched with admiration as Kamehameha thrust them aside. A person remained near the chief with a container of water for his bath; and after the spear throwers had finished and had seated themselves, Kamehameha bathed and donned a dry malo. He went up to see his cousin Kiwalao, and when they met food was made ready. Thus they met graciously.

Despite a new division of land, some of the *aliʻi*, including Kiwalaʻō and Keoua, were dissatisfied, resulting in a battle that summer near Keʻei in Kona. Keʻeaumoku, whose name means Island-Climbing Swimmer, accompanied Kamehameha to Kona. While Kamehameha was in camp, performing rituals to the war god, word came that Keʻeaumoku had been taken captive by Kiwalaʻō. Kamehameha rushed to the battlefield, as did Keʻeaumoku's eight-year-old daughter, the young chiefess Kaʻahumanu, carried on the back of Pahia, a warrior skilled at throwing stones. Kiwalaʻō hesitated before killing Keʻeaumoku, as he did not want blood to touch the *lei niho palaoa* (necklace of braided hair and whale tooth) that Keʻeaumoku was wearing. Seeing this, Pahia dropped Kaʻahumanu to the ground, picked up a stone, and struck Kiwalaʻō so forcefully on the head that he fell on top of the wounded Keʻeaumoku, who quickly cut Kiwalaʻō's throat with a shark's-tooth knife.

The result of this battle was to divide the island of Hawai'i into three independent and hostile kingdoms. Keoua retreated to his family lands in Puna and Ka'ū, where he was declared *mō'i*, or king, as successor to his brother. Kamehameha was acknowledged high chief of Kona, Kohala, and sections of Hāmākua, while Hilo and parts of Puna went to Keawemauhili. Kamehameha attacked Keoua and Keawemauhili, who were allies of Kahekili of Maui, but he was routed, escaping with what remained of his army to Laupāhoehoe, on the Hāmākua coast. While resting his men, he sailed south with a few warriors in search of people to use as sacrifices, running in upon the reef near Kea'au when he spotted some fishermen. Kamehameha jumped from his canoe to capture them, but the fishermen fled, leaving two men to defend their retreat, one of whom, encumbered with a child on his back, struggled with Kamehameha. The chief's foot slipped into a hole in the reef, and while he tried to free himself, the fisherman struck him on the head with a paddle, shattering the wood. The injured Kamehameha swam to his canoe, unaware of the names of the fishermen or their village.

In 1790, while Kamehameha was fighting on Maui, Keoua attacked Hilo. Keawemauhili was killed, allowing Keoua to add the district of Hilo to his lands of Ka'ū and Puna. He then invaded Hāmākua, north of Hilo, destroying *kalo* fields and fish ponds at Waipi'o, and plundering land that belonged to Kamehameha. Before Kamehameha could return from Maui, a sudden eruption of Kīlauea, in Keoua's own district, destroyed most of Keoua's army as it made its way south to Ka'ū, which was seen as an omen that the unpredictable fire goddess favored Kamehameha, a distinction that would serve him well throughout his life.

Both sides, exhausted after years of fighting, their supplies and ranks depleted, fell into an uneasy peace. In 1792, after sporadic skirmishes, Kamehameha sent two of his chiefs to Ka'ū to invite Keoua to Pu'ukoholā, his war *heiau* at Kawaihae, so that they could together rule peacefully over the island. Judge Fornander wrote that Kamehameha's messengers crawled before Keoua and embraced his feet:

> When the wailing was over Keoua asked them what their errand was. They said, "We have come to you, the son of our late lord and brother, to induce you to go with us to Kona to be united and reconciled with your younger brother [Kamehameha], that you two may be the kings,

Grass houses built near Kamehameha's war *heiau*, Puʻukoholā, in Kawaihae. Watercolor by Adrien Aimé Taunay, 1819. The king, who was under a *kapu*, is sitting alone before his thatched house. Image courtesy of Mark and Carolyn Blackburn

and we . . . live under you. Let the war between you two come to an end."

Mistrustful of Kamehameha, Keoua's chiefs counseled him not to go, and his *kahuna* warned him that if he went to Kawaihae he would be killed: "*Hele aku ʻoe maʻaneʻi, he waʻa kanaka; hoʻi mai ʻoe maʻō he waʻa akua.*" "When you go from here, the canoe will contain men; when you return it will be a ghostly canoe."

Although Keoua was aware of Kamehameha's ambition and duplicity, he agreed to meet with him, embarking in his double canoe, paddled by twenty-four men. It is said that in anticipation of his death, he stopped shortly before reaching Kawaihae to perform a ritual act in which he cut off the tip of his penis as a sign that he would sire no more children. As his canoe reached Kawaihae, he saw that Kamehameha's war canoes, mounted with the guns Kamehameha had begun to receive from foreign traders, were stationed around the bay, making escape impossible.

As Keoua stepped ashore he was speared to death by Keʻeaumoku, and all of his chiefs and attendants, except for one man, were killed. Keoua's body was carried up the hill to the *heiau* and sacrificed to the war god. With his murder, there was at last peace on Hawaiʻi Island. The kingdom of Kaʻū no longer existed, and the entire island belonged to Kamehameha.

> The whole land belongs to the chief,
> The chief holds the inland and the ocean;
> For him is the night, for him the day,
> For him are the seasons, the winter, the summer,
> The months, the seven stars of heaven.
> All valuable property, above and below,
> The chief holds all fixed property;
> All property that floats ashore, all fowls that light upon the land,
> The thick-shelled broad backed turtle, the dead whales cut up, and
>   the *uhu*.
> Let the chief live the highest! let him ever live a chief!
> Let him be borne with honor among the short gods and the long gods.
> Let him go forth fearlessly, the chief in possession of the island.

The Cloak of Bird Feathers

In Honolulu in the winter of 1827, Queen Kaʻahumanu, the widow of Kamehameha I, paid for the paper to print three thousand copies of the Sermon on the Mount in Hawaiian on the small press brought by Congregationalist missionaries from New England seven years earlier. The queen, the favorite of Kamehameha's twenty-two wives, was a new convert to Christianity, having been instructed by the Reverend Hiram Bingham, the leader of the First Company of missionaries (the American Board of Commissioners for Foreign Missions in Boston was ultimately to send twelve different companies to the Islands, each of about ten missionaries and lay workers, from 1820 to 1848).

There is a portrait of Kaʻahumanu at age forty-eight made by Louis Choris in 1816, and another by Jacques Arago in 1819. There are a number of descriptions of her by travelers, as well as by missionaries, but the queen herself did not learn to write until a few years before her death in 1832, and there is no evidence that she troubled to confide her history or her thoughts to a journal or diary. There are many legends and anecdotes about her in histories, chants, and songs, and while they are not always reliable sources (there are at least five different dates given for her birth), they reveal the fears and fantasies of a culture, as well as record temporal events.

By most accounts, the high chiefess Kaʻahumanu, known to John Papa ʻĪʻī as Mokualoha or Island of Love, was born March 17, 1768, in a small cave on the side of a hill in Hanā, on the island of Maui, to Namahana, the recent widow of her half brother, Kamehamehanui, king of Maui, and her husband, the high chief Keʻeaumoku of Kona.

Namahana's marriage to Keʻeaumoku caused much envy, particularly as she formally belonged to Kalaniōpuʻu with the death of her husband, and he had planned to take her as wife once her period of mourning ended.

Keʻeaumoku was described by King Kalākaua (1836–1891) in his book, *The Legends and Myths of Hawaii*:

This must have been known to Keeaumoku, who was thoroughly acquainted with the royal customs of his time: yet he paid such court to the sorrowing dowager, and so sweetly mingled his protestations of love with her sighs of grief, that she became his wife without consulting with the *moi* . . . Taking up his residence at Waihee, Keeaumoku enlarged and beautified his grounds and buildings, and established a petty court of princely etiquette and appointments. He was fond of display, and soon attracted to Waihee many of the more accomplished young chiefs of the island . . . He had carefully trained bands of musicians and dancers, and his entertainments were frequent and bountiful.

Enemies of the couple, not least of them the enraged Kalaniōpuʻu, conspired to drive them from Maui, and sometime between 1777 and 1779, during one of the many continuing wars between Hawaiʻi and Maui, Keʻeaumoku and Namahana fled to Kona with their household and attendants.

There is a legend that the infant Kaʻahumanu, wrapped in *kapa*, was left to sleep on the platform of a double canoe, but rolled unnoticed into the sea, disappearing under the waves, only to be saved at the last moment. She was said to have been much loved by her father, and by her grandmother, who told her that she was destined to be a queen to whom her relatives would one day bow in submission.

Kamehameha first admired her at a Makahiki festival (as a child, she would have seen him on the battlefield when her father cut the throat of Kiwalaʻō), and in 1785, the thirty-two-year-old chief, already in possession of two wives, had the seventeen-year-old Kaʻahumanu, whose name means the Cloak of Bird Feathers, brought to him in North Kohala, where he married her. Two rival chiefs had sought her as wife, but she was Kamehameha's prize, enabling him to align himself with some of the most sacred and thus most powerful *aliʻi* of Maui.

The missionary Hiram Bingham, not given to praising women for their beauty, wrote in 1823, when Kaʻahumanu was fifty-five years old, that she was "sprightly, and beautiful for a Polynesian, and engaging when young . . . Kamehameha was exceedingly jealous of her." She was six feet tall, and without blemish. Kamakau wrote that her arms were like the inside of a banana stalk:

... her fingers tapering, her palms pliable like *kukunene* grass, graceful in repose, her cheeks long in shape and pink as the bud of a banana stem; her eyes like those of a dove or the *moho* bird; her nose narrow and straight, in admirable proportion to her cheeks; her arched eyebrows shaped to the breadth of her forehead; her hair dark, wavy, and fine; her skin very light. Of Kamehameha's two possessions, his wife and his kingdom, she was the more beautiful.

It is said that upon their marriage, Kamehameha built a stone wall at Kauhola Point in Kohala to make a small protected cove where he could teach her to swim, although it seems unlikely that she would not have known this essential skill by adolescence. He did teach her to surf, and throughout her life she was a keen and skillful surfer. John Papa ʻĪʻī described one of her favorite surfing spots in Kohala:

Kekahau was a kamaʻaina [old-timer] of the place, and it was he who led Kaʻahumanu to the surf of Maliu... As the story goes, Kaʻahumanu and Kekakau swam or went by canoe to the spot where the surf rose. Before they left, Kekakau talked with the king about the nature of the surf and showed Kaʻahumanu the places to land, which would be signaled by the waving of a white tapa. If the tapa was moved to the right or to the left, she was to go to the side indicated before the sea rose up high and overwhelmed her. If the tapa was spread out, or perhaps wadded into a ball, the signal meant to go in on the middle of the wave.

She was said to find pleasure in the company of men, preferring them to women, and did not hesitate to show her contempt for a rival, although she took care to befriend pretty newcomers at court, turning any possible threat into a favorite companion. Women were said to be frightened of her, and did not like to enter her house.

She was passionate about games, and very good at them. She liked to fly kites, some of them twenty feet in length and seven feet wide, and so difficult to control that, once aloft, they had to be tied to the trunks of trees. Captain John Kendrick of the *Lady Washington* gave her a checkerboard in 1791, and twenty years later, when she played against officers on board the *Beaver*, an American trading vessel owned by John Jacob Astor then in port, not one of the officers could win a game against her.

One of her amusements was to make drunk two Aleutian women who had been brought by sailors from the northwest coast of America and then abandoned. The women were favorites of the queen, perhaps because she could be easy in their presence. She liked alcohol, and was able to drink when Kamehameha, frequently restricted by religious ritual, could not (later he eschewed alcohol altogether). The queen did not like the crude liquor distilled from the root of the *kī* plant, and instead kept a supply of brandy that she received in secret from Don Francisco Marín in exchange for gifts ('Ī'ī wrote with disapproval that Ka'ahumanu was overly fond of drink, and sometimes given to excess). Marín, a deserter from a Spanish ship, had bought large pieces of land from Kamehameha while serving as his translator, and quickly established vineyards, orchards, and ranches for stock-breeding. He ran a boardinghouse for sea captains, and he introduced to the Islands the damask rose, cotton, doves, and English hares, among other things. With his three Hawaiian wives, he had twenty-three children. Although Marín did not begrudge the queen his brandy, he was unwilling to share the produce or even the seeds from his orchards with Hawaiians. Charles Stewart wrote with disapproval:

> He [Marín] had introduced the grape, orange, lemon, pineapple, fig, and tamarind trees, but to a very limited extent; and seemingly from a motive entirely selfish: for he has perseveringly denied the seeds, and every means of propagation to others, and been known even secretly to destroy a growth that had been secured from them without his knowledge.

In 1792, Kamehameha moved to Kona to begin building a fleet of a thousand war canoes, living with Ka'ahumanu and his other wives and attendants in a large compound surrounded by stone walls, and separated by a gate from the lava platform and *kapu* precincts of nearby Hikiau *heiau*. Ka'ahumanu was not allowed inside the largest house, which was *kapu* to the king. Her own house was next in size, although she and Kamehameha slept in a smaller house built for that purpose. She was closely tended, lest she indulge what was said to be an amorous nature. If she so much as stepped outside the yard, she was followed by a malformed boy, the traditional bodyguard of high-ranking women, whose only task was to keep her in constant sight.

Kahekili, the most powerful chief in the Islands, killed his foster son and tortured the Oʻahu chiefs to death during his conquest of that island in 1786, becoming *aliʻi nui* of Molokaʻi, Maui, and Lānaʻi, as well as Oʻahu. (He liked to roast his enemies and to use their skulls as filth pots.) In honor of the thunder god who was his namesake, half of his body was tattooed black from the top of his head to one heel, in a style called "Cut-in-Half." His men bore the same marking, with the addition of tattoos on the insides of their eyelids. Martha Beckwith wrote that some of Kahekili's men were thought to be supernatural:

The hairless ʻOlohe people with whom the brindle dog is associated are believed to be dog men with the mystical shape-shifting powers of the demigods. They lived in caves dug into the sandhills, where they are said to have been first discovered and used by Kahekili in the eighteenth century as a division of his army. Living witnesses today report men with dogs' heads marching in the ghostly processions of dead warriors returned to revisit their old haunts on earth.

"Reine Cahoumanou," plate III in Louis Choris's *Voyage Pittoresque Autour du Monde*, 1822, Hawaiʻi State Archives

Kahekili had taken to cruising along the coast of Hawai'i Island, looting and burning villages, and desecrating *ali'i* graves. Kamehameha attacked Kahekili and his army in a sea battle off Waimanu, remembered as the Battle of the Red-Mouthed Gun, in which two Englishmen, Isaac Davis and John Young, fought alongside Kamehameha. Isaac Davis had been mate on board the trading schooner *Fair American*, under command of the son of a Captain Simon Metcalfe, whose own brig, the *Eleanor*, traded in Hawai'i. The *Fair American* was near Maui in February 1790 when a high chief named Kaopuiki stole the ship's boat. A watchman who had been asleep in the boat was killed, and the boat was quickly broken apart for its iron fastenings. Upon discovering the theft, Metcalfe, known to be a vicious and punitive man, fired on some villages ashore and took two prisoners. A *kapu* was put on the bay for three days, during which time no canoe was allowed to leave the beach. When the *kapu* was removed, the Hawaiians made for the *Eleanor* to resume trade, but Metcalfe, still enraged, ordered his guns turned on the Hawaiians, killing more than a hundred people and wounding hundreds more.

A month later, the *Fair American* was quietly captured off North Kona by one of Kamehameha's chiefs. All but one of the crew were murdered, including Metcalfe's son; the exception was Isaac Davis, whose life was spared most likely at the order of Kamehameha. The ship's guns, ammunition, and articles of trade were looted, and Davis was brought to Kamehameha, who was at Kealakekua, where Metcalfe's ship, the *Eleanor*, was then at anchor. That same morning, a party of sailors from the *Eleanor*, including the bos'n John Young, had gone ashore, where Young is said to have been separated from his shipmates. It is agreed by most historians that Young was kidnapped by Kamehameha, who needed a Westerner to teach him the use of the guns he was rapidly accumulating. Metcalfe remained in the bay for two days, firing signals in the hope of Young's return, but at last sailed without him.

Thanks to the special care taken of Isaac Davis, who was treated for his wounds, and of John Young, to whom the Hawaiians behaved with kindness and respect, the men were soon reconciled to captivity. Kamehameha eventually gave Young two high chiefesses as wives, one of them the daughter of his youngest brother. Young was a significant part of Kamehameha's unification of the Islands in 1795, having trained the king's men in the maintenance, deployment, and use of arms in battle. Known as 'Olohana because of his use of the bos'n's cry "All hands," Young was later made governor of Hawai'i Island (1802–1812), and became one of Kamehameha's most trusted friends and counselors.

In 1792, Kamehameha married his cousin Keōpūolani, a young chiefess possessed of the highest rank in the Islands, who was the daughter of his late rival, Kiwala'ō. Several years earlier, in one of the battles between chiefs, Kamehameha had forced the then eleven-year-old Keōpūolani to flee Maui with her grandmother, who was mortally ill. The chiefess, foreseeing that Kamehameha would one day be *ali'i nui*, gave him her granddaughter as a future wife. When the old woman died, Kamehameha showed his respect for her sacred lineage by knocking out his eyeteeth and having himself tattooed.

Following the death of her grandmother, the girl was taken to Keauhou near Kona where she would be kept in seclusion until she was ready to mate with Kamehameha. The navigator George Vancouver was present at a chant and *hula* performance in Kealakekua in honor of a "captive princess" who is said to have been Keōpūolani. Vancouver noticed that when her name was spoken, each person removed all clothing or ornaments above the waist. (Kamehameha himself had to remove his loincloth when he visited her.) The girl was not known for her beauty or intelligence. At her birth, a nurse had tried to switch her for a more comely baby, but a wild dog attacked the substitute child, and the scrawny Keōpūolani remained in place. What she did possess, which was of far more value than beauty, was the prostrating *kapu*. She was never a favorite wife, but she bore Kamehameha eleven children of the highest rank, three of whom lived to adulthood—Liholiho (Kamehameha II), Nāhi'ena'ena, and Kauikeaouli (Kamehameha III).

The acquisition of rank was determinate in the accruing and maintaining of kingly, and thus divine, power. When it was not sufficiently inherent, it could be obtained, in timeless expediency, through marriage. The most sacred marriage, that of a brother and sister (Samuel Kamakau wrote that a sister often sat in a brother's lap, caressing him affectionately as he chanted verses composed in her honor), was known as a thing bent onto itself, an arch, or *nī'aupi'o*, symbolized by the figure of a bow. A *nī'aupi'o* marriage increased the alliance of family gods within a family, as well as strengthened its political power. The birth of a *nī'aupi'o* child was a reenactment of the birth of the first human, and was known as a fire, a blaze, a raging heart.

Since a child inherited rank from both parents, it was possible for him to attain a higher, more sacred position than that of either his mother or father. A child of any of these unions was venerated as an *akua*, or god, with varying degrees of adoration, manifested by *kapu*. Once a child of sufficient rank was born, however, its parents were free to take a partner of his or her choice, and a child born of any subsequent union was made an attendant or counselor to his sacred half brother or sister. Lines of descent were necessarily extremely convoluted, with many ties and connections, and further complicated by the belief that a double paternity (that is, uncertainty as to which chief had sired a woman's child) could lead to an increase in rank. Martha Beckwith wrote:

> Kamehameha sought marriage alliances with blue blooded families of Maui as well as his own island, who looked upon him as a usurper against the legitimate line of out-ranking chiefs from Keawe. The Maui chiefess Kalolo was, after the affable custom of chief wives, both mother of Kiwala'o as consort of Kalaniopu'u and, by his [Kalaniopu'u's] half-brother of Kona who became the father of Kamehameha, mother to Kiwala'o's chief wife. She bore to him [Kiwala'o] a daughter, and this girl Kamehameha took as his own chief wife.

Kamehameha also married Namahana, one of Ka'ahumanu's younger sisters. Ka'ahumanu was quick-tempered and proud, like her father, but Namahana was malleable and complacent. One of her favorite diversions was to be carried through shouting crowds of delighted subjects. Known as the Child Mountain when she was a girl, she was also much larger than Ka'ahumanu.

When Ka'ahumanu's sister, Kaheiheimālie, gave birth to a daughter, Kekaūluohi, Kamehameha demanded the child as a future wife, but Kaheiheimālie, who was in love with her husband, Kamehameha's half brother and the chief priest of 'Io, a cult honoring the Hawaiian hawk, refused to give up the girl. Kamehameha then stole Kaheiheimālie, whose nickname was Coconut, from his half brother ("a very strange act on his part," wrote Kamakau), and with her, his young niece, who, it was said, would warm him in his old age. Ka'ahumanu was rather optimistically given the duty of watching over the girl until she would be ready to sleep with the king.

As the girl matured, Kaʻahumanu became lax in her care, perhaps out of spite, but more likely because it was her nature, and saw to it that the male and female attendants assigned to watch Kekaūluohi remained at the far end of her house. Any man said to be favored by Kaʻahumanu was allowed to meet the girl in secret.

Unlike his other wives, particularly Kaʻahumanu, who was impossible to control, Kaheiheimālie was faithful to him, although she remained in love with his half brother throughout her life. She is said never to have slept with another man after her marriage to the king. She was similar to Kaʻahumanu only in that she loathed gossip, her eyes turning red with anger if rumors were repeated in her presence. She required any offender to pay a pig as penalty, lest he be put into irons until "his sores festered and he was reduced to skin and bones."

Throughout these marriages of both affection and expediency, serving to solidify, and entangle, his relations with his high chiefs, many of whom were the fathers and brothers and sometimes husbands of his wives, Kaʻahumanu remained the favorite; Kamehameha's *kuʻu ʻiʻini*, or heart's desire. She in turn described him as "*Pāpale ʻai ʻāina, kuʻu aloha*," "The head-covering over the land, my beloved." Their marriage served to ensure a continuing alliance with Kaʻahumanu's powerful father and his family (she is said to have several times

A double canoe with masked men, some of whom may be priests carrying idols. Engraving after pen, ink wash, and watercolor over pencil by John Webber, 1778

dissuaded her uncles and brothers from rebelling against him). Kamakau wrote that the king "cherished her as if she were a goddess or an ivory-tooth necklace to adorn his neck. She was as carefully protected as if she were living in the sacred place of a heiau. He feared lest, if she escaped from her nest, all the fledglings also would leave it with her, hence she was carefully guarded."

Captain George Vancouver, who was midshipman with Cook in 1778, returned to the Islands during a five-year expedition undertaken once again to find a Northwest Passage to the Atlantic Ocean, stopping in the Islands for two weeks in 1792, six weeks in 1793, and ten weeks in 1794. On his first visit, Vancouver landed five cows, two ewes, and one ram at Kealakekua as a gift to Kamehameha. He gave the king more cattle the following year, and the use of his carpenters to help build a small schooner, named *Britannia*, which Kamehameha had ordered for his own use.

The foreigners who visited the Islands in the early nineteenth century were treated by the Hawaiians with care, particularly by the far-seeing Kamehameha, who perhaps did not wish to antagonize or threaten them after the death of Cook. Vancouver, like other early travelers, found much to admire in them:

> They [the Hawaiians] had been constantly with [the astronomer] Mr. Whidby in the marquee, and had acquired such a taste for our mode of living, that their utmost endeavors were expended to imitate our ways . . . Their attachment was by no means of a childish nature, or arising from novelty, it was the effect of reflection; and a consciousness of their own comparative inferiority. This directed their minds to the acquisition of useful instruction . . . Their conversation had always for its object useful information, not frivolous inquiry . . . and the pains they took to become acquainted with our language, and to be instructed in reading and writing, bespoke them to have not only a genius to acquire, but abilities to profit by instruction.

Vancouver first met Ka'ahumanu's parents, Ke'eaumoku and Namahana, when his ship *Discovery* was anchored off Kawaihae in 1792. When he discovered that Kamehameha's favorite wife was their daughter, he treated them with particular respect, and invited Ke'eaumoku to dine with him on board ship. Vancouver also asked Namahana and her fellow wives to join them, not expecting her to accept, as a *kapu* was newly in place that prohibited women from leaving land. Namahana, however, claimed that *kapu* did not apply to visits with foreigners, who were not obliged to obey it. Her sly reasoning persuaded Keʻeaumoku and she was brought to the ship in one of Vancouver's boats. Vancouver thought it would be helpful to have Keʻeaumoku and Namahana on board when he again met Kamehameha, and they accompanied him when he sailed south along the coast. Kamehameha met the ship near Kailua. The following is from the journal of Archibald Menzies, surgeon and botanist on the *Discovery*:

> A little after both vessels anchored, Kamehameha came in great state from the shore accompanied by a number of double canoes that stopped at a little distance from our stern, while the king in his canoe was paddled with great rapidity round both vessels, which occasioned no little hurry and confusion among the canoes that surrounded us to open an avenue for him. Numbers of them were overturned, and some of them nearly run over. He stood upright in the middle of the canoe with a fan in his hand, and was gracefully robed in a beautiful long cloak of yellow feathers, and his underdress consisted of a loose gown of printed cotton girdled on with a sash which he said had been given him by Captain Cook [Vancouver notes that it had been given to Kalaniopuʻu] . . . On his coming on board, he first presented a variety of feathered capes and helmets to Captain Vancouver. Then taking him by the hand to the gangway, he told him that there were ten canoes loaded with hogs for him . . . This was done with such a princely air of dignity, that it instantaneously riveted our admiration, as the manner of presenting and the magnitude of the present far exceeded anything . . . we had seen before.

In return, Vancouver gave Kamehameha a red wool cloak, trimmed with tinsel. It cannot have escaped the notice of the British that there was a great discrepancy in value between the cloaks. The Hawaiians' gift would have taken perhaps a generation to make, and required the capture and sometimes killing of tens of thousands of small birds. The feathers were sewn with a bone needle and thread to a netting made from the fiber of the *olonā* shrub, starting at the hem and working toward the neck. The cape, a sign of royal descent, marked the wearer as a representative of the gods. To give to a foreigner

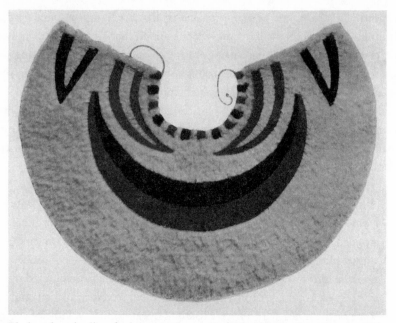

Black, red, and yellow feather cape given to Lady Franklin by Kamehameha IV in 1861, now in the Bernice Pauahi Bishop Museum, Honolulu

such a cloak (many of them now in museums throughout the world) indicated that the chiefs believed him also to be an avatar of the gods, and thus deserving of the highest honor (Kalaniōpuʻu gave seven cloaks, called *ʻahuʻula*, to Cook in 1778). The wool-and-tinsel cloak given to Kamehameha was for the English quite the opposite—not an object of great worth and significance, but a thrifty and valueless gift.

Kamehameha put on the cloak, dancing in delight at the sight of himself in a mirror, and went on deck to pace nonchalantly back and forth in view of his men in the waiting canoes, who shouted their praise and admiration. When Vancouver gave him more gifts, Kamehameha's relatives and retainers climbed noisily on board, and Kamehameha passed to them his presents, giving generously to the men, but nothing to the chiefesses. Vancouver was offended by this perceived rudeness and went to each woman to ensure that she had been given a proper present, to the amusement of Kamehameha and his chiefs. Kamehameha gave Vancouver so many gifts—mats, capes, idols, calabashes—during his time in the Islands that it was necessary to keep them in specially built storehouses.

Kamehameha asked permission to bring Ka'ahumanu, who had been waiting alongside in her own canoe, on board the ship. She appeared to Vancouver to be sixteen years old (she was more likely twenty-five). She wore a *lei niho palaoa* and was wrapped in many layers of *kapa*, folded about her waist and reaching to her knees. She was beautiful, wrote Vancouver, even by Western standards, and "undoubtedly did credit to the taste and choice of Kamaahmaah [*sic*], being one of the finest women we had yet seen on any of the islands." Vancouver noticed what appeared to be her irritation at the restrictions placed upon women by certain *kapu*, and suspected that she complied with them only because of Kamehameha. It is perhaps due to this that Vancouver stipulated that the cattle he had given to the king in 1793 not be made *kapu* to women. Ka'ahumanu's regal manner disappeared the moment that she saw her parents, when she threw herself into her father's arms.

One of Vancouver's officers noticed that although his fellow chiefs and warriors ate amply, Kamehameha, like his uncle Kalaniōpu'u, took only breadfruit and a drink of water (when he fasted before performing a religious ritual, he ate only the honey of banana flowers). Vancouver gave Kamehameha another red wool cloak—the cloaks were later named Ke'akualapu, or Ghost God, and Kekukuhe, the Bamboo Plant, and treated with reverence. The pleasant day ended when a messenger arrived from the priests to remind the king that a *kapu* would be in effect at sunset, and the visitors hastily jumped overboard and returned to shore with their gifts.

Lieutenant Thomas Manby, sailing with Vancouver, was beguiled by Hawaiian women, finding them beautiful. Charmed by their delight in jokes and games, he claimed never to have witnessed a quarrel between them. He later described Ka'ahumanu as she sat stringing beads under a tree in a small courtyard in Kamehameha's compound in Kealakekua while attendants fanned her with feathered staffs. A fresh mat was spread for him, and Ka'ahumanu sat next to him. She offered him fruit, asking one of her servants to bring some coconuts for herself and her guests. Manby would have known that women were forbidden to eat with men (they were also forbidden coconuts), but Ka'ahumanu must have known that the Hawaiian women visiting the sailors on board the foreign ships frequently ate with the sailors. She amused herself by "tying and untying his hair," as she braided it with feathers and flowers. She was fascinated by the whiteness of his complexion. "She then nearly undressed me to observe my skin," and was delighted to find that he bore a Tahitian tattoo on his leg. She sent for an old man, who

The chiefess Kaonoe, with feather *lei*, bleached hair, and tattoos. Lithograph after a drawing by Jacques Arago, 1819

examined it intently and interpreted the design to much teasing and laughter. Manby's attention to the queen must have seemed a bit too forward even
for the *ali'i*, who were impressively informal about their sexual arrangements
(unlike commoners, who tended to be monogamous), as Ka'ahumanu was
"called to order by a little deformed wretch" who would be put to death
should his charge be found in the arms of a man not her husband. She liked
to turn out the pockets of her Western friends to choose what she wanted for
her own, and when she discovered that Manby's pockets had already been
picked by one of her attendants, the guilty one was punished and dismissed
from her household.

When Vancouver returned to Kona the following year, he was distressed
to learn that Kamehameha had separated from Ka'ahumanu because of her
suspected liaison with the high chief Ka'iana. Vancouver considered Ka'iana
and his brother to be "turbulent, treacherous, and ungrateful," and believed
them responsible for the massacre of the sailors on the *Fair American*, in
which Isaac Davis had been the only survivor. King Kalākaua in his 1888
study of Ka'iana claimed that an angry Kamehameha had sent Ka'ahumanu
to live with her parents in Kealakekua. Archibald Menzies believed that
Ka'ahumanu's infidelity was not with Ka'iana but with one of her attendants
or another handsome young chief, and that Kamehameha punished him for
disloyalty by stripping him of his rank and his lands. Menzies claimed that
Ka'ahumanu had been left in disgrace in Hilo, while her parents were in
Kona at the bedside of a young son who was dying of wounds suffered in a
mock spear fight. Samuel Kamakau wrote that Ka'iana was not the lover of
Ka'ahumanu but of her mother, Namahana, and was the father of two of
Namahana's sons.

In February, Ka'ahumanu was in fact in Kealakekua when her brother
died from his wounds and Vancouver secretly arranged for her to visit his
ship to surprise Kamehameha, who was already on board. When Ka'ahumanu
arrived, Vancouver led her to Kamehameha and placed her hand in the king's
hand. Kamehameha relented at the sight of her, and embraced her, both of
them weeping. Before she left the ship, however, Ka'ahumanu asked Vancouver if he would make Kamehameha promise to stop beating her.

The American adventurer James Jarves spent the years 1840 to 1848 in
Honolulu as the editor of the *Polynesian*, a weekly newspaper. Francis Steegmuller wrote a biography of Jarves, who later became vice consul in Flor-
ence and a sketchy picture dealer, and Jarves appears as the hapless art

connoisseur in Edith Wharton's novella *False Dawn*. He described Kamehameha in his book *Scenes and Scenery in the Sandwich Islands* (1844):

> His carriage was majestic, and every action bespoke a mind which,
> under any circumstances, would have distinguished its possessor.
> His eyes were dark and piercing, in the words of one who not long
> after was well acquainted with him, he seemed capable of penetrat-
> ing the designs and reading the thoughts of those about him, before
> his glance the most courageous quailed. His general deportment
> was frank, cheerful and generous . . . His sagacious mind seized
> upon every opportunity of improvement and aggrandizement . . .
> Cook's narrative presented him as a wonderful savage, ambitious,
> brave and resolute, Vancouver's intercourse showed him in the dawn
> of a ripened intellect, as possessing all the latter qualities, yet hu-
> mane and thoughtful.

Kamehameha was, by many accounts, a violent man. The Reverend
Hiram Bingham, writing twenty years after Kamehameha's death, was told of
the king's temper by Kaheiheimālie. Bingham seems to commiserate with the
king as to the difficulties inherent in possessing more than one wife:

> How it would be possible for a barbarian warrior to manage from one
> to two dozen wives—some young, and some old—some handsome,
> and some ugly—some of high rank, and some low, without martial law
> among them, or without resorting to despotic violence . . . it would
> be . . . extremely difficult to conceive. Kalakua [Kaheiheimālie], the
> late governess of Maui, who gave me much of Kamehameha's do-
> mestic history, says of him, "He kanaka pepehi no ia; aole mea e ana
> ai kona inaina. He was a man of violence,—nothing could pacify
> his wrath." She said she was once beaten by him, with a stone, upon her
> head, till she bled profusely, when in circumstances demanding his
> kindest indulgence and care, as a husband . . . An English resident,
> who enjoyed his confidence as fully and long as any foreigner, says,
> he has seen him beat Kaahumanu with severity for the simple offence
> of speaking of a young man as "handsome" . . . Captain Douglass
> speaks of his violent temper and rashness, judging that "those about

Portrait of Hiram Bingham, from his book *A Residence of Twenty-One Years in the Sandwich Islands*, published in 1848

him feared rather than loved him;" and says, "Conceiving himself affronted, one day, by the chiefs who were on board, he kicked them all by turns, without mercy, and without resistance."

It was inconceivable to Bingham that Ka'ahumanu might have lived happily with Kamehameha: "The amount and the kind of attention which a young wife, among many, could, in the circumstance of Kaahumanu, receive from such a pagan polygamist warrior, and his heathen family, must have failed of producing much domestic happiness as her share." Bingham wrote with ill-concealed admiration that the queen had run away from her husband when they were living at Waikīkī. "Determined on making the passage to Kauai, by herself,—[she] embarked in a beautiful single canoe, and nearly accomplished her design. She was, however, brought back to Honolulu, where she complimented Captain Broughton, of the Providence, with the present of the canoe in which she had made the bold attempt."

Kamehameha and Ka'ahumanu later accompanied Vancouver to the site of Cook's death fourteen years earlier. Vancouver had been in one of the guard boats when Cook was killed, and Kamehameha took pains to assure him that he himself had not been present the morning of Cook's death, which was not true. Kamehameha was well aware of the rich and powerful kingdoms beyond the Pacific, having been visited by the armed ships of the United States, Portugal, Spain, Russia, and Britain. Mindful that at any moment, one of these powers could take possession of the Islands, he wished to cede his kingdom to the British, in the hope that they would help to repel any future foreign aggression, while retaining for the Islands the right of self-government, according to the kingdom's own laws. Observing that these powerful and wealthy nations worshipped a Christian god, he also asked Vancouver to send religious instructors from England.

It has never been clear if the well-meaning Vancouver promised Kamehameha the protection that he sought, as such an agreement would have required the ratification of Parliament, which was never given, or whether Kamehameha and his chiefs (although one might presume that John Young understood the terms and requirements of such a treaty) did not fully comprehend the meaning of cession. Andrew Bloxam, who in 1824 was a botanist on board HMS *Blonde*, wrote:

> This singular cession of the country to a power nearly at the Antipodes was not, of course, followed by any act of authority, or any apparent change in the conduct of the English to Hawaii, but it was proof of the anxious desire of Tamehameha [*sic*] for the advantage of his kingdom. His intelligent mind was aware of the incalculable superiority possessed by the Europeans and others, whose ships visited him, over his own poor Islanders. The circumstances, that the English were the first to touch there; that their vessels were the largest and most powerful; that, besides the advantages sought for themselves in procuring provisions of all kinds, they had endeavoured to improve the Islands by carrying thither new and profitable animals and vegetables; all led him to look on the British as not only the most powerful but the most friendly of the new nations they had learned to know; and he might reasonably hope that we should be as willing as able to protect them against the insults and injuries that some of the traders had offered them.

When Vancouver left the Islands, Kamehameha, Ka'ahumanu, and her cousin, Kalanimoku, were so upset that they traveled alongside his ships in canoes, following him up the coast, although Kamehameha had to return to shore before dark to conduct a religious ceremony to cleanse himself from the pollution of eating with men who had eaten with women. During these ceremonies, it was customary for the gifts that had been received from the foreigners, many of them given to women, to be laid at Kamehameha's feet so that he could claim his share. These presents accounted for much of the booty—cloth, mirrors, nails, and trinkets—that Kamehameha was rapidly accumulating in his treasure houses.

The death in 1794 of the murderous high chief Kahekili of O'ahu, who had once desecrated the graves of Hawai'i Island chiefs, caused Kamehameha great disappointment as it deprived him of the chance to kill him in battle. Kahekili left his kingdom of O'ahu, Lāna'i, Moloka'i, and Maui to his son and to his half brother, and Kamehameha shrewdly left them to fight each other while he began to gather an army. When Kahekili's son was defeated the following year by his uncle, Kamehameha acted quickly to invade Maui and Moloka'i, before sailing across the channel to O'ahu.

Kamehameha's large army and his fleet of nearly one thousand war canoes had been organized and outfitted in accordance to instructions given him by Vancouver, including the use of the redoubtable John Young as artillery commander (Vancouver wrote in his journal that the Hawaiians "could use these weapons with an adroitness that would not disgrace the generality of European soldiers"). Following Young's direction, Kamehameha's war canoes landed at Wai'alae and Waikīkī on O'ahu, and the army marched to the *pali*, or cliffs, of Nu'uanu where they defeated Kamehameha's rivals, among them the dashing Ka'iana. Ten thousand men died in the Battle of Nu'uanu, a victory for Kamehameha that at last consolidated the unruly island chiefdoms (except for distant Kaua'i and Ni'ihau) under one king. Kamehameha's triumph (the historian Ralph S. Kuykendall calls Kamehameha "one of the great men of the world"), was due in large part to the assistance of John Young and other foreigners, who had not only trained and drilled the army, but developed a winning strategy based on the use of Kamehameha's new weaponry. (Judge Fornander solemnly marked this as the closing event in the history of ancient Hawai'i.)

With the unification of six islands, there came peace after generations of war (there also came levies, and commoners complained that even the smallest patch of taro was taxed). Kamehameha moved eight thousand of his warriors and their families from the island of Hawai'i to O'ahu, where they were given grants of land, which served to vitalize and to expand agricultural production on O'ahu. Kamehameha's victory resulted in the founding of a dynasty which was to last one hundred years.

Ooro, one of Kamehameha's officers, in a feather cape with a sword. Pen and ink wash over graphite by Jacques Arago, 1819, Honolulu Museum of Art

Kamehameha and Kaʻahumanu lived at Helumoa in Waikīkī (on a present-day map, the land between the Moana Surfrider and Royal Hawaiian Hotels). The king's enclosure, surrounded by a stone wall and fences, was within a large encampment where more than two thousand people—chiefs, priests, warriors, artisans, and attendants, and their wives and children— lived in seven hundred grass houses stretching along the shore from Nuʻuanu Stream to Kakaʻako. Behind the houses were *kalo* and other cultivated fields, marked with long rows of boundary stones. The king's bodyguard, dressed in ill-fitting uniforms, drilled with muskets and rusty bayonets in a dusty parade ground.

Kamehameha's house, eighty feet long and sixty feet wide, with sandalwood posts twelve feet high, sat in a dirt clearing with thirteen smaller buildings, among them the men's eating house, a sleeping house, an audience house, and a powder magazine, as well as the houses of his close attendants. At one end was the king's *heiau*, the largest in the compound, with carved wooden gods twenty-eight feet high, the ground piled with the decaying bodies of pigs, cats, and dogs. There was also a new stone storehouse, built to hold the king's growing inventory of china, silk, coins, furniture, knives, and swords obtained through trade, extortion from foreign ships, and as tribute from his people. It was during this time on Oʻahu that five more children were born to Kamehameha, including Kaheiheimālie's daughter, Kīnaʻu, who would herself be mother of two Hawaiian kings.

When Kamehameha moved his court to Hilo the following year, Kaʻahumanu and her fellow wives, including her sister, Kaheiheimālie, traveled with him, remaining there for six years. While in Hilo, the king became enamored of Kanahoahoa, the young daughter of a chief whom Kamehameha suspected of plotting against him. It is possible that Kamehameha thought to bind the girl to him, as he wished her alliance in the long-forestalled invasion of Kauaʻi, whose king was her uncle. John Papa ʻĪʻī wrote in *Fragments of Hawaiian History*, "Kamehameha went to spend the night with Kanahoahoa, with the knowledge of the god, Kāneikaulanaʻula, and the attendant who carried it. Kamehameha dismissed the attendant, sending him to his sleeping house, where Kaʻahumanu and Kaheiheimālie were awaiting Kamehameha's return. When they asked the attendant the whereabouts of the king, he replied, 'They two are at Olo, only at Olo.'"

The two incensed women composed a chant while they waited, using the attendant's words:

We are sorry for Kāneikaulana'ula.
He flies unattended,
For they two are at Olo, only at Olo.
In the presence of Kapo, wife of Puanui,
Great is your love, it keeps your eyes on her.

Kamehameha returned that night to find the two women dancing to the chant, their fury, according to 'Ī'ī, "like the sea sweeping over the embankments of the ponds of their hearts." The king demanded to know the meaning of the song, but they refused to tell him. When he angrily insisted, they pointed to the boy who was bearer of the king's spittoon, sleeping on a nearby mat. The king, perhaps out of guilt, or embarrassment at having been caught, turned his anger on the innocent boy, and it was only through the intervention of fellow chiefs that the boy's life was saved. 'Ī'ī wondered if the king knew that what he had done—not his dalliance, but his behavior to the boy—was hardly worthy of a great king.

In 1797, Keōpūolani, Kamehameha's sacred wife, gave birth in Hilo to a son, Liholiho. As was the tradition, the king referred to the boy as his grandchild, and to Keōpūolani as his daughter, not because of his age (Kamehameha was then forty years old; Keōpūolani was nineteen), but to honor their lineage. After learning that the baby's wet nurse, required by tradition to feed the infant while naked, was neglectful, Kamehameha sent Ka'ahumanu to take the child into her care. As Liholiho's guardian, the subtle Ka'ahumanu was easily able to shape him to her liking, strengthening her already formidable position at the center of court, even though she herself had never given the king a child (it is said that one of her terms when she married him was that any children of her own would be made sole heirs to the kingdom).

When Liholiho grew older, it was difficult for him to find other children with whom to play, as they feared that their houses might be burned down, or that they would be killed if they violated a *kapu*. When Liholiho was six years old, he saw an *'ehu* (red-haired Polynesian) boy playing on the beach with other children. In imitation of the adults who fell to the ground at the approach of the prince, the children threw themselves facedown in the sand. Liholiho, wanting to play with the red-haired boy, jumped onto his back. His attendants snatched the boy to take him to the *heiau* to be killed, as he had been touched by the god-chief, but Liholiho held the boy tightly, shouting,

I'i, i'i, i'i. The boy was saved and he became Liholiho's favorite playmate, fittingly given the name Daniel I'i.

Keōpūolani, although still required to sleep with Kamehameha after each menstruation, had taken as her lover Ka'ahumanu's cousin, Kalanimoku, with whom she had no children (according to Kamakau, allowing her a lover was Kamehameha's way to control her sexually), although she bore Kamehameha a second son in 1813. The child, Kauikeaouli, was stillborn, but was miraculously prayed into life by the high priest and prophet Kapihe. In the birth chant composed for Kauikeaouli, the lines "That which is above shall be brought down; That which is below shall be lifted up" may reflect Kapihe's warning that the gods would soon be abandoned, and the high chiefs left adrift. Disregarding tradition, which allowed a high chiefess to give a newborn child to another chief to raise as his own, Keōpūolani insisted on keeping both Kauikeaouli and his sister Nāhi'ena'ena (born in 1815) close to her. The following is part of the chant composed at Kauikeaouli's birth:

> The chiefess gave birth,
> she bore in labor above,
> she lay as in a faint, a weakness at the navel.
> The afterbirth stirred at the roots, crept in darkness,
> in waves of pain came the bitter bile of the child.
> This was a month of travail,
> of gasping labor,
> a writhing to deliver the chief.
> He is this chief born of a chiefess.
>
> Now a chief shall be here above.
> Who shall be below?

After thirteen years of intimacy, Kamehameha abandoned Ka'ahumanu to live in Kona with Kaheiheimālie. The following is a chant said by Kamakau to have been composed by Ka'ahumanu in her grief:

> The husband is the one beloved.
> Weary with labor have I been for his sake,

Weary for you, O my bird-like companion.
Like a bird is Keolewa in the calm.
Wai'ale'ale rises high in the heavens,
Ha'upu is dark and green in the north,
There are groans on the plain of Koholalele.
Torn blossoms of the *kukui* are tossed about by the wind,
Tossed from their stems by the Wind-of-the-North,
The flowers are flung about at Wailua,
Hau flowers of Ka-lehua-wehe are flung in heaps.
How can you untangle what has been firmly knotted?
It cannot be unraveled, for love is deaf to reason
Until rejected, then it will listen.

In her despair, Ka'ahumanu plunged into the sea and swam six miles in the dark through shoals of sharks, from Ke'ei to Hōnaunau in south Kona.

She swam out to sea with the intention of going until her strength gave out. While in the water she saw a boy following her. She cried out to him to go back, but he kept following. Noticing that he was getting tired, she allowed him to lean on her shoulder to rest. Pity for the boy, Luahine, made her swim back to shore. So it was said that the boy was Ka'ahumanu's shoulder cover. Luahine, ke kā'awe o Ka'ahumanu.

When Kamehameha's land at Puakō in South Kohala was threatened with lava, people said that Pele had lost patience with her favorite and was punishing him for his disloyalty to Ka'ahumanu. He quickly made offerings to the goddess, and Ka'ahumanu and Kaheiheimālie loyally resolved to perish with Kamehameha should the lava overtake him. Kamakau wrote that Pele appeared to the women, dancing at the end of a troupe of goddesses, chanting, "Our husband has gone to carry the bigger load [Kaheiheimālie], while the lighter load [Ka'ahumanu] is neglected." The goddess deigned to accept the king's offerings, and the fast-moving lava was diverted into the sea.

Despite this reprieve, or perhaps because of it, Kamehameha kept Ka'ahumanu's sister with him (she was an easygoing and trustworthy woman, unlike Ka'ahumanu), but wisely gave a feast for Ka'ahumanu that was remem-

The goddess Pele's volcano of Kīlauea. Oil painting by Titian Ramsey Peale, 1842, Bernice Pauahi Bishop Museum, Honolulu

bered for generations. She lay on a couch spread with feather cloaks, amid pillows soaked with perfume, as a large feather *kāhili*, called Hawai'i Loa, which had been created in her honor, was borne before her. The hem of her *pā'ū* was carried by a line of chiefs and chiefesses, followed by Kaheiheimālie herself; then sacred Keōpūolani, and the rest of the queens. Several days were spent in dancing and feasting, during which all of the food of the surrounding countryside was consumed.

In 1812, when the American ship *Beaver*, bound for Canton, was in port, Ka'ahumanu and the king, as well as three of Kamehameha's other wives, arrived at the ship in a large double canoe with fourteen paddlers. The women lounged on the center platform, while Kamehameha sat above them, surrounded by chests of arms and a guard holding a short sword. Kamehameha was invited to dinner with the officers on board (the same men who could not beat Ka'ahumanu in a game of checkers) but the women, constrained by *kapu*, had to wait until the men were finished before going below deck to eat the raw fish, dog, and *poi* that attendants had brought from shore for them.

The officers of the *Beaver* arranged a day of racing for Kamehameha. The king, dressed in a *malo*, sat cross-legged on a platform twenty feet above the ground while guards with muskets patrolled below him. People crowded around the track to bet on a footrace between Kamehameha's nephew and a black man named Anderson, while Ka'ahumanu paraded through the crowd in a blue satin gown trimmed with gold lace, made for her in England, which is the first time that she is described in Western clothes. When Anderson won the race, there was a fight between some Hawaiians and one of the sailors, and the sailor drew a pistol. From his elevated seat, Kamehameha ordered his guards to arrest the sailor. Taking away the man's gun, the king warned him that if he started any more fights, he would have him put to death.

In 1813, angry chiefs brought to Kamehameha the fishermen who had attacked him twelve years earlier on the reef near Kea'au, and demanded that they be killed. Kamehameha had no wish to punish them, enacting instead the Law of the Splintered Paddle, which protected by decree any travelers, particularly old people, women, and children, from harm, especially from such wanton acts of violence as he himself had committed throughout his life. It was the first time in the history of the kingdom that the rights of the weak were recognized.

Kamehameha had grown rich thanks to the sale of sandalwood, sought by the Chinese for incense, and from the sale of goods taken in exchange for it, as well as the profits from the rapid growth of whaling and shipping. Harbor duties, paid by all foreign vessels entering Hawaiian ports, had increased considerably with each year, especially after Kamehameha learned that a large part of the money he made from sandalwood went to pay duty in Canton. During the height of the sandalwood trade, Kamehameha is said to have been paid hundreds of thousands of Spanish dollars—a hoard still thought to be hidden in caves and lava tubes across the Big Island.

The harvesting of sandalwood was extremely arduous work, often done in the rain, and without sufficient clothing or food for the workers, who were often left misshapen for the rest of their lives. A pit would be dug in a hillside in the shape of a ship's hold, and when it was filled, the logs, three to four feet long and stripped of bark, would be tied onto the backs of men, women, and children with *kī* leaves passed over the shoulders and under the arms, to be carried downhill to the ports where foreign ships lay waiting for their cargoes (the warehouses stored with sandalwood were said to be so fragrant that the scent carried for miles). The Kaua'i missionary Peter Gulick wrote in 1830 that he pitied the people who collected sandalwood: "They are often driven by hunger to eat wild and bitter herbs, moss, &c. and though the winter is so cold on the hills that my winter clothes will scarcely keep me comfortable, I frequently see men with no clothing except the maro [*malo*], were they not remarkably hardy, most of them would certainly perish."

In addition to the desire for sandalwood, firewood was needed by ships, resulting in the eventual clearing of much of the forests down to the last branch. The once fertile plains east of Honolulu were turned to dust, and lower Kalihi, Nuʻuanu, Makiki, and Mānoa were barren of vegetation for the next hundred years. In 1819 the commander of a French ship, Louis de Freycinet, wrote that he feared for the Hawaiians. "What will happen . . . when sandalwood, which is such a powerful attraction to greedy speculators, becomes exhausted. It is already becoming difficult to obtain, for each log has to be carried on human backs, exposed to scorching sun, across the forests and precipices, where there are no roads. The forests are being destroyed, and it seems that no one is going to take care of replanting them for a long time." By 1829, Hawaiian sandalwood forests had disappeared.

With the employment of native people to serve the increasing number of foreigners, agriculture and fishing began to fall into neglect, and there was a decline in ritual ceremonies, including the performance of sacred and social *hula*, as well as those sports and games that Hawaiians no longer had the time or inclination to play. People began to go hungry and to fall sick. Although the feudal system that had served the *aliʻi* for centuries had been harsh, the exploitation of tenants and workers increased with the headlong rush to capitalism. The chiefs acquired new desires, which demanded a different kind of labor from their people. Since the time of Cook, *haoles* had provided the Hawaiians with the iron they needed to make tools, nails, weapons, and fishhooks. A warrior class had once been necessary to maintain the high chiefs, but with the coming of guns and the new forms of battle introduced by foreigners, war had become far more expensive as well as dangerous, and thus less frequent. With peace came a preoccupation, if not an obsession, with consumption. Rather than high-ranking women or land or fame on the battlefield, it was bolts of silk, schooners, Chinese furniture, porcelain, carpets, and imported alcohol that the chiefs desired, acquired without thought of expense or utility. The missionary Peter Gulick wrote, "This propensity to buy, seems indeed, to be deeply rooted in most of the chiefs . . . However bitterly [the traders] may complain, of dilatory payments, and want of veracity, and integrity in the natives, they urge upon them things which they do not want; and for which, they have no means of paying, but by imposing new burdens upon the people."

After the plundering of the sandalwood forests, the *ali'i* relied for income on the export of horses, hides, and tallow, which were less profitable than sandalwood. The association with foreigners, either on ships or with the men opening stores, brothels, and lumber yards, awakened in the *ali'i* a taste for foreign goods, however, which in turn stimulated other cravings and needs, and served to weaken their traditional sense of responsibility. Copper, canvas, naval stores, wine and spirits, furniture, steel, iron, soap, and paint were imported from the United States. From China came tea, cotton, and silk. Tahiti and the South Pacific traded tortoiseshell, mother-of-pearl, pearls, and sugar (until the Americans started their own plantations). French ships from Bordeaux carried ironware to Chile, Mexico, and Peru, and brought what cargo remained across the Pacific. California, the Northwest, and Canada sent salmon, lumber, furs, skins, and hides. From Mexico came specie and bullion, which were the monies favored for commerce. Sereno Bishop, the son of the missionary Artemas Bishop, wrote that his father remembered well the old chief John Adams Kuakini who was governor of Hawai'i Island:

> Kona district was the residence of quite a number of chiefs . . . who were supported by the labor of their many serfs from the produce of the rich uplands. Occasionally a chair or a camphor trunk might be seen in the nice thatched cottages of such natives of rank, besides the mats, tapas, calabashes, and wooden bowls and trays which constituted their furniture. Cloth of any kind was scarce. Kuakini was disposed to monopolize such trade as came from occasional whalers touching at Kaawaloa. He possessed vast quantities of foreign goods stored up in his warehouses, while his people were naked. I often heard my father tell of once seeing one of Kuakini's large double canoes loaded deep with bales of broad cloths and Chinese silks and satins which had become damaged by long storage. They were carried out and dumped into the ocean. Probably they had been purchased . . . with the sandalwood which, in the twenties was such a mine of wealth to the chiefs.

James Jarves described life at court when the prestige accruing from the possession of foreign goods was at its height:

A few of the chiefs had attempted crude imitations of foreign houses, but most of them were lodged in more ample and better-constructed straw huts than the common sort. Some were really very neat and attractive in their way, and far more convenient and comfortable to their owners than the most ambitious experiments of those who had thrown away their money upon foreign mechanics. The exterior of these were, in general, more or less dilapidated, and the grounds about them parched and barren. Their interior presented an incongruous mixture of white and native habits and articles. Huge state-beds to look at, and piles of fine cool mats to sleep upon. Chairs and sofas backed rigidly and uselessly against the walls while their owners squatted upon the floors. Velvets and porcelain were snubbed by tapas and calabashes. Fleas and other vermin reveled among the sweets of cologne and otto [*sic*] of roses. At dinner, you might be served, one day, reclining on the ground with baked dog or live fish, by your own fingers, from a common wooden platter; and the next, sit comfortably upright at a high table, horrified at the rapacity and awkwardness with which your aristocratic hosts devoured pate de foie gras with the aid of silver forks, and engulfed champagne from the costliest crystal.

It was said that the thought of the island of Kaua'i, unconquered and independent, was for Kamehameha like a sea urchin spine in his side. In 1802, after six years of preparation, he moved with a large entourage and nearly a thousand war canoes, each a hundred feet long and three feet deep (his army of seven thousand men also had twenty-one schooners, forty swivel guns, and six mortars), from Hilo to Lahaina, on Maui, to prepare for a second invasion of Kaua'i (the first attempt was in 1796, when Kamehameha's fleet of eight hundred canoes, seemingly abandoned by the fire goddess, was stopped by a tremendous storm in the dangerous channel between Kaua'i and O'ahu).

While in Lahaina, Kamehameha enlisted two fugitives escaped from an Australian penal colony to build for Ka'ahumanu the first Western-style house in the Islands. The two-story redbrick house of four rooms was set on a point overlooking the sea, and Ka'ahumanu became one of the few *ali'i* ever to be comfortable living in the foreign style. Kamakau described her during this period (she was then thirty-four years old) as imposingly grand. He thought that she had grown proud, as the chiefs obeyed her commands without question. She insisted that the finest patterns of *kapa* and the fattest hog, dog, chicken, or fish, as well as the most fragrant seaweed, be first offered to her (Kamakau adds that this may have been true only after Kamehameha's death).

In 1804, after living on food supplied by the Maui chiefs, or "eating the land," as it was called, Kamehameha moved his court from Lahaina to Oʻahu in the last stages of preparation before attacking Kauaʻi. As he assembled his army, however, there was an outbreak of plague, which killed many of his chiefs and warriors. Hundreds of bodies were washed to sea each day from the beaches of Waikīkī. Kamakau wrote that those who contracted it died very quickly:

> It was a very virulent pestilence . . . A person on the highway would die before he could reach home. One might go for food and water and die so suddenly that those at home did not know what had happened. The body turned black at death. A few died a lingering death, but never longer than twenty-four hours; if they were able to hold out for a day they had a fair chance to live. Those who lived generally lost their hair, hence the illness was called "Head Stripped Bare."

Kamehameha himself was ill, but recovered. When Kaʻahumanu's father, the high chief Keʻeaumoku, lay dying, a weeping Kamehameha asked him if there was anyone strong enough to take the kingdom from him. Keʻeaumoku is said to have answered that Kamehameha need fear only Kaʻahumanu. He reminded the king that her intervention in various plots against him over the years had helped to keep him in power. If she were ever to ally herself with another man, there was the chance that he would rise against Kamehameha, bringing along the many powerful chiefs who were her relatives and adherents.

Kaʻahumanu's grief at the death of her father was very great. For the rest of her life, she kept his bones next to her sleeping platform on a feather mattress given to her by a sea captain, ensuring that her father's *mana* would be in her care as his spirit assumed the nature of a family god. This is the mourning chant that Kaʻahumanu wrote at her father's death:

> Like a peal of thunder is your tread
> Reverberating to the presence of Wakea,

Here is the divine child of a multitude of sacred offspring,
My father and chief,
My beloved companion,
My loved one.
I am breathless with grieving for you.
I weep for my companion in the cold,
My companion of the chilly rain.
The chill encircles me,
The cold surrounds me,
Purple with cold not rejected,
Only two places to find warmth—
The bed mate at home,
The tapa covering is the second warmth,
Found in the bosom of a companion.
It is there, it is there, it is there.

Treating Keʻeaumoku's warning with the seriousness it deserved, Kamehameha declared Kaʻahumanu *kapu* to all persons other than himself. The following proverb from Mary Kawena Pukui's book of Hawaiian sayings, *ʻŌlelo Noʻeau*, refers to the unification of Maui, Molokaʻi, Oʻahu, Lānaʻi, Hawaiʻi, and Kahoʻolawe in 1795:

Eonu moku a Kamehameha ua
Noa ia ʻoukou,
Akā o ka hiku
O ka moku ua
Kapu ia naʻu.

Six of Kamehameha's islands
Are free to you,
But the seventh [Kaʻahumanu] is *kapu*,
And is for me alone.

The *kapu* meant that should Kaʻahumanu be caught in adultery, her lover would be killed and his body given in sacrifice to the gods, although she herself would be spared. If any person, including Kamehameha's own relatives, were to start a quarrel with any of Kaʻahumanu's family, he, too, would be put to death. Kamehameha assigned the somewhat fraught responsibility of guarding her, given her sensuous and willful nature, to two of his men, who, it may be surmised, were not always successful in their task.

Kamehameha also gave Ka'ahumanu the right of *pu'uhonua*, which allowed her to grant sanctuary to anyone who sought her protection, and the power to repeal a death sentence, making her person, while forbidden to anyone but the king, a place of refuge where men, women, children, fugitives from battle, and criminals could find safety. The lands that Ka'ahumanu had inherited and that Kamehameha had given her were also deemed places of refuge. (Kamakau, who valued Ka'ahumanu at half the worth of her husband's kingdom, wrote that Kamehameha dealt out death and Ka'ahumanu saved from death.) The king's gift threatened the dominance of the priests, as it lessened the religious significance of refuge, once found only at *heiau* and special sacred sites, at the same time that it increased Ka'ahumanu's already estimable power. The role once played by gods and priests within *kapu* precincts was henceforth to be shared with a woman. In addition, she was awarded her father's place at the king's councils, a privilege which should by tradition have gone to one of her brothers.

In 1809, when Kamehameha was no longer young, but still possessed the physique and strength of a warrior ("without the flabbiness of age," wrote Kamakau), he at last married Kekāuluohi, the daughter of Kaheiheimālie and his half brother, whom he had claimed at birth. Kekāuluohi, who had a light complexion and husky voice, had spent her childhood studying genealogy chants, although Ka'ahumanu, whose responsibility it had been to guard her, had allowed her to meet in secret any man who pleased Ka'ahumanu, which tended to keep the girl from her studies. (At the death of Kamehameha ten years later, she married his son, Liholiho, who in turn gave her to one of his friends, to whom she bore a son, Lunalilo, who became king in 1873.)

That year, Ka'ahumanu's mother, Namahana, died in Honolulu. A mourner hurried to town from Waialua on the north shore so that she could be buried with the chiefess, sharing her grave, as was the custom, but Ka'ahumanu and her brothers would not permit it. This is Ka'ahumanu's death chant for her mother:

> My mother in the house well-peopled,
> House into whose shelter we entered
> To rest from the heat of the way,

Diamond Head at Waikīkī. Oil on canvas by Enoch Wood Perry, Jr., ca. 1865, Bernice Pauahi Bishop Museum, Honolulu

Love to my mother who has gone,
Leaving me wandering on the mountainside.
You are the woman consumed by the wind
Consumed by the trade wind,
Consumed, consumed, consumed with love . . .

Despite the *kapu* on her body, Kaʻahumanu began a love affair with Kanihonui, the nineteen-year-old son of Kamehameha's half sister. A favorite of Kamehameha, he had lived in the king's house since childhood, and was said to be the most beautiful man in the kingdom—a description used for all of Kaʻahumanu's lovers. The queen met him in secret whenever Kamehameha conducted rites in the *heiau*, but a guard of the sleeping house, aware that he would be killed if he did not report it, told the king, and Kanihonui was promptly strangled to death in Papaʻenaʻena *heiau* on the slope of Diamond Head (the stones of the temple were later used to build a residence for Lunalilo in Waikīkī).

The surf was particularly high on the day of Kanihonui's death, and Kaʻahumanu asked that a holiday be granted so that the court could surf at Kapua, near Diamond Head (still a popular surfing spot, now known as First

Break). As Kaʻahumanu rode her board to shore, she could see the *heiau* where the body of her lover lay rotting on the altar, and the smoke as the sacrificial fires were lighted. Kaʻahumanu, who blamed her disloyalty to Kamehameha on foreigners' alcohol, angrily determined to take the kingdom from her husband on behalf of Liholiho, whom she had raised from childhood. John Papa ʻĪʻī wrote that Kaʻahumanu, surrounded by her chiefs, wailed in rage as she watched the smoke:

> Kalanimoku [Kamehameha's commander-in-chief and prime minister of the kingdom] was there, watching over his grieving cousin. While the young chief [Liholiho] and a group of chiefs were in their presence, Kalanimoku asked, "What do you think? Shall we wrest the kingdom from your father, make you king, and put him to death?" Liholiho bowed his head in meditation . . . and answered, "I do not want my father to die." This reply brought forth the admiration of all the chiefs.

Although perhaps not the admiration of Kaʻahumanu. Kamakau believed that while it was wrong of the king to put Kanihonui to death, there had been talk of rebellion, and Kamehameha had been forced to kill him in order to frighten the restive chiefs.

At the end of 1812, Kamehameha and his court left Honolulu to return to his compound at Kamakahonu in Kailua. ʻĪʻī described the settlement, with its lovely cove:

> It was a gathering place for those who went swimming and a place where the surf rolled in and dashed on land when it was rough. It was deep enough there for boats to land when the tide was high, and when it was ebb tide the boats came up close to its rocky pahoehoe [smooth lava] side. From there the sea was shallow as far as the spring of Honuaula, where there was a house site on a raised pavement. There the young chief [Liholiho] lived. A Hale o Lono [*heiau*] faced directly toward the upland, and toward the north there was a bed of pahoe-

hoe which reached to the sea, where there was a surfing place for children . . . Later, a heiau was built there by the king.

In 1815, the British trader *Columbia*, carrying furs to China, anchored in Kailua Bay. Its chief officer, Peter Corney, described the king and his followers:

Tameamah [Kamehameha] was dressed in a coloured shirt, velveteen breeches, red waistcoat, large military shoes, and worsted stockings, a black silk handkerchief around his neck, no coat: he is a tall, stout, athletic man, nose rather flat, thick lips, the upper one turned up; an open countenance, with three of his lower front teeth gone . . . The canoes collected from all parts, and, in a short time, there were no fewer than eighty of them, with from three to ten men in each, and some hundreds of men, women, and children swimming about the ship, regardless of the sharks . . . Captain Robson, being rather alarmed at having so many on board, told the king to send them ashore. He took a handspike in his hand, and said a few words, and in a moment the men flew out of the ship in all directions.

A year later, Otto von Kotzebue, on board the Russian ship *Rurick*, called on Ka'ahumanu at Kamakahonu. The queen was seated on a large pile of *kapa* mats with her husband's lesser wives on either side. An interpreter sat nearby to translate her many questions. Despite the *kapu* that prohibited women from eating food that had not been prepared by men, she asked her female attendant for a watermelon, cut it herself, and handed a piece to Kotzebue, an act for which her servant could have been executed. Her hospitality impressed the foreigners, who perhaps were not aware that inattention to one's guests was considered so rude by Hawaiians that it would be discussed for years. The captain, who declined using her pipe, watched as she shared it with her women, who seemed to be solely interested in combing and dressing their hair. Ka'ahumanu wore her hair short, cropped with a shark's-tooth knife, as was the fashion (a woman's hair was cut after the birth of her first child, but Ka'ahumanu was childless), with a lock on her forehead shaped into a little curl and held in place with juice made from roots and tree gum. The hair around her face had been bleached blond with lime and *kī* juice (men dressed their hair with a paste made of clay or lime, which was rolled

Chiefess wearing a *lei niho palaoa*. Lithograph from a drawing by Louis Choris, 1816, Honolulu Museum of Art

into small balls and moistened in the mouth before applying it to the hair). Kotzebue did not find her particularly handsome, but he considered Hawaiian women in general to be fat and charmless. He did allow, however, that the queen had a uniquely male understanding that guaranteed her domination of all things. Ka'ahumanu asked after Captain Vancouver, and when Kotzebue told her that he had long been dead, she was very upset.

Camille de Roquefeuil, a French naval officer, met Kamehameha and his family in 1819, the year of the king's death. Roquefeuil was disappointed by the king's acquisitive nature. Mary Ellen Birkett translates from Roquefeuil's book *Journal d'un Voyage autour du Monde pendant les années 1816, 1817, 1818, et 1819* in *The Hawaiian Journal of History*:

> [Kamehameha's] bearing showed signs of the prodigious strength with which he had been endowed. He wore the kind of European clothes that our artisans wear in winter; his appearance was clean and decent. A serious and searching gaze was the distinguishing feature of his countenance. As for his character, satisfied ambition seemed to have procured insatiable avarice . . . Tameamea [*sic*] asked me about my voyage and about our cargo, and was rather disappointed when I told him that it did not contain luxury goods.

Kamehameha I, from a watercolor by Louis Choris, ca. 1817

The following day, wrote Roquefeuil, the king's son, Liholiho, and several of Liholiho's wives, as well as one of Kamehameha's wives, along with courtiers and attendants, visited his ship. "Although the pilot had stayed on board to police the ship during the prince's visit, we noticed that a few small items were missing."

Kamehameha at age sixty-five continued his habit of nimbly deflecting the spears thrown at him by his warriors as he took his vigorous walks up and down the hillsides, his men lying in wait for him, poised to hurl spears at his approach. Although he had learned to converse in English, he could not write. He had heard the rumor that the Tahitian chiefs had become Christian, but he showed no interest in the purported mercies of a Christian god. He is said to have told a *haole* with whom he was walking one day that if the man were to jump from a nearby bluff only to be saved by his god, he would consider conversion. A disingenuous argument, as it is unlikely that Kamehameha's own gods would have troubled to save him had he happened to jump, but it impressed the foreigner.

The Russian navigator Vasily Golovnin described Kamehameha's audience hall at Kawaihae:

> The King . . . was standing by the corner of his house . . . and invited us into his "dining room." . . . There we saw on one side, a huge trunk which contained hand arms . . . next to it, a mahogany bureau of European workmanship, two mahogany tables—one large leaf-table and one round; the latter was covered with a blue napkin and on it stood a quart of rum, a decanter half filled with red wine, a large glass of water and three or four smaller empty glasses. Next to the table stood an armchair and two or three straight chairs, also of European make. Two very ordinary mirrors . . . hung on the wall, and under them, leaning against the wall, stood several guns, cutlasses, and spears. This half . . . was covered with grass mats, while the floor of the other half was bare and contained an ordinary ship's cast iron stove, in which a fire was burning, and an assortment of dishes in the corner.

When Kamehameha fell ill in the spring of 1819, the Spanish adventurer Francisco de Marín, known for his skill at healing (he hoarded a private dispensary of foreign herbs and medicine), sailed to Kona to treat the king, but he could do nothing for him. When the native healers conceded that Kamehameha was not responding to their own treatments, he was carried from his house to a small shack of *ʻōhiʻa* wood that had been made for him in his illness, which required a human sacrifice. Upon hearing this, people ran to hide in the bush, only the chiefs remaining in attendance, but Kamehameha forbade the priests to make a sacrifice. He then instructed Kaʻahumanu that no human beings should be made to serve as his companions in the grave—not out of mercy but as an acknowledgement of the rights of ownership, as with his death, all men would become the property of Liholiho.

After three days in which he grew weaker, he was carried to his own sleeping house to die. One of the chiefs asked for his last instructions: " 'We are all here, your younger brothers, your chiefs, your foreigner [John Young]. Give us a word.' 'For what purpose?' asked Kamehameha. And then he whispered, *E naʻi wale no ʻoukou i koʻu pono, ʻaʻole e pau.* 'You can seek out all of the benefits I have given you and find them without number.' " John Young, who had served Kamehameha for almost twenty years as political and military adviser, as well as trusted friend, put his arms around the king's neck and kissed him. A chief asked to be given the care of his bones, and the king consented. Kamehameha died at three o'clock in the morning, May 8, 1819.

The chiefs quarreled over his body, many of them desiring to take it. One chief suggested that they eat it, as it would be impossible to hide it. Kaʻahumanu said, "This body is not ours; ours was the breath, the body

The king's *heiau* in Kealakekua, with an *ʻanuʻu* tower hung with offerings, tall wooden images, and the carcass of a sacrificed pig. Engraving after a drawing by Jacques Arago, 1822

belongs to one of the chiefs." The corpse was taken to nearby 'Ahu'ena *heiau*, and a pig was cooked as a sacrifice to preserve the king's soul so that it would live on as a guardian spirit. Five hundred dogs were sacrificed as his bones were burned. Liholiho had been defiled by touching his father's body, and a prayer was chanted for his purification.

> Here is the food offered, here is the food offered in your favor,
> Here is the food for the sin offering; let him be hidden,
> Let him go and play,
> Here let there be mourning,
> For the dead and for his heir,
> Let him be accepted where he is laid to rest,
> Let him go in peace,
> Let him go in silence.

Ka'ahumanu cut herself and burned her body, symbols of dying with her husband, and she and the other female chiefs had sexual intercourse with random strangers, without regard to rank, which served to emphasize the triumph of life over death. Wailing men and women broke their teeth, tattooed their tongues, and burned their skin (if a man hesitated to knock out a tooth, his wife did it for him while he slept). Usually only one tooth was removed at the death of a chief, but there were few men born before the arrival of the missionaries with a full set. The loss of teeth affected men's speech, and many older Hawaiians spoke with a lisp. Cutting one or both ears was also a gesture of intense grief, and the tongue was tattooed with a black spot or line. The head was shaved close, with a strip of hair down the center of the head, not unlike a modern Mohawk, or a small round spot was shaved on the crown, like the tonsure of a monk. Some shaved their heads on one side, leaving long the hair on the other side, which often reached eighteen inches. A chief's attendants and dependents followed his example and shaved their heads and mutilated themselves in imitation of him.

The rituals of mourning understandably caused astonishment, if not horror, in foreigners like James Jarves:

> The hair was shaved or cut close, teeth knocked out and sometimes the ears were mangled. Some tattooed their tongues in a corresponding manner to the other parts of their bodies. Frequently the flesh was

cut or burnt, eyes scooped out, and other even more painful personal outrages inflicted. But these usages, however shocking they may appear, were innocent compared with the horrid saturnalia which immediately followed the death of a chief of the highest rank. Then the most unbounded license prevailed; law and restraint were cast aside, and the whole people appeared more like demons than human beings. Every vice and crime was allowed. Property was destroyed, houses fired and old feuds revived and avenged. Gambling, theft and murder were as open as the day; clothing was cast aside as a useless incumbrance [sic]; drunkenness and promiscuous prostitution prevailed throughout the land, no women, excepting the widows of the deceased, being exempt from the grossest violation. There was no passion however lewd, or desire however wicked, but could be gratified with impunity during the continuance of this period, which, happily, from its own violence soon spent itself. No other nation was ever witness to a custom which so entirely threw off all moral and legal restraints and incited the evil passions to unresisted riot and wanton debauchery.

Jarves was wrong, as the early observers were wrong about a number of things. The Hawaiian ritual of mourning was shared by other cultures, serving to incorporate the past into the present and the present into the past, creating anew, over and over again, a cosmology without end. The missionary Lucy Thurston, who arrived in the Islands five months after Kamehameha's death, terrified by warnings that she would be bewitched, robbed, and even eaten, described in her journal what she had been told of the traditional chaos that followed the king's death:

They went upon the idea that their grief was so great, that they knew not what they did. They were let thoroughly loose, without law or restraint, and so gave themselves up to every evil, that they acted more like devils incarnate, than like human beings . . . Their grass-thatched cottages were left empty; their last vestige of clothing thrown aside; and such scenes of wholesale and frantic excesses exhibited in the open face of day, as would make darkness pale. A tornado swept over the nation, making it drunk with abominations . . . It was among their more decent and innocent extravagances that they burned their faces with fire, in large, permanent, semi-circular figures, and with stones knocked out their front teeth.

Since it was believed that Kamehameha's death could only have been caused by sorcery, fire pits of stone, bordered by tall poles hung with strips of white *kapa*, were built for a ritual of detection, while the priests searched for the evildoer who had prayed the king to death. Ka'ahumanu's brother, Ke'eaumoku, known to foreigners as George Cox, broke one of the poles

Ke'eaumoku, Governor Cox of Maui, on board the *Uranie* under Louis de Freycinet. Watercolor and pen over pencil by Adrien Taunay the Younger, 1819, Honolulu Museum of Art

while drunk, causing suspicion to fall on their family. He had long been contemptuous of the priests, openly denouncing them as liars, and he remained defiant despite the rumors, which were quickly suppressed.

Kamehameha's body, as befitting that of a great king, was wrapped in leaves of banana, mulberry, and *kalo*, laid in a shallow trench a foot deep, and covered with soil. A fire was lighted the length of the grave and kept burning for ten days, during which time chants and prayers were recited without pause. The grave was then opened and the bones cleaned. The flesh, internal organs, and other parts of the body were taken in secret after dark and thrown into the sea, during which time no commoner was allowed to leave his house or he would be killed. The priests then arranged his bones in the shape of a body and wrapped them in white *kapa*, which marked the end of the period of defilement. The hiding place of Kamehameha's bones, said to be along the Kona coast or in Kohala, has never been found.

As Liholiho had been violated by the presence of his father's corpse, he sailed north to Kawaihae and remained there with his cousin, Kekuaokalani, who held to the old beliefs and encouraged Liholiho to resist the requests of his foster mother, Kaʻahumanu, and his mother, Keōpūolani, to return to Kona. "Your grandfather [Kamehameha] left . . . the care of the government to you, of the [war] god to me, and each of us to look to the other . . . Let us remain. There is food in the uplands and fish in the sea, and if a messenger is again sent by your *kahu* face to face, let him fear death in the bush."

Despite his cousin's advice, Liholiho sailed to Kailua, where Kaʻahumanu was waiting for him. Holding Kamehameha's favorite spear, she was dressed in the dead king's feather cloak and war helmet, lest there be any lingering hope that Liholiho might rule the kingdom alone. Behind her stood Queen Keōpūolani with her two young children, Kauikeaouli and Nāhiʻenaʻena, and Hewahewa, the head priest. Liholiho, wearing his own helmet and feather cloak over a red-and-gold British soldier's uniform, arrived in silence with his honor guard. Kamakau wrote that Kaʻahumanu greeted Liholiho with the words, "O Heavenly One! I speak to you the commands of your grandfather [father]. Here are the chiefs, here are the people of your ancestors; here are your guns; here are your lands. But we two shall share the rule of the land."

Liholiho was twenty-one years old. He was more than six feet tall, although not as tall as his father, corpulent, and handsome (as was the tradition, his skull had been carefully molded and elongated by massage in childhood), with long black hair that reached his shoulders. He had inherited the light golden skin of his mother, Keōpūolani, rather than Kamehameha's darker coloring, as well as the prostrating *kapu*, which obliged men to keep their heads lower than his own. Kamehameha is said to have called him Kuʻumakamae, or "My Treasure," and the boy had been raised with great tenderness. The traditional training of a high chief in the art of war had not been given him, in part because warfare was no longer a matter of hand-to-hand combat, and because his father's unification of the Islands in 1795 had ended the long years of fighting. He had been instructed in his ceremonial religious duties, but had not been taught the practical duties of governing. He must have understood that without the support of Kaʻahumanu and her family, he would not have the power to hold the kingdom. He would be the ceremonial figurehead, and Kaʻahumanu would rule. In her forthright and fearless way, Kaʻahumanu had created for herself the new position of *kuhina nui*, or regent. Whether Kamehameha had indeed asked her to assume this powerful position is not known for certain, but no one dared question her claim.

During the ceremony, Keōpūolani gestured to Liholiho, putting her hand to her mouth to indicate her wish that he eat with the women. David Malo wrote that it was a very curious thing for a *kapu* chiefess to do, "one for whom these tabus were made and who had the benefit of them." Keōpūolani then asked Liholiho for permission to eat with his five-year-old brother, Kauikeaouli (the future Kamehameha III). Liholiho obediently sent the boy to her later that afternoon, and fled to sea with his favorites, sailing in his two-masted canoe to take refuge once again in Kawaihae, sending messengers every few days to Kona to fetch rum.

Although it was customary for a short while after the death of a chief to indulge in free eating, Kaʻahumanu proclaimed that men and women could henceforth eat food cooked in the same ovens, and could eat out of the same bowl (it was rumored that she herself had been eating shark meat and pork as early as 1810), although she took care that it was not a royal decree—those who chose to keep the old *kapu* were free to do so. Keōpūolani quickly made clear her allegiance to Kaʻahumanu, despite her fear that Kaʻahumanu's orders would cause Kaʻahumanu to be punished by the gods.

Kaʻahumanu and a retinue of chiefs loyal to her journeyed by canoe to Kawaihae where they were determined to conclude the terms, as one-sided as they were, of her regency. John Young, who lived in Kawaihae with his

Hawaiian wife, asked Captain Louis de Freycinet, commander of a French scientific expedition then in port, to reconcile the chiefs. Liholiho stood alone and apart, as he remained under a *kapu* (Liholiho's cousin, Kekuaokalani, refused to attend). Freycinet, unaware of the subtleties of court etiquette, was surprised to see that no one rose to greet the queen when she arrived, "draped with some grace" in gray silk, and followed by servants bearing *kāhili* and European parasols. The chiefs paid not the least attention to her, even though the entire company had been waiting in the heat for hours.

Ka'ahumanu was known for her straightforward opinions, but her lack of inhibition in expressing them was an unusual and unsettling trait in a culture in which most thought was concealed in allusion and metaphor. Freycinet was impressed when she revealed a sophisticated understanding of the competition for territory and markets in European nations, and he assured Ka'ahumanu and Liholiho that his presence in the Islands had nothing to do with the wish of France to secure the Sandwich Islands, which the late king had believed to be under the protection of England, thanks to his earlier agreement with Vancouver. Liholiho accepted the full terms of their shared power. Ka'ahumanu and her chiefs returned to Kailua, and Liholiho sailed to nearby Honokāhau to dedicate a *heiau*.

Ka'ahumanu's earlier declaration that men and women could eat food prepared in the same oven had caused consternation, and while there was no active dissent, there was growing instability and anxiety at court. Determined to end the chiefs' indecision and confusion, she sent a message to Liholiho, busy on his round of religious ceremonies and feasts: "Place a shield of ti leaves before your god when you arrive in Kona," meaning that he should free the *kapu* of the war god Kūkā'ilimoku, which had been given to his cousin Kekuaokalani by Kamehameha upon his death, and release his people from restraint and fear.

Liholiho was too drunk to answer, and for two days sailed back and forth along the Kona coast. Seeing that the wind had died, preventing Liholiho from fleeing farther north, Ka'ahumanu sent her chiefs after him in a double canoe, waiting for him with his mother and other chiefesses, while the chiefs and foreign men who were visiting sat together on mats. At last, on the fourth day of October—the third night of the new moon and thus sacred to Kūkā'ilimoku—Liholiho was brought to her, taking his place with the men to celebrate the feast she had made in his honor.

Dancer wearing anklets of dogs' teeth. Lithograph after a pen and sepia wash drawing by John Webber, 1779

In the midst of the dancing and chanting, he suddenly rose from his place. Walking slowly to the women, he made a circle around them. He then walked around the men, before returning to the women to sit down with them. Six months after the death of his father, and with the urging of his stepmother and guardian and the quiet persuasion of his mother, the king ate with the women, bringing to an end a thousand years of *kapu*.

The shocked assembly clapped their hands and shouted, "*Ai noa! Ai noa!*" "Free eating!" To the astonishment of many, the king was not struck dead as he called for the destruction of sacred precincts and *heiau*. He himself appeared relieved—perhaps he, too, had feared that he would be killed—and danced and sang with the performers.

The chiefs and priests might still be feared, but the gods had been dispossessed of their fearsome power. The high priest Hewahewa did as Ka'ahumanu bid and set fire to more than one hundred wooden images in a nearby *heiau*. Pork was taken to outlying villages and given to both male and female commoners to eat. Hiram Bingham wrote that messengers were sent as far as Kaua'i to proclaim the abolition of *kapu*: "Kaumualii [the king of Kaua'i] readily renounced tabu, and the ceremonial restraints on eating, smoking, drinking, and sleeping, were no longer enforced by the king and his supporters. The governmental sacrifices ceased, and licentiousness and revelry abounded."

A moral crisis is inevitable when a people lose their belief in myth, as it is the link with that part of the psyche that is independent of and beyond consciousness. Without their gods, the Hawaiians were suddenly alone, with neither the old nor the new; lost in a profound uncertainty that left them particularly vulnerable to the god Jehovah, who was bearing down on them—the First Company of Congregationalist missionaries left Boston for the Sandwich Islands five months after the death of Kamehameha and one month before the abolition of *kapu*, crossing two oceans while Liholiho restlessly tacked up and down the west coast of Hawai'i. In later documents and oral histories, this period, called 'Ai noa, was referred to as the time they placed a *kapu* on the temples, rendering the overthrow of the gods itself a sacred ritual.

The *kapu* that were part of the Hawaiian belief system demanded ethical and behavioral obligations. The subjugation of the Hawaiians by their priests and rulers was enacted in service of the gods—ritual acts intended to redeem men from chaos—and was thus both pure and purifying. "Because of that loss, both chiefs and commoners became like voyagers adrift on the trackless sea, without sight of the stars above to guide them."

Toward the end of Kamehameha's reign, an attitude of lassitude, if not negligence, in respect to *kapu*, especially those regarding food, had been increasingly evident, although as late as 1818 two men were sacrificed at Kealakekua for wearing the *malo* of a chief and for entering a house that was *kapu*. To retain control of the lucrative trade with foreigners (as well as to render certain favorite surfing spots exclusive to the *ali'i*), Kamehameha had used *kapu* for purposes other than religion, imposing it whenever he found it to his advantage, whether for greed, sport, or governance.

Since the time of the first white men, however, Hawaiians, in particular women, had broken many of the *kapu*, often in the company of foreigners, and there had been no divine wrath or punishment, and little persecution by mortal men. After foreign ships began to frequent the Islands at the end of the eighteenth century, women, taking care not to be discovered, secretly swam at night to the foreign ships to eat pork and shark flesh with the sailors. The shipwrecked Scots sail maker Archibald Campbell, who remained in Honolulu for several years after his rescue to make canvas for Kamehameha, wrote in his memoir, *A Voyage Round the World from 1806 to 1812*, that he once came upon Queen Ka'ahumanu herself eating meat. She begged him not to betray her, explaining that it would be as much as her life was worth.

Otto von Kotzebue, the captain of a Russian ship of exploration, wrote in his book, *Voyage of Discovery* (1830), that although he saw the body of a woman floating in Honolulu harbor, killed for entering a men's eating house while drunk, he was several times invited by Hawaiian women to eat dog with them, which he declined to do—the anthropologist Marshall Sahlins suggests that it was because dog was not to his liking, rather than fear of the death sentence that would await the women were they caught eating with him. During that same visit, chiefs and chiefesses boarded Kotzebue's ship to dine together. The Russians served pig that had not been consecrated, which had thus defiled the rest of the food when it was cooked in the same fire. Even the chiefs watched while the Russians had their dinner, taking only little bites of crackers, fruit, and cheese. The chiefesses who were present, which was in itself a violation of *kapu*, drank along with the men but did not eat, making frequent toasts to Kamehameha I and the emperor of Russia.

The seemingly sudden abandonment of sacred ritual, shrewdly manipulated by Ka'ahumanu, was the culmination of the actions of many women who had for some time realized, thanks in part to the arrival of the British navy in 1778, that the gods were not paying as much attention to them as they had been led to believe. Many of the chiefs were also aware that King Pōmare II of Tahiti had overthrown *kapu* without consequence to his person or his kingdom. Over the years, foreigners had done their part, too, in undermining *kapu* by their attempts to convince Hawaiians of the injustice of its seemingly arbitrary rules.

There are a number of theories as to how two women, Keōpūolani and Ka'ahumanu, with the support of chiefs loyal to them, could so easily have ended the *kapu* system and abolished the gods whom they once served. Some believe that it was an attempt by Ka'ahumanu and her followers to control the distribution of land that traditionally followed the death of a king, and to solidify the newly established supremacy of the Kamehameha family. Hiram Bingham wrote, "Kaahumanu desired equal privilege with men, in respect to eating and drinking, and, therefore, wished the termination of those distinctions and restraints which were felt to be degrading to her and Keopuolani, and to her royal sisters, and royal step-daughters." Dr. Rufus Anderson of the missionary board in Boston could not help but view the death of the gods as an act of divine politics. "It is thought that Kaahumanu, the strong-minded dowager queen, favoured the changes in order to remove unreasonable disabilities from her sex . . . But an unseen Power, though they knew it not, was preparing them for the speedy introduction of a better religion."

With the death of the gods, it became increasingly difficult if not impossible for the *ali'i* to justify claims of their own divinity. In abandoning the gods, the chiefs lost the source of their great power, their *mana*, and their ability to impose meaning, however questionable, on the customs of the land. Mary Kawena Pukui believed that one of the more immediate effects of this upheaval was an increase in the indifference already felt by many *ali'i* to the concerns and needs of the people. There were chiefs, of course, who looked after their people—there is a saying, *E 'ōpū ali'i*, which means to have the kindness and generosity of a chief—but the power gained through lineage and rank was not always used to the benefit of the Hawaiian people.

The historian and professor of microbiology O. A. Bushnell writes, "the extreme geographical isolation of Hawai'i (the closest land—Alaska—is 2,000 miles to the north, and the Philippines are 4,500 miles to the west) made its people unacquainted with any other way of living and thinking than their own. Because they were denied the opportunity to share their experience and the accumulating wisdom of other societies, the Hawaiians had nothing with which to compare the social system they had developed in their centuries of isolation. Nothing but their intelligence to lighten their ignorance, and only respect for the gods (and fear of the gods' surrogates on earth) to restrain their egotism."

Unlike Islam, Judaism, and Christianity, which are founded on a philosophical structure that is under constant study and even scrutiny, the religion of the Hawaiians was not based on doctrine. The importance of ancestors grew from their supposed ability to provide protection, just as *kapu* were in place to protect men from all that they could not control or understand. In abolishing the gods and with them a system of *kapu* that had served to determine the behavior, spiritual and mundane, of both chiefs and commoners, the *ali'i* relinquished the stability and order that come with tradition, and the organizing structure, even if restrictive, of social relationships and responsibilities.

To add to the chaos that ensued from the overthrow of the gods, the *ali'i* did not offer anything in its place. Even the wise Ka'ahumanu did not bother to fill the emptiness that ensued. A year after the abolishment of *kapu*, a missionary noticed in surprising sympathy, perhaps because the man was a priest like himself, a group of boys teasing a *kahuna* whose displeasure only a few months earlier would have resulted in their deaths. "Now as he comes along the boys mock him by getting a stick of wood, and saying some of his former prayers to it to deride it."

Despite the abolishment of the gods, many Hawaiians resisted the new order. While some busied themselves with the dismantling of the old system, others refused to give up their gods and their rites. Wooden statues were taken from *heiau* and family altars and hidden in caves and lava tubes, or buried in the earth, which accounts in part for the scarcity of Hawaiian religious artifacts. The *akua* continued to be worshipped, as were the bones of dead chiefs and ancestors. The forests continued to offer refuge to the spirits who had lived in the trees and streams for generations. As late as 1890 in Ka'ū, a morning prayer, called the Coming of Pele, was said to the goddess each day before first light. In the same year, a traveler on Maui noticed a

Hawaiian man by the side of the road who was said to be "a victim of the 'Hoodoo' . . . His enemy had willed him to die, and die he must." Along the coast, one may still find stone images of fish gods. Pele, the fire goddess, is venerated to this day.

Those chiefs who were antagonistic to Ka'ahumanu and her followers, for religious as well as political reasons, soon joined Liholiho's cousin Kekuao-kalani, who wished to kill all foreigners and to restore the old gods. When Kekuaokalani and his followers gathered at Kealakekua Bay, where Captain Cook had died, Ka'ahumanu sent to Honolulu for guns, powder, and cannon. Keōpūolani, who was once unable to show herself in daylight lest her shadow fall upon a being less sacred than herself, sailed to Kealakekua in the hope of swaying the rebels. When her efforts came to nothing, Ka'ahumanu's warriors, led by the prime minister, Kalanimoku, attacked the rebels. Kekuaokalani and his wife Manono were killed (it is said that Manono covered her fallen husband's body with his feather cloak and fought alone until she was hit in the temple by a musket ball). The outnumbered forces were slaughtered by Ka'ahumanu's warriors, whose war canoes were mounted with swivel guns and commanded by the queen herself in feather cape and helmet. Captain Cook had recorded the speed of a Hawaiian canoe in calm water at seven knots an hour, adding that a double canoe under full sail, with fifty men, was quickly able to circle his own ship as it lay at anchor. The sight of a fleet of war canoes racing toward shore, filled with warriors in fluttering gourd helmets, must have been terrifying, and with the new and unfamiliar guns, it would have been impossible to prevail against it. One of the defeated chiefs fled to Ka'ahumanu in search of mercy, and his life was spared, although she confiscated his lands. With the defeat of Kekuaokalani, little more was heard of the old gods.

That same year, the French artist Jacques Arago, sailing with Louis de Freycinet aboard the *Uranie*, visited some of the queens:

> I found . . . [the queens] at the door, lying on a bundle of cloth; never have I seen such women. They were not more than five feet six inches in height, but so dreadfully fat as to be out of all proportion. Their countenances were mild; and they were elegantly tattooed; one of

them had even her tongue tattooed. Their familiarity had not that air of licentiousness which characterizes the women of the lower classes. They allowed themselves however to be very freely handled; and he who should lay his hand on the bosom of one, would be thought very deficient in politeness if he were to forget the other.

In one of Choris's portraits of Ka'ahumanu, who was then about fifty years old, she is seated on a mat, wrapped in yards of finely printed *kapa*, as she is fanned by a dwarf. The queen customarily wore *pā'ū* made from mulberry bark, rather than silk from the numerous bolts of cloth kept in the small house in Honolulu, cluttered with calabashes and little Chinese trinkets, that she shared with Kamehameha's other widows. While Arago found Ka'ahumanu to be very fat, she was still thinner than the other queens. "Her face is interesting; her eyes were heavy from a slight indisposition, her manner very engaging ... Her body bears the marks of a great number of burns and incisions she inflicted on herself at the death of her husband."

Arago, an amiable and easy gentleman, was very interested in women's breasts, as is evident in his journal and in his drawings ("the busts of these females seems in general to rival every thing which the ancients have told us ... It is neither too large nor too small, but firm and separated"), as well as by local methods of corporal punishment and execution. He quickly found favor with the Hawaiians, perhaps because he obligingly entertained them with juggling and magic tricks.

The King [Liholiho] gave me a pack of French cards: I readily complied, and, novice as I am in this art, I was very much amused at the surprise of the officers, and particularly at the unmeaning look of the King. His wife requested me in the most polite manner to teach her some of the tricks; I consented, and had the pleasure of seeing her practice some of them with great dexterity. This lady is the sister of her husband. In her manners she has something childish, soft, and even simple; which is, however, in her not unbecoming. The presence of the King puts no restraint on the demonstrations of her affection, or on her tender caresses. All the strangers who please her are examined by her pretty hands; and they are allowed to judge for themselves of the elasticity of her bosom, and the fineness of her skin ... Every sleight-of-hand trick which I performed, was rewarded by a fresh proof of her pleasure and gratitude. I confess I was very sorry not to know more . . . I would strongly recommend to strangers who go to Owhyhee [Hawai'i], and wish to pass some agreeable moments there, to get acquainted with this interesting female.

Tattooing was done with the bones of a bird, sharpened into points and attached to a handle, which were held against the skin and tapped lightly with a wooden rod. A liquid taken from burned *kukui* nuts and mixed with sugarcane juice was then inserted in the punctures. When healed, a black ridge remained, which grew less prominent with age. William Ellis, an English missionary who arrived in Hawai'i after seven years of mission work in Tahiti, described the tattooing done to Queen Kamāmalu, the lovely daughter of Kaheiheimālie, after the death of Keōpūolani, the mother of her husband, Liholiho:

The artist first immersed the face of the instrument, which was a quarter of an inch wide, and set with a number of small fish-bones, into the colouring matter, placed it on her tongue, and giving it a quick and smart stroke with a small rod in his right hand, punctured the skin, and injected the dye at the same time. Her tongue bled much, and a few moments after I entered she made a sign for him to desist. She emptied her mouth of the blood, and then held her hands to it to counteract the pain. As soon as it appeared to have subsided a little, she said, He eha nui no, he nui roa ra kuu aroha! Pain, great indeed; but greater my affection.

When the tattoos were not in honor of dead chiefs or relatives, the designs were most commonly birds, lizards, triangles, and diamonds. Following the introduction of the animals to the Islands by Cook and Vancouver, tattoos of goats were much prized. William Ellis described Mahoa, his guide on an expedition to a volcano:

He was rather a singular looking little man, between forty and fifty years of age. A thick bunch of long, black, curling hair shaded his wrinkled forehead; and another bunch of the same kind hung down behind each of his ears. The rest of his head was cropped as short as shears could make it. His small black eyes were ornamented with tattooed vandyke semicircles. Two goats, impressed in the same indelible manner, stood rampant over each brow, one, like the supporter of a coat of arms, stood on each side of his nose, and two more guarded the corners of his mouth. The upper part of his beard was shaven close, but that which grew under his chin was drawn together, braided for an inch or two, and then tied in a knot, while the extremities of the knot spread out in curls like a tassel.

Arago clearly found Kaʻahumanu intriguing, and was not surprised by the respect that the late king had shown her. During one visit, she asked Arago if he'd like a drink of beer, and touched her own glass to his when he toasted the new king. Now and then, female attendants presented her with a small calabash, filled with flowers and discreetly tied in a handkerchief, into which she would spit. She smoked a large German pipe of dark wood trimmed in brass, which hung handily at her side when she was not using it, which was almost never. Arago wrote that Kaʻahumanu asked him to tattoo her:

> Her legs, the palm of her left hand, and her tongue . . . [were] elegantly tattooed . . . [and] the designs which ornamented her voluminous breasts . . . traced with a perfect taste. She was tattooed on the tongue; the name of Tamehameha, the date of his death, could be read on her arms; the sole of her feet and the palm of her hands, so delicate, carried figures which I suspect were traced by the artist of the expedition commanded by Kotzebue . . . When I finished my work, she begged me to ornament her with several new designs, and Rives informed me that she strongly desired a hunters horn on her posterior, and a figure of Tamehameha on the shoulder, to which I consented with great pleasure.

Rose de Freycinet, the wife of Louis de Freycinet, who in 1817 had been smuggled on board his ship when it left France, wrote in her journal that except for Liholiho's wife and half-sister, Kamāmalu, and Kaʻahumanu, only the young women were handsome:

> All the others were old or ugly. Louis found them all lying flat on their stomachs, with their chins resting on small cushions, in keeping

with local custom, and surrounded by servants armed with feather fly-swats. Kaoumanou [Ka'ahumanu] claimed to be sick and liked to inspire a lot more pity than one was inclined to feel for her, seeing how well she looked . . . Kamahamarou [Kamāmalu] . . . is tall and pretty; she has two other sisters among the five wives of the King [Liholiho, Kamehameha II] . . . One of these . . . was also one of his father's wives. I thought that all these women knew how to drape their saris with a great deal of elegance and grace and that, despite their bronzed complexions, the young ones in particular could well be regarded as beautiful.

One Great Caravanserai

Soon after the death of Captain Cook, it became known among seamen and merchants that the Islands provided a cheap source of provisions and fittings, and a seemingly endless supply of native sailors. The trip from New England to the Sandwich Islands, which once took six months, could be done, given good winds, in 110 days. The wharves of Honolulu and Lahaina were crowded with shouting factors, ship's chandlers, sandalwood agents, and sea captains selling and buying their cargoes, old schooners, and new ships on credit. The first American whaling ships appeared in the Pacific as early as 1791, when whales were beginning to grow scarce in the Atlantic, hunting off the coast of Chile and moving west across the ocean. Hundreds of ships and thousands of seamen waited in port each winter for the seasonal migrations of whales from the Arctic and the southern Pacific, as did the many merchants and factors dependent on the whalers and the growing fur trade with China.

The Islands were one of the last stops for runaway sailors, and every foreign vessel left port missing several of its original crew. Hawaiian men, known for their strength and good nature, were often hired to replace them, paid in goods after they were charged for the cold-weather jackets, shoes, and trousers that they would need in Asia and on the northwest coast of America.

The Sandwich Islands became one great caravanserai for flitting ships; and, without being asked, Hawaiians were thrust into many new roles—as hosts, chandlers, panders, and whores, foremost among them, to mariners from countries half a world away in space and 5,000 years in time . . . Inasmuch as their chiefs had been using them for centuries, commoners never thought to complain. Captains and chiefs alike exploited them, as provisioners, laborers, servants . . . and deckhands shanghaied or recruited ... In exchange for these varied services, foreigners usually paid in goods or in coins, with incidental supplements in germs and genes.

By the start of the nineteenth century, Honolulu was full of deserters, repo men, escaped convicts, traders, seamen, and beachcombers. This excerpt is from a short story by Robert Louis Stevenson, "The Ebb Tide," and although he is describing Papeete, it could easily be Honolulu:

> Throughout the island world of the Pacific, scattered men of many European races and from almost every grade of society carry activity and disseminate disease. Some prosper, some vegetate. Some have mounted the steps of thrones and owned islands and navies. Others again must marry for a livelihood; a strapping, merry, chocolate-coloured dame supports them in sheer idleness; and, dressed like natives, but still retaining some foreign element of gait or attitude, still perhaps with some relic (such as a single eye-glass) of the officer and gentleman, they sprawl in palm-leafed verandahs.

The sail maker Archibald Campbell knew sixty white men living in Honolulu in 1810, many of whom had found work with Kamehameha and the chiefs as blacksmiths, carpenters, gunners, shipwrights, gardeners, quack doctors, and translators. During the almost fifty years between Cook's landing in the Islands and the arrival of the missionaries in 1820, there had been a steady and growing association with foreigners, and writing and reading, as well as the strange Christian god, were not unknown to the Hawaiians. The Hawaiians, no longer in awe of foreigners, had quickly learned to view white men as creatures to be exploited. They had also learned the use and efficiency of guns, and they could not have enough of them, even if the arms were often defective. For some time, it was *kapu* to trade pigs to foreign ships for anything *but* guns, and there were frequent attacks on the shore parties of merchant ships and warships by Hawaiian men looking for them. Otto von Kotzebue wrote:

> The Sandwich Islanders are engaged in constant intercourse with foreign sailors, mostly of licentious characters, who indeed profess the Christian religion; but brought hither by the desire of gain, or the

necessity of laying in provisions for their ships, are generally wholly occupied in driving crafty bargains, and certainly are no way instrumental in inspiring the islands with ideas of religion or morality, but on the contrary, set them examples which have a direct tendency to deprave their minds.

Not only were foreign ships provisioned, but the exhausted crews used the ports of Lahaina, Hilo, and Honolulu as havens in which to recover from their arduous journeys, and the long months at sea without women. Native men were quick to offer their women to foreigners in exchange for goods.

At noon a single proa [canoe] came off to us: the crew consisted of four Sandwich Islanders, large and well made, one of whom came on board, and danced with much gaiety and agility. Their features had a character of ferocity; and yet their manners were mild and timid. Some other canoes with a single outrigger arrived one after another; several of the natives, who steered them, invited us to profit by the opportunity, and not to refuse the caresses of their wives, who were almost naked and disgustingly ugly. We did not think it right to yield to these pressing invitations; though I am persuaded that the refusal of the sailors was only dictated by the certainty, that at the anchorage they would get hold of some more bewitching *Laises* [*sic*] with whom they might make up for lost time, and be rewarded for the delay.

Hawaiian women could not be kept from the ships, even though some of the ship's masters feared the spread of venereal disease—not by the sailors, but by the women. Girls swarmed noisily across the rigging, below decks, and in the hold, and it became necessary for a ship to fire a gun at sunrise so that the sailors could muster for work unmolested, and another gun at sunset when the women were allowed to return. Jacques Arago, one of the more sophisticated observers, was surprised by the behavior of Hawaiian women and particularly their men, amoral by European standards only because of the complicity of men in the sexual availability of their women:

Their indecent gestures, and their motions still more indecent, were intended to provoke desire, and make us ashamed of our self-command . . . It was pardonable in a European, and particularly in a

Young woman of the Sandwich Islands. Engraving by John Sherwin, after a drawing by John Webber, 1779

Frenchman, to suppose that the coquette profited by the absence of her husband to seek admirers; and that the caresses she bestowed on those who accosted her were unknown to the husband, whom we pitied sincerely for his good faith and confidence. But we were ere long convinced that the husbands . . . set them an example of noble generosity.

In his journal of his visit to the Sandwich Islands in 1821, only one year after the abolition of *kapu*, the English traveler Gilbert Mathison came upon thirty women living happily on ships with sailors:

> [The women] seemed unwilling to quit the ship. At length, when we had advanced about a mile out of the harbor, they took a most tender leave of their respective sweethearts, and with loud laughter and cries, and huzzas from the crew, leaped overboard in one instant into the sea. There they remained swimming and diving, and playing about the ship, like so many mermaids in their native element, until a breeze sprung up; and as we bounded merrily before it, women and canoes, and houses and the land itself, gradually disappeared from our view.

Many of the sailors who abandoned ship were moved to desert because of women. Foreigners often married native women, preferably those with lineage and thus some land—John Young, Isaac Davis, and Don Francisco Marín all had Hawaiian wives. It was not only the women who were captivating. The *haole* wife of Kamehameha's gardener, a Welshman named William Davis, was stolen from him by a Hawaiian man.

The only seeming reason for the existence of Honolulu was its harbor. The town was fetid, dry, barren, and hot. Its residents were thirsty and they smelled bad. Although bacteria and the viruses that cause enteric fevers and dysentery, parasites, and pathogenic amoebas festered in the water and the soil, and thus in the food, there was no thought of building a public water system by either the chiefs or the government. There was no fresh water other than the muddy and polluted Nu'uanu Stream, a few springs, and a handful of brackish wells. Rainwater was collected in barrels and tanks for washing and bathing (and sometimes drinking), and water was drawn as needed from irrigation ditches or *kalo* patches. O. A. Bushnell described Honolulu in 1815:

> Commoners, if they still were concerned about grooming their persons, bathed perforce in the dirty river or in the turbid harbor, amid the refuse dumped overboard from ships moored there. Chiefs, and perhaps the more favored among their retainers . . . enjoyed the few spring-fed ponds . . . Scavenging pigs, dogs, goats, cats, rats, and chickens devoured whatever was edible, leaving the residue to be trampled into the dirt, or just to lie there until it disintegrated . . . Pollution took many forms: haole excrement, and with that haole germs, was not the only abomination . . . Rubbish, junk, the debris of wrapping, crates, barrels, papers, jute bags, and rags; empty bottles, jugs, jars, crocks, shards of glass; the scabrous shops, warehouses and sheds; the raucous rancid grogshops and whorehouses; the two "inns"; the dismantled hulks of dead ships rotting in the harbor; the one pitiable cemetery . . . in which the husks of dead haoles were dumped and soon forgotten . . . made of Honolulu . . . [a] midden, alive with maggots, flies, vermin, and . . . the least admirable specimens of mankind, foulmouthed, diseased, and indomitable, lurching through the town in search of rum and women.

Most Hawaiians and *haoles* lived near the port or alongside Nuʻuanu Stream in grass huts and a handful of stone or adobe houses. There were no straight streets, certainly none paved, until 1838. There were saltwater fish ponds to the north and south of the town, but the surrounding land was mostly swamp until the Army Corps of Engineers drained it a few years before the Second World War. There were no artesian wells until 1879, and between the swamp and the mountains was a dusty flatland, known as the Plains. The town itself was without trees and the chiefs built their thatched houses in the groves of coconut palms that lined nearby Waikīkī Beach. There were four general stores with warehouses, a few inns, numerous grogshops, ramshackle stalls selling cheap street food, and many whorehouses. The only government building was a newly finished fort, begun in 1815 when Kamehameha engaged some Russians from a scientific expedition to construct what he thought would be a storehouse against the side of Pakaka *heiau*, using stones from the temple. The Russians had been dismissed when the

View of Honolulu from *kalo* patches. Engraving after a watercolor by R. Beechey of HMS *Blossom*, 1826

king realized that they were building a fort with coral walls twenty feet thick, leaving the work unfinished, although later he himself used it as an armory and prison, much as the Russians had intended.

When the First Company of missionaries arrived in the Islands in 1820, there were two thousand people in Honolulu, two hundred of whom were foreigners. The following is a description of the mission compound in Honolulu, which was forbidden to commoners, written by Levi Chamberlain. "Mr. B" is Hiram Bingham, leader of the First Company; "Wititi" is Waikīkī.

No. 1 is the house for public worship, school and social prayer, and a part of it affords a study and lodging room for Mr. B. It is 28 ft. long and 20 wide, has two doors and three windows. The window that appears at the south end looks out towards the open sea, which is about a mile distant. The door at the opposite end opens toward the mountain and towards the road leading from the village eastward to Wititi. No. 2 is a dwelling house, it has one door and three windows, two rooms, one for a lodging room for Mrs. Loomis, and the other for orphan girls. No. 3 is a dwelling house occupied by Capt. Chamberlain and family, it has one door, four windows and three rooms. No. 4 is a store house about 30 ft. square . . . No. 5 is a dwelling now occupied by Dr. Wiliems and unfortunate British seamen, but intended for a lodging house for John Honorii and orphan boys. No. 6 is a small cooking house where the stoves and a large boiler are set up. This is covered with mortar. No. 7 is a Ranai [lānaʻi] or open building connecting the doors of these houses, having itself three entrances, two on the south side and one to the east end. No. 8, the spring of water.

From the time of Kamehameha I and the introduction in 1791 of alcohol by a Captain James Maxwell, an Englishman from New Zealand who is said to have given Kamehameha his first taste of rum, drunkenness was a grave threat to the Hawaiians. Several men who had escaped from penal colonies in New South Wales were given land in return for services to Kamehameha, and lost no time in setting up stills to make alcohol from sugarcane. Don Marín was making beer and wine in Honolulu in 1815, and by 1820 there were several small but busy distilleries. Men, women, and children drank, gin being the favorite drink of the *aliʻi*, and thus the most fashionable. Visitors wrote that parties of drunken sailors and natives were commonplace, and that Hawaiians would purchase a cask of spirits and spend a day or two drinking until it was empty. *ʻAwa* had traditionally been grown for fermentation, but its effect was narcotic and soporific, unlike rum and gin. The use of *ʻawa*, thought to be a cure for corpulence and other conditions, did not cease entirely, but became far less common. Alcohol made from the *kī* plant was called *ʻōkolehao*, its name taken from the iron stills in which it was made, but it, too, was less prized than the foreigners' alcohol.

Kamehameha II and later Kamehameha III, both enthusiastic drinkers, were encouraged by the foreign merchants to drink as often and as much as possible, as it was greatly to the traders' advantage to have the king drunk and inattentive to affairs of state or matters of business. The missionaries themselves were not without a modest liking for alcohol. In 1826, Hiram Bingham bought seven and a half gallons of wine, an equally large amount of rum, and two gallons of gin; the teacher Samuel Ruggles bought a mere one-and-a-quarter gallons of brandy and two and a quarter gallons of wine.

By 1844, there were five hundred whaling ships anchored in Hawaiian ports, all in need of meat, fresh fruit and vegetables, firewood, salt, and water. The foreigners themselves all wanted something—the merchants needed sandalwood; the whalers sought oil and native sailors to replace sick or deserting men; and the scientists and explorers descending upon the Islands from different countries needed samples and specimens, taking away everything of interest that they could find—rocks, insects, plants, and not least, increasingly rare ethnographic artifacts.

A Pilgrim and a Stranger

In the early years of the nineteenth century, a wave of piety swept through the Protestant seminaries and churches of New England, their members troubled by a new and growing awareness of the legions of heathens living in sin at the far reaches of the world. Conversion of the damned suddenly seemed not only possible, but a responsibility, and at the Andover Theological Seminary, a center of missionary ardor, a group of zealous young men swore to undertake as their life's work the saving of pagan souls.

The unlikely arrival in New Haven in 1809 of two young Hawaiians, Henry Opukaha'ia (called Obookiah by the Americans) and Thomas Hopu, aroused the curiosity of young seminarians at the Yale Divinity School. Opukaha'ia, who had run away to sea as a boy after his parents were killed in one of the wars between chiefs, had been stranded in New Haven by a sea captain under whom he had served. Without work or a place to live, he was found crying on the steps of a building at Yale, and was persuaded by theology students to study the Bible with them. Under their tutelage, he became an eager and attentive church member. His death of typhus in 1818 was a great shock to the Foreign Mission in Cornwall, Connecticut, where he had been training as a missionary to serve in his native country. Thomas Hopu had also been at sea, serving as cabin boy on the same ship that conscripted Opukaha'ia, sailing to China and around the Horn to New Haven, and as a marine in the War of 1812.

One year after the death of Opukaha'ia, a party of ministers, schoolmasters, a farmer, a printer, and a doctor, and their wives (the Board required that missionaries be married), along with Thomas Hopu and four other young Hawaiian men, left Boston on board the brig *Thaddeus* on a mission to the Sandwich Islands.

One of the clergymen on the *Thaddeus* was thirty-three-year-old Asa Thurston, born in Fitchburg, Massachusetts. Admired for his great strength and courage (he was six feet, eight inches tall, with a long nose and chin), he had thought it a compliment to be considered a bully at Yale, where he had demonstrated such intellectual promise that his teachers encouraged him to enter Andover Theological Seminary. Lucy Goodale, his new wife, was born in 1795 in Marlborough, Massachusetts. She described in her journal her courtship and marriage to Asa Thurston, three months before the embarkation of the First Company of missionaries:

> The gentleman proposed as the companion of my life is Mr. Thurston, member of the senior class, in Andover Theological Institution. He had recently become an accepted missionary of the American Board of Commissioners for Foreign Missions . . . This has all come suddenly upon him. Now that he knows the situation he is called to fill, he has no personal knowledge of one who is both willing and qualified to go with him to a foreign land. Some of his classmates were admitted to his private confidence. One of them, in passing back and forth, had been entertained at Dean Goodale's. They spoke of his daughter Lucy as being fitted for such a position. It proved a hinge to act upon . . . most closely and seriously during the last year, he has pressed the subject on my consideration, of personally engaging in the missionary enterprise. What could I say? We thoroughly discussed the subject, after which I gave permission for a visit. Next week on Thursday is the anticipated, dreaded interview of final decision . . . Last night I could neither eat, nor close my eyes in sleep.

She could have said no, of course. Instead, Lucy wrote to her father, a deacon in the local church, for advice. Dean Goodale answered that he had "consecrated her to God, and though such a separation would be most trying to nature, yet the thing proceeded from the Lord; his will be done." She worriedly wrote again to ask if he were advising her to go "for life to a foreign heathen land?" and he answered that it was for her to choose, "apart from your father." Thurston visited Lucy at her family's farm, and in a week's time they pledged themselves to each other as "close companions in the race of life, consecrating . . . their all to a life's work among the heathen." The women in the Goodale family gathered to prepare Lucy's trousseau—ten loose and twelve fitted dresses of calico and gingham, four thin and two flannel petticoats, twenty-four nightdresses, twenty-five sets of underwear, aprons, handkerchiefs, shawls, and stockings. One of her sisters felt that Lucy's wedding was like a funeral, and a neighbor's hired hand fretted that she would be eaten by cannibals.

In the little band on board the *Thaddeus* with the Thurstons were Sybil and Reverend Hiram Bingham; Samuel Ruggles, a teacher, and his wife, Nancy; Thomas Holman, a physician, and his elegant wife, Lucia (she was instantly disliked by the others for hoarding the sweets and oranges her brother had given her as a parting gift); Samuel Whitney, a teacher, and his wife, Mercy; Daniel Chamberlain, a farmer, with his wife, Jerusha, and their five children; and Elisha Loomis, a printer, and his wife, Maria. The four Hawaiian men accompanying them were William Kanui, John Honolii, Thomas Hopu, and George Humehume (named Tamoree by the Americans). Humehume was the lost son of Kaumuali'i, the king of Kaua'i. In 1804, Kaumuali'i had asked a visiting sea captain to see that his six-year-old son was educated in America, giving him eight thousand dollars to pay the boy's expenses and tuition. The boy, whose story resembles a fairy tale, spent several years at sea before arriving in Rhode Island, where the captain, unable to care for him, left him penniless in the care of a schoolteacher. He later served in the United States Navy until his discharge, when he met the other Hawaiian boys living in New England. He was befriended by the Congregationalist minister with whom he lodged, and began to study Scripture. Lucy Thurston was extremely shocked when she discovered that the prince was, in her words, illegitimate—an early indication of the misunderstandings that were soon to confound both the Hawaiians and the missionaries.

Most of the diaries kept by the missionaries on board the *Thaddeus* dutifully begin on the first day of their journey, October 23, 1819, and then fall silent until taken up a few weeks later, the writers too seasick to commit another word until the middle of November. When she recovered, Mercy Whitney made a schedule of her day's activities:

5:00 private devotion and sewing
7:30–9 breakfast and exercise
9–12 writing and study

12–1 recitation and conversation
1–2 dinner and private devotion
2–5 writing and reading
5–6 study of the Hawaiian language
6–7:30 tea, conversation, and exercise
7:30–9:30 private and family devotion

In a letter dated December 20, two months after the *kapu* system in the Sandwich Islands was overthrown and the Hawaiian gods and their temples destroyed, Lucy Thurston wrote to her father from the *Thaddeus*. The ship was twenty-four feet wide and eighty-five feet long, and it would be three months before it reached the Sandwich Islands:

> Chests, trunks, bundles, bags &c., were piled into our little room six feet square, until no place was left on the floor for the sole of one's foot . . . With such narrow limits, and such confined air, it might be compared to a dungeon. This was with me a gloomy season, in which I felt myself a pilgrim and a stranger . . . Our whole family, with the exception of the natives, were all under the horrors of seasickness, some thrown on their mattresses, others seated in clusters, hanging one upon another, while here and there individuals leaned on the railing, or supported themselves by hanging upon a rope . . . We had entered a new school.

Daniel Chamberlain wrote that the small cabins were so packed with their belongings that it was necessary to walk bent in two, crawling over chests and trunks on their hands and knees, and banging their heads against the walls and ceiling. Halfway through the journey, Samuel Ruggles was exultant to collect three pints of drinking water from the tip of his umbrella. At the end of January, in the Le Maire Strait, near Tierra del Fuego, the ship was blown off course by high winds. Lucy Thurston wrote:

> Sails were taken down and we were carried before the wind. The incessant and violent rocking of the vessel keeps me here laid prostrate upon my couch. Oh, the luxury in feeble health of reclining on a bed with tranquility and ease! But I must not, I will not repine. Even now,

though tears bedew my cheeks, I wish not for an alteration in my present situation or future prospects. When I look forward to that land of darkness, whither I am bound, and reflect on the degradation and misery of its inhabitants, follow them into the eternal world, and forward to the great day of retribution, all my petty sufferings dwindle to a point, and I exclaim, What have I to say of trials, I, who can press to my bosom the word of God.

Lucy asked the captain of the *Thaddeus* if the lives of the missionaries would be in danger in the Islands. He answered that while the natives were addicted to alcohol, which resulted in an occasional "bold assault," the only threat of which she should beware was that of poisoning. "When they conceive a dislike, no intimation is given, but by these means they secretly seize on the first opportunity to accomplish their fatal purpose." Theft, too, added the captain, could be a bit of a difficulty. He arrived on one visit with twenty-four shirts and left a few weeks later with three. It is not surprising that Lucy was terrified.

We were taught that unprovoked, the natives of these islands conspired the death of the great navigator, Capt. Cook, cut off vessels, murdered crews, and chewed the flesh of their enemies as the sweetest titbit of revenge. Conversing with the captain of our vessel, a few weeks before reaching these islands, in 1820, he remarked that he must get his guns out, for it was not safe to approach these islands without being in a state of defense. "What," I replied, "leave us, a feeble company, in a defenseless state, among a people you cannot approach without fire-arms?" "Ah," said he, shaking his head, "it is not *my* wish to leave you in such circumstances."

On the 158th day, the missionaries saw the island of Hawai'i looming before them. The coastal village of Kawaihae was visible from a porthole, and Lucy watched apprehensively as a canoe of "chattering natives with animated countenances" approached the ship. The canoe pulled alongside and the Hawaiians handed Lucy a banana. When she grabbed hold of it and tentatively passed them a biscuit in return, the natives called out, *"Wahine maika'i,"* or "Good woman." She impulsively threw them more biscuits, and when she repeated the word *wahine*, they shouted in delight. "Thus, after sailing eighteen thousand miles," Lucy wrote in her journal, "I met, for the first time, those children of nature alone."

Not so frightening, after all. But certainly repellent. The missionaries could not have landed in a place more unsettling, or more provocative to their untried souls, than the Sandwich Islands. Led to believe that they would find cannibals, sorcerers, murderers, and thieves, they must have been relieved to discover that the heathens were only repulsive. Instead of terror, there was revulsion and ignorance: "The appearance of destitution, degradation, and barbarism, among the chattering, and almost naked savages, whose heads and feet, and much of their sunburnt swarthy skins, were bare, was appalling . . . Some of our number, with gushing tears, turned away from the spectacle."

Anchoring off Kawaihae, the captain sent a boat ashore with one of the officers, who returned with the astonishing news that the great Kamehameha was dead, *kapu* abolished, idols destroyed, and temples demolished. The new king, Kamehameha II (Liholiho), was living thirty miles down the coast at Kailua. The high chief Kalanimoku, a cousin of Ka'ahumanu's, sent to the *Thaddeus* presents of coconuts, bananas, breadfruit, sweet potatoes, and two hogs. Men in canoes bartered fruit for knives, a pair of scissors, and some fishhooks. Kalanimoku, whom the English had nicknamed Billy Pitt (after the British prime minister William Pitt) for his skillful statesmanship, soon arrived on a canopied double canoe with his wife, Likelike, and Namahana and Kaheiheimālie. Perhaps out of respect to the foreigners, the women, who were close to three hundred pounds each, wore shifts of Indian cotton over their *pā'ū*.

The missionaries may have been disgusted by what they saw, but the Hawaiians were curious, and even amused. They had never seen a white woman. "Crowds gathered, and one and another exclaimed, 'How white the women are!' 'What bright-colored eyes!' 'What strange hats, not at all like the tall hats of the men!' 'What long necks! but pleasing to look at!' 'What pinched-in bodies!' 'What tight clothing above and wide below!'" They asked the *haole* women to loosen their hair, so that they could comb and braid it, and some of the women obliged them. When the chiefesses asked the women to join them in cards, however, the missionaries explained that in America, ladies did not play cards, causing the Hawaiians to wonder that such a *kapu* could be imposed on white women. Accustomed to the smiling faces of

The compound of Kalanimoku. Engraving after a pencil drawing by Alphonse Pellion, 1819

amorous sailors, the Hawaiians were soon bewildered by the solemnity of the strangers, while the missionaries, irritated by the constant chatter and laughter of the Hawaiians, were suspicious of their sudden explosions of laughter, convinced that native translators were deliberately altering their words.

At the invitation of the Americans, Kalanimoku and several of the royal women went on board the *Thaddeus*. Lucy Thurston described the queens in her journal:

> Trammeled with clothes and seated on chairs, the queens were out of their element. They divested themselves of their outer dresses. Then the one stretched herself full length upon a bench, and the others sat down upon the deck. Mattresses were then brought for them to recline in their own way. After reaching the cabin . . . one of the queens divested herself of her only remaining dress, simply retaining her pa-u. While we were opening wide our eyes, she looked as self-possessed and easy as though sitting in the shades of Eden.

The *Thaddeus* sailed south from Kawaihae to Kona with the chiefs, numerous queens, and attendants on board, some of whom slept on deck. One of Liholiho's wives demanded that the women make her a white cambric dress like they themselves wore, insisting that they finish it before they reached Kona, as she wished to wear it to surprise her husband. It took the women two days of stitching (they did not sew on the Sabbath), but when the *Thaddeus* arrived in Kona, the queen wore her new dress ashore to the screams and cheers of hundreds of her subjects. The women also gave her a lace cap and scarf, which they had brought from America as gifts. Shortly after their arrival in Kona, Lucia Holman visited what remained of 'Ahu'ena, the *heiau* used for human sacrifice by Kamehameha I when he lived at Kamakahonu, and which had been destroyed by order of Ka'ahumanu:

> It was sure enough in ruins, and such a scene of devastation, I never before beheld. There appeared to me to have been stone (solid lava) enough among the ruins of the temple, to build a city—4 of the wooden gods are left for curiosity . . . In a large ohale (or house) near by lies buried the bones of the Great Tamahamaah [*sic*]—with a cross on each side, signifying Tarboo, (or no admittance). Upon this sacred ground was no common person allowed to step his foot.

Kuakini, a younger brother of Ka'ahumanu's, was the first person to greet the missionaries in Kona. He was very tall and very big, and wore a traditional *malo* with a short cloak, known as a *kīhei*, thrown around his huge shoulders. He was notorious even among the generous Hawaiians for his extravagance. According to Kamakau, Kuakini was also a patron of thieves, keeping men solely to plunder ships and the stores of foreign merchants. Kuakini had once written to the president of the United States in the hope of exchanging names with him, and although Adams did not answer, Kuakini had adopted the name of John Adams. He invited the missionaries to a feast at his house, but they refused his invitation. Thomas Hopu, surprised by their rudeness, advised them to reconsider, and they reluctantly agreed to attend. Although there was ample and varied food, the missionaries declined to eat. Kuakini even had wine for them, but they took only demure sips of coconut water. He was an accomplished dancer and kept the finest troupe of dancers in the kingdom, but the missionaries ignored his invitation to watch a performance. Hiram Bingham and Asa Thurston left the feast early, announcing that in future they only wished to meet with the king.

With Hopu serving as intermediary and with the help of John Young, Bingham and Thurston at last met Liholiho. They arrived while he was eating

Namahana, six feet, two inches tall, one of the widows of Kamehameha I and sister to Kaʻahumanu. Lithograph after a watercolor by L. Massard, ca. 1830

The high chief Kuakini, independent-minded brother of Kaʻahumanu, known for his generosity and love of pleasure. Drawing by William Ellis from his book, *A Journal of a Tour Around Hawaii*, 1822

dinner with his five wives, two of whom were his sisters, and one of whom had been married to his father. Refusing to be seated, the missionaries read aloud formal letters from the Board in Boston. One can imagine—or perhaps not—the reaction of the king and his queens to the dry and somewhat naïve instructions of the Board. The Prudential Committee also sent a letter of confidential advice for the First Company, which was not read aloud. It contained surprisingly benign, although ultimately ineffective instructions, particularly concerning involvement in the kingdom's politics:

> Your views are to be limited to the low, narrow scale, but you are to open your hearts wide and set your goals high. You are to aim at nothing short of covering these islands with fruitful fields, and pleasant dwellings and schools and churches, and of raising up the whole people to an elevated state of Christian civilization. You are to obtain an adequate language of the people; to make them acquainted with letters, to give them the Bible, with skill to read it ... to introduce and get into extended operation and influence among them, the arts and institutions and usages of civilized life and society; and you are to abstain from all interference with local and political interests of the people and to inculcate the duties of justice, moderation, forbearance, truth and universal kindness. Do all in your power to make men of every class good, wise and happy.

Out of fear of Kaʻahumanu, or perhaps an instinctive foreboding, Liholiho refused to give the missionaries permission to land in the Islands. Although his father had asked Vancouver to send religious instructors, it had been in the interest of increasing the wealth of his kingdom, not his chances of salvation. Liholiho told Bingham that Kaʻahumanu was away fishing, and he could not make a decision without her. Lucy Thurston wrote in her journal that the missionaries then invited the king and his family to dinner on the *Thaddeus*. The king came to the ship in a double canoe of twenty paddlers and a large number of attendants.

> The king was introduced to the first white women, and they to the first king, that each had ever seen. His dress on the occasion was a girdle, a green silk scarf put on under the left arm, brought up and knotted over the right shoulder, a chain of gold around his neck

and over his chest, and a wreath of yellow flowers upon his head. The next day several of the brothers and sisters of the Mission went ashore, hoping that social intercourse might give weight to the scale that was then poising [*sic*]. They visited the palace. Ten or fifteen armed soldiers stood without, and although it was ten or eleven o'clock in the forenoon, we found him on whom devolved the government of a nation, three or four of his chiefs, and five or six of his attendants, prostrate on their mats, wrapped in deep slumbers.

Hiram Bingham was shocked that Liholiho wore no shoes, stockings, pants, or gloves, although Thomas Hopu had warned the chiefs and chiefesses to dress with care when they called on the missionaries. As the *ali'i* were accustomed to wearing Western clothes (merchants had long supplied them with suits, and bolts of cloth for gowns), most of them obligingly appeared for their daily visits in gowns of Chinese silk and striped taffeta, brocade jackets, and heavy velvet waistcoats, which were stifling in the heat. Some of the *ali'i*, hoping to please the *haoles*, evoked instead their private ridicule by their odd assortment of clothes—one of many melancholy ironies that was to ensure they remained unknown to one another. In his memoir, Charles Stewart described a "monstrously large" chiefess dressed in white muslin, "thick woodsman's shoes, and no stockings, a heavy silver-headed cane in her hand, and an immense French *chapeau* on her head!"

Over the next week, the missionaries waited for the king's decision, confident of the sanctity of their mission (to their irritation, the chiefs were easily distracted, at one point by a troupe of musicians), as they made excursions on shore, sailed up and down the coast on the *Thaddeus*, and visited with the Hawaiians. As the moon rose one evening, Asa Thurston and Hiram Bingham climbed to the maintop of the *Thaddeus*, and while their wives, the captain and crew, and the *ali'i* of Hawai'i Island watched in silence, loudly shouted the hymn they had sung at their ordainment in New England and again at Park Street Church when they left Boston.

Head of the Church Triumphant,
We joyfully adore thee:
Till thou appear,
The members here,
Shall sing like those in glory:

We lift our hearts and voices,
In blest anticipation,
And cry aloud,
And give to God
The praise of our salvation.

The royal women and their chiefs and attendants arrived at the ship each morning, seated under Chinese umbrellas on the platforms of large double canoes as they were fanned by a dozen men. The redoubtable Hiram Bingham was impressed by the agility and physical grace of the paddlers, if little else:

Ten athletic men in each of the coupled canoes making regular, rapid, and effective strokes, all on one side for a while then, changing at a signal in exact time, all on the other. Each raising his head erect and lifting one hand high to throw the paddle forward . . . dipping their blades and bowing simultaneously . . . making the brine boil and giving great speed to their novel seacraft. These grandees and their ambitious rowers gave us a pleasing indication of the physical capacity, at least, of the people whom we were desirous to enlighten.

The missionary wives sewed a dress for the queen mother, Keōpūolani, that so delighted her that she ordered more for her attendants and herself, waiting as the foreign women, unused to the dry heat of Kona, dazedly cut and stitched her a wardrobe. The chiefesses and queens were particularly taken with the Chamberlains' young daughter and decided to adopt her, or *hanaʻi* her, a practice common in Hawaiian families. To their surprise, the Chamberlains refused, but reluctantly agreed to let the child be taken ashore for the night, a gesture that helped to convince the queens that the missionaries meant them no harm. Lucia Holman, the prettiest of the missionary wives, wrote that one of the queens "got me into her lap, and felt me from head to foot and said I must cow-cow and be nooe-nooe, i.e., I must eat and grow larger." When Lucia walked with Nancy Ruggles and Maria Loomis on shore, the Hawaiians surrounded them, touching and poking them with curiosity.

When the missionaries learned that Kaʻahumanu had at last returned from fishing, they went on shore to discover the chiefs at a feast to welcome her home. Ka'ahumanu lay on a large mat in a yellow satin *pā'ū* with a purple satin *kihei* over her shoulders, wearing a *lei* of *maile* leaves, and a band of yellow feathers low on her forehead. Her attendants fanned her and scratched her back, while the chiefs waited in line to greet her. It was the first time that the missionaries saw the *hula*—hundreds of dancing men and women, shouting and clapping, the men wearing thick anklets of rattling dogs' teeth. The women dancers were bare-breasted, in *kapa pā'ū* and feather anklets. Daniel Chamberlain wrote that he had never in his life seen anything so Satanic.

Ka'ahumanu showed neither interest in nor disdain for the missionaries. She was aloof and grand, as was her way, allowing them to touch only her little finger when they attempted to take her hands in greeting, and commanded the *haole* women to make dresses for her and her women.

Although the *ali'i* knew that Tahiti had adopted the Christian faith, Liholiho had no interest in the new god. The idea of a heavenly kingdom had not excited much curiosity in his father or the old chiefs, either, except for Ka'ahumanu's cousin, the always independent Kalanimoku, who had been impetuously baptized by a French chaplain in 1819. After endless talk, and the intervention of John Young, who favored allowing the missionaries to stay, Liholiho and the chiefs, satisfied that the odd white men did not intend war (in part because they had brought their wives with them), decided that the missionaries could remain in the Islands for one year.

Liholiho told Bingham that a number of chiefs were keen to learn to read English, fortunately for the missionaries, as he had also declared the learning of English *kapu* to anyone but *ali'i* (Bingham believed that Liholiho did not want commoners to learn to read, as it would distract them from cutting sandalwood, the profits of which the king needed to pay his debts). In the past, traders had often taken advantage of the chiefs, and it must have occurred to Liholiho and his counselors that the missionaries would be useful as intermediaries, and helpful in drafting promissory notes. Liholiho insisted that Dr. Holman and his wife live in Kailua with his court, along with two of the Hawaiian scholars from New England, Thomas Hopu and William Kanui, who would serve as interpreters. It was decided by ballot that Asa and Lucy Thurston would also remain in Kailua, and Lucy watched in distress as the *Thaddeus* disappeared, headed for Honolulu. "At evening twilight," she wrote, "we sundered ourselves . . . from the dear old brig, and from civilization."

Kailua was a village of grass houses built around the bay and on the surrounding hillside, with a population of perhaps three thousand people. Two buildings made of coral served as storehouses. The Thurstons' traditional thatched hut of one room was "an abode of most uncouth and humble character," wrote Lucy. It sat on an expanse of black lava, overlooking the ocean, where nothing grew but a few dusty stalks of tobacco, some prickly bushes, and an occasional frayed coconut tree. The nearest source of water was a spring five miles distant. "We had entered a pathway that made it wisdom to take things as they came,—and to take them by the smooth handle," Lucy wrote in a letter.

For the first few nights, the king sent men to guard the Thurstons' grass house, and they watched in curiosity as Asa and Lucy struggled to pile blankets atop their trunks and boxes to make beds. Troubled by the incessant yelping of dogs, Lucy found it difficult to sleep:

> Between one and two hundred were thrown in groups on the ground, utterly unable to move, having their fore-legs brought over their backs and bound together. Some had burst the bands that confined their mouths, and some had expired. Their piteous moans would excite the compassion of any heart. Natives considered baked dog a great delicacy . . . They never offer it to foreigners . . . Once they mischievously attached a pig's head to a dog's body, and thus inveigled foreigners to partake of it.

The dogs that kept Lucy awake for two days with their cries were being fattened for the feast honoring the first anniversary of the death of Kamehameha. There was another far more provocative annoyance, however. "A secret enemy . . . lying in ambush," wrote Lucy. "It was the flea."

Queen Kamāmalu soon sent the Thurstons two carved Chinese beds, and the king gave them a circular Chinese table with six drawers, which would be used by the Thurstons and their children for more than twenty years. The king also gave them their own *kalo* patch, explaining that when the taro was gone, he would give them another. Each morning, attendants brought them fish, *kalo*, and sweet potatoes on pewter platters. The king invited them to a feast, and Queen Kamāmalu asked Lucy if she could borrow a dress for the celebration, but they could not find anything to fit her:

> [Kamāmalu], however, according to court ceremony, so arranged a native-cloth pau, a yard wide, with ten folds, as to be enveloped round the middle with seventy thicknesses. To array herself in this unwieldy attire, the long cloth was spread out on the ground, when, beginning at one end, she laid her body across it, and rolled herself over and over till she had rolled the whole around her. Two attendants followed her, one bearing up the end of this cumbrous robe of state, and the other waving over her head an elegant nodding flybrush of beautiful plumes, its long handle completely covered with little tortoise-shell rings of various colors. Her head was ornamented with a graceful yellow wreath of elegant feathers, of great value, from the fact that after a mountain bird has been caught in a snare, just two small feathers of rare beauty, one under each wing, could be obtained from it. A mountain vine, with green leaves, small and lustrous, was the only drapery which went to deck and cover her neck and the upper part of her person ... After this ... her majesty lay down again upon the ground and unrolled the cloth by reversing the process of clothing.

Liholiho had promised to supply them with water, brought to them in calabashes, but he had not realized how much they would need, resulting in a shortage of water and a quarrel between the Thurstons and the Holmans. (Holman, who was a physician, would angrily quit the mission seven months after his arrival. His wife Lucia wrote in an indignant letter that "fruits and vegetables, everything that these Islands produce, taste *heathenish*.")

For the first month, the Thurstons' grass house was surrounded by hundreds of people, gathered at the low door to peer inside and to gossip loudly about them in Hawaiian. The Thurstons pretended to ignore them, wasting no time in setting up classes for instruction in religion and, what was more relevant to their plan to convert the Hawaiians through the written word, classes in reading and writing. Lucy wrote that the king seemed interested at first: "For several months his majesty kept foremost in learning, then the pleasures of the cup caused his books to be quite neglected. Some of the queens were ambitious, and made good progress, but they met with serious interruptions, going from place to place with their intoxicated husband."

Liholiho saw to it, however, that his brother and heir, the seven-year-old Kauikeaouli, attended classes regularly, threatening punishment if the child neglected his schoolwork. He also asked Thurston to teach two young men named Kahuhu and Iʻi (perhaps the boy with red hair whom he had saved from death as a child), explaining that it would be the same as teaching himself, as through them he would discover what it meant to learn. The king saw that the two young men were always dressed in white, in a manner acceptable to the foreigners. When he returned from a sailing trip of several months, he went straight to the Thurstons' house to hear his favorites recite their lessons. Delighted with their progress, the king shook Thurston's hand, and kissed it. Thurston, encouraged by the king's enthusiasm and the quickness and eagerness of his students, received permission from him to teach persons other than the *aliʻi*.

One day, Lucy was teaching Kauikeaouli, who was accompanied by twelve of his attendants, when a drunken priest ran into the Thurstons' house and promptly removed his loincloth.

Before I was aware every individual had left the house and yard. The priest and I stood face to face, alone. As he advanced, I receded. Thus we performed many evolutions around the room. In a retired corner stood a high post bedstead. He threw himself upon the bed and seemed to enjoy the luxury of rolling from side to side upon its white covering... I went out at one front door, and he after me. I entered the other front door and he after me. Thus out and in, out and in ... Having a substantial stick in my hand, I gave the fellow a severe blow across the arm ... Loss and pain together so enraged him that he picked up clubs and threw them at me ... In my flight, I swiftly ran through the crowd ... straight toward the palace where Mr. Thurston was teaching... I had not proceeded far ... before I met my husband. The prince and his attendants, being frightened at the appearance of the priest, ran to tell Hopu ... As long as action was required, my strength, courage and self-possession were equal to the emergency. But when I sat down in my own dwelling, safe beneath the protection of my husband, there was a mighty reaction. Then came prostration, trembling and tears. In fifteen minutes the house was filled with scholars and their numerous trains of attendants. The queens were very sympathizing. With tears they often tenderly embraced me, joined noses and said: "Very great is our love to you." . . . Two of our devoted pupils, John Ii and James Kahuhu, for a fortnight slept beneath our roof, with deadly weapons by their pillows . . . The king would have put the priest to death; but Mr. Thurston restrained him.

Lucy later added a note to her journal explaining that it was the only known instance when a missionary lady received an insult from a Hawaiian.

That spring, Liholiho decided to move his court to Honolulu, and wished the missionaries to accompany him. (Bingham had written to the Thurstons after Lucy's misadventure with the priest that in his view, they were "no longer considered as reasonably secure," and had encouraged them to come to Honolulu, but they had remained in Kailua.) Seven months after their arrival, the Thurstons dutifully sailed to the capital, a distance of 147 nautical miles, on one of the leaking, stinking schooners that carried passengers and livestock between islands.

Four hundred and seventy-five souls were on the brig, and with the exception of a few individuals, all were then above deck. Several hundred calabashes, containing poi, fish, water, &c., provisions for the passage, occupied not a little room, while a large number of dogs, with here and there a nest of puppies, served to fill up the crevices . . . We were treated with a great deal of kindness, fresh meat, &c. my hands, fingers, nails, and every part of dress, were examined and felt of with the utmost minuteness. They were all good, very good.

Lucy was relieved to see Hiram Bingham waiting for their boat on the beach at Waikīkī: "Then rose to our view a village of thatched huts. It was bare of trees save groves of cocoa-nuts on the margin of the shore. Beyond stretched an extensive plain, open on one side to the sea, otherwise hemmed in with an amphitheatre of mountains, some of the nearest as naked of trees as the village . . . the more remote were dressed with nature's richest, most verdant robes."

In a letter of Sunday, May 5, 1821, sent to the Board in Boston, missionaries described the welcome given them in Honolulu by Queen Ka'ahumanu:

Kaahoomanoo said to us, "We bid you welcome to our islands;—our hearts are glad you come—very glad. We are glad too you come on

Taboo day [Sunday], and have been with us in worship . . . She then offered to send a waggon [*sic*] back with us . . . She sent a large company of men to carry us on their backs through some standing water . . . While we were waiting for our boat, several hundred natives collected around us, and nothing was heard but their hoarse voices telling each other the story of our arrival.

Liholiho and his court, wandering from island to island with no object save pleasure, and ease from their tedium, eventually followed the Thurstons to Honolulu. The king continued to be a trial to Ka'ahumanu, taxing her patience and strength of will. While making one of her first formal visits to Hiram Bingham, she asked him to pray for Liholiho in his waywardness. She confided that, by all accounts, the king was by nature attracted to everything bad, leaving out that it was she who had raised him. Liholiho and the royal family, including Ka'ahumanu, called on the Thurstons soon after the king arrived in Honolulu, where the missionaries lived in far more comfort than in Kona. The king and his attendants examined everything in the mission house with the deepest interest.

An improvement of window frames and wooden shutters had been introduced into our own personal cottage of one room . . . To a common dining chair, the only one we possessed, Mr. Thurston had attached rockers, arms, and a high back . . . All was pronounced to be very good, and the hands that produced them *very* skillful. The king felt the bed. Finding it a mattress, he sought farther and entered another cottage. There the feather bed had just been stripped. Unceremoniously he threw himself upon it and rolled from side to side in a jovial manner, that he might the more fully experience its soft delights. In passing out they met with our hand cart. The king took a seat in the bottom of it, and thus backwards was drawn by his servants with speed to the village. A large retinue of attendants, his wives, and an armed guard, all scampered across the plain to keep up with his majesty, their loose garments flying in the trade wind.

Although clearly impressed by feather beds, Liholiho continued to pay little attention to the missionaries themselves; perhaps too little. He had helped to free the Islands of one religion, and may not have been eager to adopt another so quickly, especially as it might interfere with his amusements. When Hiram Bingham pressed him, he asked for five years in which to indulge himself, after which he would become a good man. He teased Kamāmalu, who was fond of the missionaries, that if they were to accept the foreigners' god he would be allowed only one wife, and it would not be she (she was his half-sister). When the missionaries tried to entice him to learn to read by writing his name on a board, he is reported to have stared at it and said, "It looks neither like myself nor any other man." During a visit to Kamāmalu, however, Otto von Kotzebue found the stairs to her rooms crowded with adults and children, whom the queen was gamely helping in their lessons. Some of the old people among them, however, "with an affectation of extreme diligence," held their spelling books upside down.

After the abolishment of the gods and the complex system of ritual that accompanied them, as well as the end of warfare, there was not very much for the *ali'i* to do. They had yet to take an interest in government, or in a system in which influence and power were not dependent on rank and lineage. The missionaries wasted little time in discouraging (and would soon forbid) gambling, dancing, surfing, sea bathing, or even watching the *hula*, arranging it so that the only approved pastimes were attendance at church, and classes in reading and writing. With the new Christian *kapu* imposed by the missionaries, the *ali'i* were even more adrift than they had been. Before they quite realized it, rules had been established as restrictive as some of the old *kapu*, although their violation would only bring eternal damnation, rather than the more immediate ritual strangulation. When the *ali'i* were not in church (the chiefesses went several times a day, not out of sanctity, but curiosity and a wish to please the missionaries) or learning to read and write, the women lay about on piles of mats and listened to stories told them by their chanters, while the chiefs went fishing.

The American traveler Gilbert Mathison disliked the missionaries from the start, not on behalf of the Hawaiians, but as an adventurer who found that the Islands would become necessarily less exotic under their influence. He complained that mock battles had been abandoned, and lamented that the sudden view of a fleet of a thousand canoes filled with warriors in gourd helmets would never again be seen. James Jarves wrote that even singing had become an objectionable pastime:

The consummate profligacy of attempting to dance would certainly find no mercy. On Sundays, no cooking is permitted, nor must even a fire be kindled; nothing, in short, must be done; the whole day is devoted to prayer, with how much piety may be easily imagined . . . Their white instructors in taking away their games, dances, festivals, and wars, had given them nothing in return as an outlet for their animal energies. A polka or waltz was proscribed, as the devices of the devil. Theatricals were something else. Horse-races were no better than hell's tournaments. Even smoking was made a capital sin, and tattoo-ing was the mark of the beast. National songs and festivals all smacked of eternal damnation. There was absolutely nothing left to the poor native for the indulgence of his physical forces, or the development of his intellectual, but that which he hated most, hard labor and theo-logical reading.

As commoners, too, began to attend school and to spend long hours in Sunday worship, the old patterns were further undermined. The fixed sea-sons for fishing and planting were disregarded, and the extensive *kalo* fields, once well cultivated and productive, lay in weeds. Even the mode of dress was affected. Titus Coan, a member of the Seventh Company of missionaries, which arrived in 1835, was worried by the harm done to natives by their adoption of foreign dress. Hawaiians wore to church, "two pairs of panta-loons over a thick woolen shirt, with tight boots, and a thick coat . . . over all . . . panting with heat and wet with perspiration." There quickly developed a certain church etiquette—the grandest of the *ali'i* did not arrive until after Service had begun, causing a disturbance with the sound of their carts, and the cheers of the commoners who awaited them in the street. Their good-natured progression down the aisle as they nodded and gestured to friends in the congregation occasioned shouts of laughter as their costumes, flower adornments, and hats were admired. Ephraim Eveleth wrote that he and his fellow priests sometimes preached to five thousand people at a gathering, particularly during the period known as the Revival, in 1838.

Some Hawaiians approved of the mission, confessing that they had lived in evil times, but now required learning and salvation. Others had heard rumors that on those islands in the Pacific where foreigners had married natives, the indigenous population had begun to disappear. They worried that it might happen in their own islands, and that they, too,

Missionaries preaching in a grove of *kukui* trees. Engraving from Charles Wilkes's *Narrative of the United States Exploring Expedition*, 1845

would cease to exist as a people. Hiram Bingham was discouraged by the initial resistance of the Hawaiians to what he considered the only path to redemption:

> How often have the chiefs and people of the Sandwich Islands been represented as easily influenced and moulded to one's will! Their ready compliance was doubtless in reference to that which they had not physical strength to resist. But in respect to the course the Bible marks out, the case was different. The missionaries found that the conflict between the light of Christianity and the darkness of heathenism was no momentary struggle. Even those who were desirous to be instructed, clung with great tenacity to their heathen customs, and their heathen pleasures. Multitudes passed away quickly to the grave before such impression could be made on them, and others resisted for years all the endeavors of missionaries to reclaim them.

The missionary William Ellis described a conversation that he had with several Hawaiians about their former beliefs:

The natives were very desirous to shew us the place where the image of Tairi the war-god stood, and told us that frequently in the evening he used to be seen flying about in the neighbourhood, in the form of a luminous substance like a flame, or like the tail of a comet. We told them that the luminous appearance which they saw was an occurrence common to other countries, and produced by natural causes: that the natives of the Sandwich Islands . . . whenever they observed such a phenomenon, supposed it to be Tane [Kāne], one of their gods, taking his flight from one marae to another, or passing through the district seeking whom he might destroy, and were consequently filled with terror; but now, they wondered how they could ever have given way to such fears . . . We asked them if they did not see the same appearances now, though the god had been destroyed and his worship discontinued? They said, "No; it has not been seen since the abolition of idolatry."

It is hardly surprising that there were misunderstandings. The missionaries were not temperamentally given to allusion or irony, while the Hawaiians were known for their playful use of language, which was replete with double-meaning (*kaona*), sexual references, and jokes, particularly in chants and songs. The missionaries were confused, for one example, when elders scolded young women who sat with their legs apart with the admonition "*Keke!*" which means "The teeth are exposed!" Martha Beckwith complained that the subtlety of Hawaiian informants often impeded her field work. She wrote in *The Kumulipo*, "This obscurity of language is why the Hawaiian taunts the foreigner who tries to interpret his lore. 'Always keep something back' is the thought in the mind of every native informant, however helpful he may seem and really wishes to be in his relation with the foreign inquirer."

The Hawaiians, generous to the point of profligacy, were confused by the abstemious eating habits of the missionaries. Hawaiians also found incomprehensible the Christian idea of fasting—they could not understand why a god would possibly want anyone to go willingly without food. To suffer with hunger would surely cause a god displeasure, rather than do him honor. The high chief Auwai and his wife called on Charles Stewart one winter evening in Lahaina, and were distressed by the seeming meagerness of the Stewarts' table, described by Stewart in 1824:

This evening, Auwai and wife returned our call. They came in while we were at the tea table, but could not be prevailed on to join us.—We could not but be amused at the evident reason—the poverty of our board in their eyes. A plate of toast, with a little force meat, were the only articles, besides the tea service, on the table, which ... appeared to them a most scanty repast ... 'Aroha ino ia oukou (great is our compassion for you) burst from their lips, and they hastened their return to send us some fish and potatoes immediately.

For Hawaiians, everything, intrinsically and ritualistically, had its own particular place. Certain *kapa* used for clothing, or bedsheets, belonged strictly *ma luna*, or above, just as other things had to be kept *ma lalo*, or below, causing the Hawaiians to disapprove of the *haole* custom of using sheets indiscriminately on the top and bottom of a bed. Some *kapa* were meant only for the torso, and others for the hips. Mary Kawena Pukui remembered that one of her cousins, who was a *kumu* (teacher) of *hula*, chided a student for draping her skirt carelessly over her shoulder: "What belongs above should stay above, and what belongs below should stay below."

Ali'i women were surprised by the amount of domestic work done by missionary women, who, in addition to teaching school and caring for the sick, grew and prepared food, laundered, cleaned, and tended children. The Hawaiians rightly felt that the mission women were overburdened with work, and lonely in their self-willed solitude. (Lucy Thurston understood that she was an exile twice over, "first from my country, and then from the people among whom I sojourn.") According to Charles Stewart, the missionaries appeared woefully cold-hearted to the Hawaiians, as evidenced by their stiff manner of greeting one another (shaking hands), and their habit of simply nodding their heads in meeting or parting. Real or simulated weeping was commonly used by the Hawaiians to express joy, the sight of which was sometimes an embarrassment to foreigners. Louis de Freycinet described in his journal a chief who traveled from Kawaihae to Kealakekua on the Big Island, a distance of fifty miles, to call on Kuakini:

As soon as these chiefs got together, they embraced each other in the manner of the country [touching noses], then started to sob while rolling on the ground and uttering loud cries with all the outward manifestations of profound grief. After this overflow of lamentations, which always last longer with women than with men, people resume their gaiety and their ordinary occupations as if nothing had happened.

Thanks to the missionaries' unfortunate sense of disdain, something that the Hawaiians rarely felt toward the missionaries, they were unable to recognize the instinctive elegance and refinement of Hawaiians. In the annual report of the Board of American Missions, however, the contrast between the reception received by missionaries in Hawai'i and those in the American Northwest is marked—the missionaries in what was to become Oregon Territory were murdered immediately upon their arrival.

Since their arrival in Honolulu, the missionaries had tried to win permission from Liholiho to construct a frame house that had been sent in segments from Boston, but the king, frequently drunk when they called on him, dismissed or ignored their requests. Albertine Loomis, the granddaughter of Albert Loomis, of the First Company, wrote that one afternoon Boki, the younger brother of Kalanimoku and governor of O'ahu, "ushered the callers into his [Liholiho's] palace. At the far end of the room lay His Majesty, in a malo of bright green silk, a half-empty bottle in his hand. With Kamāmalu on the mat were another of Boki's wives, Liliha, and some O'ahu chiefs and chiefesses. The women fondled lap dogs and ate with unmistakable relish the fleas they picked from them. One cuddled a young pig." Liholiho fell asleep as the missionaries made their plea, and they left in silence.

In the summer of 1821, Liholiho sailed from Honolulu in a state of drunkenness to visit the windward side of the island. Once at sea, however, he ordered his captain to take the small and crowded boat across the dangerous channel to Kaua'i, arriving after a night of high seas at Waimea, the village where Captain Cook had first landed more than forty years earlier. The Kaua'i chiefs were not surprised to see Liholiho. They were well aware of his late father's long desire to conquer the island, the only kingdom to remain independent through generations of warfare, and there had been reports that Liholiho and his chiefs had set out on other occasions for Kaua'i, without ever making it across the channel. Ten years earlier, at the instigation of foreign traders who wished to increase trade between the islands, Kaumuali'i and Kamehameha had at last come to an agreement in which the Kaua'i king

High chief Boki, governor of O'ahu, and Hekili, minister of the navy, on board the *Kamchatka* under Golovnin. Watercolor over pencil by Mikhail Tikhanov, 1818, Academy of Arts, St. Petersburg

relinquished his sovereignty, paying a yearly tribute of *kapa*, fruit, hogs, and calabashes to Kamehameha in return for retaining control of the island. As a vassal state, Kaua'i no longer presented a military threat to the unified kingdom that Liholiho had inherited.

As the king arrived without cannon or soldiers, but had brought along his wives (not unlike the missionaries), he was welcomed by Kaumuali'i, who immediately sent *lele*, or messengers, to reassure the chiefs of O'ahu that the king had arrived safely. Kaumuali'i, confident that his small kingdom was in no danger, sought to honor Liholiho and his entourage by conducting them on a six-week-long progress around the island. One afternoon, Liholiho announced that he wished to repay the king's generosity and invited Kaumuali'i on board his yacht, secretly giving orders to sail. When Kaumuali'i realized that he had been tricked, he shouted to his men on shore. His chiefs chased after the schooner in canoes, but lost sight of the darkened boat in the night, and Kaumuali'i was taken to O'ahu.

Historians question whether Ka'ahumanu was an accomplice in the abduction of Kaumuali'i, and whether she had deliberately allowed Liholiho

Red feather *mahiole* of King Kaumuali'i of Kaua'i, from William T. Bingham's *Hawaiian Feather Work*, 1899

out of her keeping. She may have been distracted by the completion of her new two-story frame house near Honolulu harbor, furnished in the Western style with two doors, chandeliers, mahogany tables, and Chinese sofas. The house remained empty, however, when the queen suddenly moved to the north shore, announcing that she would remain there for several months. She returned unexpectedly to Honolulu with the arrival of Liholiho and his prisoner, and three days later, while accompanying Kaumualiʻi on a visit to Hiram and Sybil Bingham, demanded that he marry her. The forty-three-year-old king, a man known to be mild in temper and happy in his marriage to the high chiefess Kapule, had no choice but to agree. Kaumualiʻi and Kaʻahumanu, lying side by side on a low platform piled with thirty mats of the finest weave and covered by a blanket of black *kapa* to signify their union, were married that same night before a gathering of chiefs. The marriage served to unite the royal family of Kauaʻi with high-ranking Maui and Hawaiʻi chiefs, and ended the possibility of conflict, as unlikely as it was, with the only island still to remain unconquered.

A short time later, Kaʻahumanu also married Kaumualiʻi's son, Kealiʻiahonui, further distressing Kapule. (Albertine Loomis writes that Kapule was also married to Kealiʻiahonui, who was her step-son, and that she much preferred him to his father.) Not surprisingly, Kealiʻiahonui, who was seven feet tall, was said to be the best-looking man in the Islands, in spite of missing his front teeth, which he had earlier knocked out while mourning the death of his new wife's late husband, Kamehameha I. James Jarves wrote that Kaʻahumanu soon held "both father and son in her chains, which were not silken." At the time of her second marriage, Kaʻahumanu was perhaps fifty-three years old, and still beautiful, despite her arrogant demeanor, riding to church with Kaumualiʻi wearing shell combs and feathers in her hair, in a wagon drawn by fifteen men.

Unlike most of the chiefs, Kaumualiʻi was slight of build, with skin and features said to be like those of a white man. He was known for his elegance, dressing in cashmere waistcoats, white silk stockings, and black velvet pantaloons from which hung a gold watch with seals and ornaments. He spoke English well, having learned it from merchants. As a captive husband who longed for his wife on Kauaʻi, he busied himself in studying the Bible. Stewart, who thought that the king in his melancholy resembled King James I, found Kaumualiʻi to be "the most Christian person in the nation . . . I have never heard a word, nor witnessed in him a look or action, unbecoming a prince, or, what is far more important, inconsistent with the character of a professedly pious man." Kaumuali'i once asked Bingham for a blessing on his food, infuriating the jealous Ka'ahumanu, who threw a heavy pot at his head, which was deflected by a startled Bingham at the last moment. It comes as no surprise that Kaumuali'i is said to have disliked his new wife, and a frustrated Ka'ahumanu, not used to resistance, complained that he did not return her possibly real affection. Perhaps in an attempt to please her new husband, she abandoned her *pā'ū* to wear striped satin gowns, white muslin shawls, and leghorn bonnets rather than her customary *kapa* skirt and wreaths of feathers and flowers. In her new finery, she surprised and amused the *haole* women with both her grandeur and her lack of modesty. Lucy Thurston sat with the queen at a tea given by the Binghams for some of the chiefs, and officers of the *Dolphin*, then in port:

> The time passed pleasantly until nine o'clock, when it was announced that our queen, Ka'ahumanu, was tired, and wanted to go home. She arose (I never saw her look so tall), gathered up the ample folds of her black silk dress, even to the very waist, holding a portion on each arm, and exposing a beautiful undergarment of pink satin. Thus she stood . . . while we gathered around her to bid her good night.

Despite the teachings of her new friends, Ka'ahumanu still preferred to spend the Sabbath swimming and surfing, rather than in church. She stopped one Sunday at the Binghams after a day in the ocean, and settled comfortably on a sofa next to Lucy Thurston. She happened to be naked. "In the presence of them and their wives, she entered the sitting room. With the ease and self possession of royalty, she took a seat on the settee, and carried on conversation with freedom. Did I say she came from the bathing place?—She came as it were from Eden, in the dress of innocence." Ka'ahumanu treated the missionaries like spoiled favorite children, taking the women into her lap whenever it pleased her. Now and again, in the tradition of *hānai*, a chiefess would nonchalantly demand that one of the missionary children be given to her. A daughter of Kamehameha I asked for four-year-old Persis Thurston, and the high chiefess Kīna'u asked for one of the Judd children, without success.

At least in the beginning, the Hawaiians were enthralled by the fiery sermons and joyous hymns of the Christians. Hawaiians were good students in part because of the familiarity of recitation and the repetition of phrases, a system of teaching that happened to be favored by Bingham, who claimed to insist on a genuine understanding of Christian doctrine before the possibility of baptism. Bingham's habit was to ask his students the same question over and over again, in the hope that "in a few days they will be able to recollect the answers required and . . . become experienced people," which does not have much to do with sincere understanding. *Watt's Catechism, Webster's Spelling Book*, and the New Testament were used for instruction, and most students learned the alphabet within a week, some of them using the spines of sea urchins as pencils. The lessons were often set to old chants, which were repeated in unison: "*Mai mālama hou i nā akua lā-au.*" "Keep no more wooden gods."

Although the missionaries had brought a printing press with them on the *Thaddeus*, it was not used until almost two years after their arrival, when a spelling book was printed in Hawaiian (its first words were "*He aloha ke Akua*," or "God is love"). Liholiho visited the printing house to pull the lever himself when the sheets were printed, and was surprised to see a piece of clean white paper suddenly covered with what he realized were words in his language. He ordered one hundred of the primers to give to friends and attendants, and asked that his five wives resume their lessons. The following year, eighty thousand Bible tracts were printed, as well as a translation of the Gospel of St. Matthew.

As the Hawaiians grew accustomed to the inherent strangeness of the new faith, they were baptized by the hundreds, and although it was often only temporary, became devoted members of the Moral Societies that were quickly established. The respite from boredom, at least among the *ali'i*, must have been a relief and a diversion. Lucy Thurston, writing fifty years after her arrival in the Islands, unintentionally reveals a surprising sensitivity to a perceived slight:

> Soon after the printing of the first sheets of the spelling book in the Hawaiian language, a missionary was sitting at a table in his own house, with a chief, teaching him the rudiments of his own language. The chief grasped at an idea he wished to communicate. So turning to his attendants, seated on the mat, he said, "The consonant is a man, the vowel is a woman; put them together, they make something; apart they are nothing at all." We, who are more thoroughly instructed, know that a vowel makes a perfect syllable by itself. It is a consonant only, that makes nothing at all, standing alone.

Lucy Thurston reading the Bible on her *lāna'i*, from Charles Nordhoff's *Northern California, Oregon and Sandwich Islands*, 1875

In March 1823, when Ka'ahumanu's brother Kahekili died in Honolulu, Kaumuali'i convinced Ka'ahumanu to give him a Christian funeral and to bury him in one of the expensive caskets sold by a local *haole* merchant. Samuel Kamakau wrote that Governor Kuakini of the Big Island, who was Kahekili and Ka'ahumanu's brother, sailed to Honolulu for the service. Before the funeral, which was to be conducted by Bingham, six of Kuakini's men were seen to remove a heavy object from the casket, wrap it in mats, and load it into a canoe, which was paddled across the harbor to Kuakini's waiting yacht. The mischievous chiefs were curious to see if the Christian god would reveal to Bingham that the coffin was empty. When Bingham appeared not to know that the body had been stolen, the delighted Kuakini had the body stripped and burned and the bones hidden, as was the traditional way.

That same year, Keōpūolani moved with her court to Lahaina. In the hope of establishing a congregation there, she wrote to Bingham for help, and he sent the missionaries Charles Stewart and William Richards to her. Stewart, who much preferred Lahaina to Honolulu, wrote that "the entire district, stretching nearly three miles along the sea-side, is covered with luxuriant groves, not only of the cocoanut . . . but also of the breadfruit and the kou . . . while the banana plant, kapa, and sugar-cane are abundant and extend almost to the beach, on which a fine surf constantly rolls."

The morning after the arrival of the two men, Keōpūolani ordered that schools be established in the households of the chiefs. At the end of the first week, Stewart was surprised to find the Hawaiians already spelling, reading, and writing, meeting in groups of ten to thirty people from morning to night, "whether in their houses, or in the grove, whether strolling on the beach, or I might almost add sporting in the surf." He was disappointed, however, to discover that the queen and her eight-year-old daughter, Princess Nāhiʻenaʻena, continued to patronize dancers and musicians, although he was relieved to learn that the dancing was "slow and graceful, and, in this instance, free from indelicacy of action."

In May 1823, the missionaries and many of the foreign residents were invited to a feast in Honolulu that would last ten days, marking the fourth anniversary of the death of Kamehameha. For the Second Company of missionaries who arrived from Boston that April, it would have been their first sight of the Hawaiian court. Liholiho invited one hundred guests, including the missionaries, who insisted on beginning the feast with Divine Service. The tables were set with a combination of gourds and calabashes, blue and white china, and crystal wine glasses. Thousands of people

The procession in 1823 marking the anniversary of the death of Kamehameha I, with Queen Kamāmalu sitting in a whale boat, as described by Charles Stewart. From Ephraim Eveleth's *History of the Sandwich Islands*, 1829

gathered at the king's compound to watch the feasting. The guests, both native and foreign, had been asked to wear black Western clothes, although warriors in feather capes and *malo* stood on guard in the yard. When Nāhiʻenaʻena arrived, Liholiho helped to pull her four-wheeled carriage onto the lawn, then carried her on his back to her chair next to their brother, Kauikeaouli, with the words, "This is my sister, the daughter of Kamehameha."

Charles Stewart, who wrote the following description, was both dismayed and excited by the haphazard procession of chiefs roaming through the dusty streets of Honolulu. Clusters of dancers and musicians randomly joined the entourage of a favorite chief, noisily surrounding him and causing him to lose his way, only to rush to the next group. Stewart wondered if there was another nation in Christendom that could produce such haphazard magnificence:

> Black had been given out as the *court dress*, and every article of that hue in the place, satin, silk, crape, velvet, and cloth, was immediately bought: and those who were not fortunate enough to secure any of these, purchased pieces of black silk handkerchiefs, and had them made into dresses ... Tamehamaru [Kamāmalu] in satin and lace sustained the part of mistress of ceremonies ... While at table, a procession of four hundred natives, the inhabitants of eight districts of Oahu, passed before the party, and deposited a tax, *in kind*, at the feet of the king. They were all dressed in white native cloth, and made a handsome appearance as they marched in single file ... The ceremonies ... were altogether *Hawaiian* in their character; and highly interesting as an exhibition of ancient customs, which it is probable will soon be lost for ever in the light of civilization and Christianity, now rapidly dawning on the nation. The most intelligent and influential of the chiefs and people, already speak of the *"time of dark hearts;"* and I believe are sincerely desirous of abolishing every unprofitable practice which had its birth in the ignorance of former days.

Stewart goes on to describe the arrival of the queens:

> Tameha-maru ... [sat on] an elegantly modelled *whale boat*, fastened firmly to a platform or frame of light spars, thirty feet long by twelve

wide; and borne on the heads or shoulders of seventy men. The boat was lined, and the whole platform covered, first with fine imported broadcloth, and then with beautiful patterns of tapa . . . of a variety of figures and rich colours. The men supporting the whole were formed into a solid body, so that the outer rows only at the sides and ends were seen; and all forming these, wore the splendid scarlet and yellow feather cloaks and helmets . . . than which scarce any thing can appear more superb . . . The only dress of the queen was a scarlet silk *pau*, or native petticoat, and a coronet of feathers. She was seated in the middle of the boat, and screened from the sun by an immense Chinese umbrella of scarlet damask, richly ornamented with gilding, fringe, and tassels, and supported by a chief standing behind her in a scarlet maro or girdle, and feather helmet. On one quarter of the boat stood Karaimoko [Kalanimoku] the prime minister; and on the other, *Naihi*, the national orator; both also in maros of scarlet silk and helmets of feathers, and each bearing a kahile or feathered staff of state, near thirty feet in height . . . The queens Kinau and Kekau-onohi presented themselves in much the same manner as Tameha-maru; but instead of whaleboats had for their seats *double canoes*. Pau-ahi, another of the wives of Riho-Riho, after passing in the procession with her retinue, alighted from the couch on which she had been borne, set fire to it and all its expensive trappings, and then threw into the flames the whole of her dress, except a single handkerchief to cast around her . . . She was immediately imitated by all her attendants . . . and entire pieces of broadcloth, were thus consumed . . . It was to commemorate a narrow escape from death by fire, while an infant: a circumstance from which she derives her name . . . One [queen] wore *seventy-two* yards of kerseymere . . . one half being scarlet and the other orange. It was wrapped round her figure, till her arms were supported horizontally by the bulk; and the remainder was formed into a train supported by persons appointed for the purpose. The young prince and princess, Kauikeaouli and Kinau, wore the native dress, maro and pau, of scarlet silk. Their *vehicle* consisted of *four field-bedsteads* of Chinese wood and workmanship, lashed together side by side, covered with handsome native cloth, and ornamented with canopies and drapery of yellow figured moreen. Two chiefs of rank bore their kahiles; and Hoapiri [Hoapili] and Kaikioeva, their

step-father and guardian, in scarlet maros, followed them as servants:
the one bearing a calabash of *raw fish*, and a calabash of *poe*, and the
other a *dish of baked dog*, for the refreshment of the young favou-
rites . . . The king [Liholiho] and his suite made but a sorry exhibition.
They were nearly naked, mounted on horses without saddles, and so
much intoxicated as scarce to be able to retain their seats as they scampered from place to place in all the disorder of a troop of baccha-
nalians. A bodyguard of fifty or sixty men, in shabby uniforms,
attempted by a running march to keep near the person of their sover-
eign, while hundreds of ragged natives, filling the air with their hoot-
ings and shouting, followed in the chase. Companies of singing and
dancing girls and men, consisting of many hundreds, met the procession in different places, encircling the highest chiefs, and shouting
their praise in enthusiastic adulations. The dull and monotonous
sounds of the native drum and calabash, the wild notes of their
songs . . . and the pulsations, on the ground, of the tread of thousands
in the dance, reached us even at the Missionary enclosure.

Later that year, Liholiho amused himself with the building of a palace of
thatched grass with wooden doors, and windows with shutters. Traditional
mats covered the floor, and crystal chandeliers dangled from the ridgepoles.
Gilt mirrors and engravings of English naval battles, as well as two life-sized
portraits of Liholiho, were on the walls. There were Chinese sofas in crimson
brocade, and mahogany tables for eating, and for playing cards. On one of Stewart's visits, the king's favorite wife, the graceful Kamāmalu, sat at a long table
with an attendant at each end, recording in ledgers the levies collected from
a long line of commoners, come to pay their taxes. In order to build the palace,
the king had assessed the high chiefs fifty dollars; foreign traders and shopkeepers were charged twenty dollars; and commoners contributed whatever
small fees they could afford. Although the palace was *kapu*, the curious could
pay one Spanish dollar for a quick tour.

The journal of Don Francisco de Marín, kept from 1809 to 1826, has
many entries that day after day record the king's drunkenness. The following
is from 1823: "8 October. The King is drinking." "9 October. Today they talk
much of expelling all white men out of this island. The King is drinking."
"22 October. The King is drunk." "23 October. The King is drinking."

"24 October. The King is sick." The king was often found on a sofa of silk velvet, wearing a chintz *malo* as his servants fanned him. If he was not drunk, he was recovering from the excesses of drink, while Kamāmalu fed him cups of tea for his nausea. The king had begun to suffer from convulsions induced by alcohol, accompanied by paralysis and bleeding from the mouth. He was treated by Hawaiian doctors as well as the mission doctors, but during one attack, he sat cross-legged on the ground for two weeks, collecting pieces of straw and other twigs to present ceremoniously to his wives and attendants. Sybil Bingham, who admired him, despaired of ever converting him to Christianity:

> The early habits of Rihoriho did not warrant any great expecta-
> tions. His natural disposition was frank, and humane. The natives
> always spoke of him as good-natured, except when he was under
> the influence of ardent spirits; his manners were perfectly free, at the
> same time dignified, and always agreeable to those who were about
> him. His mind was naturally inquisitive. The questions he usually
> presented . . . were by no means trifling; and his memory was reten-
> tive. His general knowledge of the world was much greater than could
> have been expected. I have heard him entertain a party of chiefs for
> hours together, with accounts of different parts of the earth, describ-
> ing the extensive lakes, the mountains, and mines of North and South
> America; the elephants and inhabitants of India; the houses, manu-
> factures, &c. of England, with no small accuracy, considering he had
> never seen them. He had a great thirst for knowledge, and was diligent
> in his studies . . . Mr. Bingham and myself were his daily teachers, and
> have often been surprised at his unwearied perseverance . . . We do not
> know that Christianity exerted any decisive influence on his heart . . .
> Though generous in his disposition, and humane in his conduct . . . he
> was addicted to intoxication; whether from natural inclination, or
> the influence and example of others, is not now to be determined;
> frequently, to my own knowledge, it has been entirely from the latter.

That spring, there were rumors that the king was dying at his retreat in Waikīkī, and weeping crowds rushed with Hiram Bingham to see him. This account is from a letter written to the Mission Board in Boston:

His guards assembled around him with swords and muskets; and the multitude, surrounding the house, made the grove to resound with their loud wailing. His mother [Keōpūolani] and Kaahumanu, Tamoree [Kaumuali'i], and the principal chiefs, his wives and particular friends, [stood] round his couch in tears . . . He had been seized suddenly with an alarming fit, first red, then pale, and stiff with spasm, and shaken with convulsions, with interrupted and difficult respiration, attended with vomiting, and followed by profuse perspiration. He emitted considerable blood from the mouth . . . Early in the morning a convenient bed was spread upon a double canoe, and the king was laid upon it, to be removed to Honoruru [Honolulu], with the principal chiefs.

To everyone's surprise, Liholiho recovered, and in March he wrote to the Board to thank them for sending Mr. Bingham and Mr. Thurston to the Islands: "Spontaneous was your love in thinking of us . . . Had you not sent hither the teachers, extreme mental darkness would even now have pervaded all our islands. But no. You have kindly compassionated us;—and the people of our islands are becoming enlightened. Grateful affection to you all."

After the death of Keōpūolani in Lahaina, Liholiho and Kamāmalu, perhaps mistrustful of the intentions of the Americans regarding their small but strategically located kingdom, and perhaps looking for something to ease Liholiho's increasing restlessness, decided to visit King George IV of England to seek advice as to the best form of government for the Islands. King George had given Liholiho a present of a schooner, the *Prince Regent*, and Liholiho also wished to thank him in person. Perhaps unaware of his father's earlier cession of the Islands to Vancouver, or mindful that it had not taken effect, Liholiho had written the king a thank-you letter in which he made known his wish "to place his Sandwich Islands under the protection of the British crown . . . [given] the confidence I place in your Majesty's wisdom and judgment."

In November, against the counsel of his chiefs, Liholiho was lifted by his bearers into the cutter that would carry him across the harbor to the English whaler, *L'Aigle*, bound for London. Sailing with him were Kamāmalu; the high chief Boki and his wife, Liliha; his interpreter, Kānehoa, who was the son of John Young; four young chiefs; and a large number of attendants and servants. Stewart wrote that Kamāmalu hesitated on shore until the last moment:

She arose from the mat on which she had been reclining, embraced her mother [Kaheiheimālie] and other relations most affectionately, and passed through the crowd . . . The people fell down on their knees as she walked along pressing and saluting at her feet, frequently bathing them with tears of unfeigned sorrow.

Thousands of moaning and chanting people waded after her as she boarded a pinnace. She implored them to stop weeping: "I am going to a distant land, and perhaps we shall not meet again."

Kamakau wrote that the ship fell below the horizon, "as if dropping into its grave." Out of sight of land, a disappointed Liholiho confessed that he had expected the people to prevent them from leaving. It had eventually become clear to him, however, that no one was going to stop them (in port, a chief who had proposed holding them had the clothes ripped from his body by outraged Hawaiians). Liholiho is said to have remarked with a sigh, "They have long despised us."

Over the years, Ka'ahumanu had maintained her position as regent with little effort. Any dissension in the kingdom was between the missionaries and those chiefs who had not yet succumbed to Christianity, or who had ceded their diminishing power to *haole* traders. Thanks to Keōpūolani's baptism shortly before her death, many of the chiefs had converted, relinquishing many of their hereditary prerogatives, including the right to order a man's death. Ka'ahumanu did not hesitate to take advantage of Liholiho's absence to issue reforms that the missionaries had been quietly pressing her to make for some time. A few months after the king's sailing, she summoned a counsel of high chiefs to declare her intention to follow the teachings of the missionaries, and to further the instruction of her people with more books, more schools, and more native teachers. Overnight, thatched longhouses were turned into schoolrooms, and landlords were punished if they did not comply with the new law to provide additional teachers. When Ka'ahumanu was visiting Kaua'i, she wrote to ask "the posse of Longnecks to send some more books down here. Many are the people—few are the books. I want . . . 800 Hawaiian books to be sent hither . . . By and by, perhaps, we shall be wise." The new schoolhouses each held one hundred students. Lessons were taught by native teachers who stood on raised platforms to shout the letters of the alphabet, which were then repeated by the students. The schools were easily found, it is said, because of the noise filling the lanes around them. According to Kotzebue, however, the busy scene was full of melancholy: "Every sort of gaiety is forbidden."

Hiram Bingham was surprised by the ease with which Ka'ahumanu issued the new laws, and her assumption of absolute power in the king's absence. Among her advisers were the guardian of the royal children, Hoapili (stepfather to Kauikeaouli and Nāhi'ena'ena), and Kīna'u, a daughter of Kamehameha who did not share the sacred rank of Nāhi'ena'ena, her half-sister. Bingham realized that he had miscalculated, having spent the previous year trying to win the trust of the king through his prime minister. Years later, when writing his memoir, he conceded his mistake: "We had not the means of knowing fully the standing and influence of Kaahumanu, and perhaps lost time and opportunities on that account; but we soon learned to appreciate her importance in the nation."

Laura Judd, the wife of the physician Gerrit P. Judd, who later arrived

Laura Judd, wife of the physician
Dr. Gerrit P. Judd of the Third
Company of missionaries (1828),
with her daughter, Juliet Isabel.
Oil painting by James Gay Sawkins,
1850, Mission Houses Museum,
Honolulu

with the Third Company, did not make Bingham's mistake. She was attentive to the queen, and won her regard:

> After dinner she [Ka'ahumanu] reclined on a sofa, and received vari-
> ous presents sent by [the missionaries'] friends from Boston. Mr. Bing-
> ham read letters from Messrs. Stewart, Loomis and Ellis to her. She
> listened attentively, her tears flowed freely, and she could only articu-
> late the expression, Aloha ino (Love intense). At four o'clock she said
> she was tired, and must go home; accordingly her retinue was sum-
> moned, some twenty in number, one bearing the kahili, another an
> umbrella, still another her spittoon. She took us each by the hand,
> and kissed each one in the Hawaiian style, by placing her nose against
> our cheeks, and giving a sniff, as one would indicate the fragrance of
> flowers . . . She seated her immense stateliness in her carriage, which is
> a light hand-cart, painted turquoise blue, spread with fine mats, and
> several beautiful damask and velvet covered cushions. It was drawn by
> six stout men, who grasped the ropes in pairs, and marched off as if
> proud of the royal burden. The old lady rides backward, with her feet
> hanging down behind the cart, which is certainly a safe, if not conve-
> nient, mode of traveling.

Two daughters, Persis and Lucy, were born to the Thurstons during their time
in Honolulu. (Two more children, Asa and Sarah, were later born in Kailua.)
Although sometimes dismayed by the domestic practices of the Hawaiians, Lucy
no longer suffered from the fear of cannibalism and poison spells that had once
troubled her, even if the arrival of an American ship was still cause for rejoicing:

> It was evening twilight [in Honolulu] . . . From the outer door into the
> sitting room, proceeded these words: "Good evening, Mr. Thurston."
> It was a voice never to be forgotten. We were newly transplanted exotics.
> We had not then taken root. We were in the heart of the nation, shut
> up to a strange dialect, without associates, and without foreigners for
> neighbors. English words, in cultivated tones, fell with strange power
> upon the ear, and upon the heart. So it was when an American vessel
> visited our port. We heard words, and experienced deeds of kindness.

God bless mariners. They are the links that connect us to the
father-land. The white sails of the ship were again unfurled to the
breeze, and the only vestige around us of civilization had passed away.

It was an occasion that proved to be troubling as well as exhilarating, as the
Hawaiian women, to Lucy's dismay, openly and without shame availed themselves of the company of the sailors:

A whole sisterhood, embracing fifteen or twenty, assembled and took
seats in a conspicuous part of the village to display themselves. Before
the arrival of that ship, they were simply attired in native cloth. After
her sailing, each one was arrayed in a foreign article, obtained from
that very ship. Their own relatives and friends, perhaps fathers or
brothers, or husbands, had paddled off that whole company of women
and girls, to spend the night on board that ship, specially for the grati-
fication of its inmates. When they returned, each one flaunted her
base reward of foreign cloth.

Near the end of the Thurstons' stay in Honolulu, Maria Loomis was
knocked to the ground by a Hawaiian on horseback whose intention, he explained, was only to give her a little scare, but her injury was sufficient to keep
her in bed for several days. Lucy was furious at the affront, and even more
incensed by the gift of a shawl from the rider—the kind of enticement, she
wrote, that tempted "many of the down-trodden women of the land into sin."
(It seems that she did not remember this when she later amended her journal
to note that she herself had suffered the only offense known to have been
rendered a missionary woman by a Hawaiian.)

At the end of 1823, the Thurstons were asked to return to their station at
Kailua, accompanied by the Reverend and Mrs. Artemas Bishop (Elizabeth
Edwards married Bishop with the intention of joining her old school friend
Lucy in the Islands). The trip between islands was difficult—the masters of
the small schooners were often drunk, and the boats themselves perilously
overcrowded and filthy.

During the night the natives kept dropping in until the cabin was
crowded. With dead-lights closed, so much heat and confined air, it
seemed almost suffocating. Disregarding quietude, even during the

hours where nature calls for rest, their united songs and chit-chat, went to form a prolonged clamor. Such were the circumstances in which we were called to resign ourselves to sea-sickness; such the state in which the two little ones were demanding the care and sympathy by night and by day; yet had circumstances permitted, I should myself have been prostrate. I survived the voyage; nor with all my sufferings did I once dream it otherwise, save when all in the gloom of midnight, a tumult on deck would arouse us from short "disturbed repose," with apprehensions that the vessel was foundering.

Charles Stewart wrote in his journal of the Thurstons' departure from Lahaina, where they stayed with the Stewarts for a week on their way to the Big Island. "I admired the spirit with which Mrs. Thurston . . . sprang into a rude canoe with her two children . . . No preparation appearing to have been made on board the brig, to hoist her on deck in a chair, which is usually done, she intrepidly mounted the ship's quarter by the manropes, and stood ready to wave us a distant farewell."

In Kona, the Thurstons began the building of a large thatched house behind the native village, a third of a mile from the ocean. It sat within a five-acre enclosure, surrounded by a stone wall six feet high. On the property was a large cave which gave the house its name—Laniākea, or Broad Heavens.

Our old people tell us of the time in their childhood, when they were aroused from their midnight slumbers, to see red hot balls hurled into the air from out of the crater on this mountain [Hualālai]. Torrents of molten lava flowed from crater to coast, extended the shore farther out into the sea, and encrusted the surface of the earth . . . Along the coast for two miles back, it is sterile; but there is a belt that is very rich, about a mile wide at the foot of the mountain, which is dotted here and there with the kukui, breadfruit and orange, all splendid trees . . . Above this fertile belt is quite a width of forest, after which the bare sides of the mountain rise to a peak. It stands toward the rising sun. These distant scenes . . . are ever to be enjoyed.

Lucy made the house as comfortable as was within her modest means. Sheets of *kapa* lined the walls and ceiling, and *lau hala* mats lay on the dirt floor over a layer of clean straw. There were the odd pieces of furniture that the Thurstons had managed to bring with them from New England; gifts from the king and queens; books; workbaskets; glass bottles for flowers; a small mirror; and the plates, saucers, glasses, and bowls given to them by sympathetic sea captains (not one piece of the china brought by the missionaries in large crates on the *Thaddeus* was unbroken when they arrived). The Board sent beef, bread, flour, molasses, and pork from New England, but the provisions often arrived so rotten that flour had to be chipped from a barrel with an axe. The smell of the meat was so rank that it was impossible to remain in the house while it was boiled. Lucy allowed her daughters to sell their extra homemade butter—they could earn more than a dollar a pound—in order to buy schoolbooks for themselves, but when the Board learned of the girls' profits (which envious missionary could have reported them?), the amount was deducted from Thurston's already minuscule salary. If a shipment of victuals was late in arriving, the missionaries went hungry, and had to ask for credit from the merchants in order to buy food. The missionaries were dependent on the occasional presents of food and household supplies—rice, soap, dried fruit, tea, firewood, and candles, among other small treasures—given them by the sea captains and traders, as well as the many gifts of food from their generous neighbors.

Within the Thurstons' enclosed yard was another thatched house, with yet a second wall, where the Thurston children were confined so that they would not be corrupted by association with Hawaiians. The Thurstons' fellow missionary, Fanny Gulick, later wrote that Lucy believed the second wall necessary, "because if she [Lucy] had but one wall, the natives would climb up outside, and converse with the children, but by having two, it was impossible as they would not dare to come over the outer one." A rule was made that "No child might speak to a native, and no native might speak to a child, babyhood excepted . . . [There were] separate rooms and yards for children, and separate rooms and yards for natives."

> There is no entrance to the yard through the wall, but a door into it from our bed room . . . The children can from thence into the bed room, and so out into their own yard and place of recreation, having without interference, the enjoyment of freedom and action. I, left in the sitting room, devoted to the natives, am still porter to the only door that leads into the children's special enclosure, and have the satisfied feeling of their being safe, beyond the reach of native

influence . . . The first rule to be attended to with regard to children is that they *must not speak* the native language. It is an easy thing to *make* such a law, but it is a mother's duty to guard it from being violated, and to form in her children *fixed habits* of doing as they are required . . . They are never left to the care of natives after reaching the age of prattling. No intercourse whatever should exist between children and heathen. On this point I am very particular.

Lucy taught her children in the morning (grammar, geography, history, arithmetic, philosophy, and chemistry; Thurston taught them singing and Latin). Classes for Hawaiian students were held later in the day. Asa was physically enormous, with a long white beard, and a melodious voice; he was so fluent in Hawaiian that people gathered at his house simply to hear him speak their language—it was said to be impossible to tell that he was not one of them. At meal times, however, only the tersest of requests and instructions were uttered to the servants in Hawaiian.

Lucy believed, as did most of the missionaries, that their children should be sent to relatives and even strangers in America to attend school as soon as they were old enough, which often was as young as seven years of age. While it was a torment for them to do so, their fear of corruption was greater than their attachment, despite constant proof of the dignity and disinterested kindness of Hawaiians. "None but He who knoweth the unutterable feelings of tenderness and love which I have felt for my child," wrote Lucy, "knows the corresponding agony which the prospect of separation has produced."

The fear of corruption did not apply to white female adolescents, oddly enough, as Lucy naïvely assumed that the characters of her girl children had by then been sufficiently molded to her liking:

> When our eldest daughters were twelve and fourteen years of age, their habits were so formed, and their principles so established, that we gave them permission to learn the native language from pure sources. They were instructed in it by their parents, allowed access to Hawaiian books, attended on their father's ministry, became teachers in the Sabbath school, also in the day school, and each had a chamber in which she gathered her own Sabbath school class around her for religious exercises. They were allowed to come in contact with native assistant teachers, under school regulations, but not as associates.

In later years, Lucy placed the blame for sending away her children on the warnings of William Ellis, the English clergyman who had spent six years in Tahiti before he arrived in Hawai'i. Like others of the missionaries, she had been frightened out of her wits by Ellis, who claimed to have seen in Tahiti corruption so foul that he could not bring himself to describe it (in a report to the London Missionary Society in 1819, it was claimed that every Tahitian girl over the age of twelve had been violated, and that husbands and wives were so given to sexual license that they freely abandoned their children to gratify their lust).

No one of us had conceived the idea that children with unformed characters must be separated from the people to whom we were sent. Those children were in full connection with the native children of our family boarding school, in their studies, in their amusements, and in their employments. When our English missionary friends came [William Ellis], they saw at a glance that we had begun upon a wrong tack with our own children. They spread before us the developments and experiences of missionary life for thirty years at the Society Islands. Some items of intelligence were most startling in their character. The earth seemed to be receding from beneath our feet, with no firm foundation remaining on which to stand.

Henry Lyman, son of the Hilo missionaries Sarah and David Lyman (and whose brother Rufus married a Chinese-Hawaiian woman), wrote in his memoir, *Hawaiian Yesterdays* (1906), that Ellis's stories of lascivious Tahitians had a very harmful effect:

[In the Sandwich Islands] the little ones were therefore kept as far as possible away from the natives ... On one occasion, as I find from my mother's journal, she was in great distress at finding that I understood the meaning of her order to a native servant to close the door. The only way to escape these evils, during the early days of missionary work, was to send the children to their relatives in America ... Torn shrieking from their mothers' arms, the wailing infants were hurried away, around Cape Horn, and sent to live among strangers, in order to preserve them from contaminating contact with the Hawaiians.

Not all the missionaries were as fearful as Lucy Thurston. Mary Ann Alexander, the wife of the Reverend William P. Alexander, who was stationed at Waiʻoli on the windward side of Oʻahu, wrote that they had very little furniture when they first set up house in 1832—a settee and a table and chairs brought from America, but no cooking stove. "We lived three years in this house. I never was happier than during those years. It was delightful to live with my doors open and to have no fears of the people around me." Mrs. Alexander bore five sons and four daughters, all of whom went to the Punahou School in Honolulu, which was established by Kamehameha III in 1841 for the children of missionaries. In his memoir, *Mission Life in Hawaii* (1888), William Alexander wrote of the joy he felt at the children's return each summer at the end of the school year:

> [The] homecoming of these children, and of those of the associate teachers, in vacations, by a tedious voyage with much seasickness, in small, slow-sailing craft, was a great event at Lahainaluna. A white flag at the mast-head, the usual sign of missionaries or of their children, announced their coming; and long before they reached the port, horses were ready for them at the beach . . . The time of vacations passed quickly for the children, in baths in the sea, rambles in the valleys, and excursions to the summits of the mountains.

One wonders if Alexander was aware that flags of white *kapa* were once used to signify a *kapu*.

Alexander wrote in a letter to one of his sons at school in the United States: "My dear son . . . the steamer brought home our dear ones, from Punahou school, who, weather-bound, had already lost one week of the short vacation . . . Altogether the tender cords of our souls are so set a-vibrating that we spent the balance of the day in a sort of dreamy delirium. Oh, shall we be ever allowed to see you all at home together once more?" Alexander is full of longing and love, but he has little fear of natives corrupting the souls (or bodies) of his children.

The missionaries, already distressed by the sight of public defecation, had been further disturbed to discover that Hawaiian children openly observed the sexual relations of adults (children themselves were sexually active from the age of ten or twelve), and they were horrified by stories about, and the occasional visible evidence of, the past punishment of children for the violation of *kapu*. Lucy described a Hawaiian girl of eight years old:

> Her erect figure, clear smooth skin, regular features, slightly curling hair, and full black eye, with the long black fringes of its covering, made her a good specimen of the loveliness of childhood. But the beauty . . . was marred by violence. The ball of her right eye had been scooped out entirely, so that the full-orbed eye of death in its gentle sleep, was far less revolting than that concave appearance. "My child, how DID you lose your eye?" "I ate a banana." Had she been of mature years, her life would have been taken.

Although some dispute that infanticide was practiced by the Hawaiians, there is sufficient evidence in the form of journals and memoirs, as well as a law against it issued by Ka'ahumanu, to believe that it was not uncommon. The Hawaiians practiced intanticide when a child was born to a *kauwā* partner, to a person much lower in rank than a parent who was a chief or chiefess, or when a child was born to a person disliked by the family (when a child was killed at birth, it was called an *'ōmilomilo*, or child strangling). In 1819, Louis de Freycinet was surprised to discover that unwanted infants were left to die or strangled by their parents, as he found the Hawaiians to be quiet and kind people: "Under the slightest pretext, the father and mother have the right to destroy the fruit of their union . . . Aside from abortions, the perils of which women brave with complete indifference, they have been known to strangle their newborn and even bury them alive, sometimes right next to their own beds."

For the young men of the mission, many of them fresh from the schoolrooms of New England seminaries, the physical ease and freedom of Hawaiian women must have been very disturbing, even if they were afforded some protection by a sense of their own superiority, and their fear and mistrust of pleasure, which helped to turn any latent desire into disgust. Rufus Anderson of the American Board of Commissions of Foreign Missions wrote in 1864 of the comportment of the Hawaiians, particularly the women:

> The dress of the natives of that period was very simple, consisting of a malo for the male, and a pa'u for the female . . . Children of both sexes

were entirely naked till they were nine or ten years old. In bathing in the sea, or sporting in the surf, no articles of clothing were ever worn; and females were accustomed to leave their pa'u at their residences, and pass on through the village to the shore, and return in the same manner; and if they were individuals of high rank they would not infrequently call at the residence of the missionary to pay their respects, and send a servant to bring the pa'u, and put it on in the missionary's presence.

In his journal, Hiram Bingham described a ceremony he witnessed at the compound of the high chief Boki, where hundreds of male and female dancers had gathered to sing and dance ten days earlier in a celebration that would continue for several months. The dancers, wearing *malo* and *pā'ū*, and adorned with leaves, flowers, bracelets, and anklets were insufficiently clothed for Bingham, and he condemned the dancers as incitements to lust. A statue of Laka, goddess of the *hula*, stood at the entrance to Boki's yard, and the dancers bedecked her image each day with flowers and leaves, further upsetting Bingham, who complained to Boki that the idolatrous image should be removed. Boki, with his customary humor, told Bingham that he was

Men dancing in anklets made with dogs' teeth. Lithograph by Louis Choris, 1822, Honolulu Museum of Art

welcome to the statue when the *hula* ceremonies were complete. Boki agreed, however, that the dancers, if allowed to dance undisturbed each morning and night, would attend the mission school by day.

It had once been acceptable, even pragmatic, for *haole* seamen and traders to keep native mistresses, not unlike the domestic arrangements and love matches of the British merchants and company officials of the East India Company in eighteenth- and nineteenth-century Bengal. A liaison or marriage to a Hawaiian woman had once been considered advantageous, particularly if a woman had *ali'i* blood and the land that often accompanied rank. It was only with the coming of the missionaries that it became disreputable for a *haole* to live with a native woman. The disapproval of the missionaries did little, however, to affect the small group of local white and, later, Asian men, who were regarded with hostility for their drinking and general bad morals, which presumably included their relationships with Hawaiian women, with whom they lived openly, and sired children.

It is no surprise that in missionary families, marriages with Hawaiians or Asians were rare. An exception was the marriage in 1866 of Rufus Lyman, the son of David and Sarah Lyman, to Hualani Ahung, who had a Chinese father and Cherokee-Hawaiian mother (in many records, her Chinese name is replaced with the name Rebecca Brickwood, thanks to her mother's

Young dancer with bleached hair and tattoos of goats. Lithograph by Nicolas-Eustache Maurin, after Jacques Arago, 1819

second marriage to the *haole* postmaster of Honolulu). The son of the Hawai'i Island missionary John D. Paris married a woman descended from the ruling chiefs of Maui, named Kailikolamaikapaliokaukini. When a visiting friend of Clarissa Armstrong, wife of the Reverend Richard Armstrong, announced that he was marrying a Hawaiian woman and staying in the Islands, Mrs. Armstrong was horrified:

> O what feelings of *sorrow, contempt* etc filled my breast. I have done nothing scarcely this P.M. but . . . weep for the folly, of one I watched over as a brother. A member of our family, and we keeping him from temptations, and the[n] without asking even our advice, is going headlong into folly, and I fear what is worse!! What will his poor mother say when she hears he is *married* to a *heathen*, who like the rest, regards not the truth, or the 7th commandment.

The Reverend George Rowell, stationed at Waimea on Kaua'i, was accused of adultery with his female parishioners by a Hawaiian woman in his church. His wife remained loyal to him, despite his dismissal and the efforts of the missionaries to turn her against him. In 1852, the Reverend Samuel G. Dwight, who had kept a school on Moloka'i for six years, was accused of lewd behavior with his young female students, and expelled from the church by unanimous vote. He married a Hawaiian girl named Anna, and became a dairy farmer.

Lucy's chores and responsibilities left little time for the isolation felt by missionary wives. Although there were hard work and deprivation, there were also moments of joy. Henry Lyman described the delight that entered his parents' lives when they taught their Hawaiian students to play music:

> For a number of years my father was the only teacher, though my mother usually gave the boys lessons in writing and singing. Under her instruction, the native boys became fairly good vocalists. After a time a musical sea-captain presented her with an old flute; and she very soon learned enough to teach her pupils how to play on the instrument. The young people took very kindly to this new form of music, and began to make for themselves fifes and flutes from the jointed

reeds of the hollow bamboo. Gifts of an accordion and a violoncello were utilized in the same way; and before the lapse of many years my parents had the satisfaction of hearing from their scholars all the music that could be reasonably desired.

Laura Judd described her day at the mission house in Honolulu in a letter to relatives in New England:

My mornings are devoted to the cares of my family, and I am ambitious to be an exemplary wife, and mother and housekeeper ... My afternoons are principally devoted to teaching native schools. I have two under my care, one composed of Masters of ships, to whom I teach Geography, Arithmetic, the Scriptures, on the verse a day system. Infant school catechism, a little that, this &c. the other consists of thirty native females employed as teachers in the Infant school at the station and the sabbath school ... I am obliged to make all the maps I use, which is quite a tax on my time. I have ... a circle of females several evenings in a week to read and explain the scriptures to them and have already found it an interesting and profitable exercise. I love to visit from house to house, as I can command time for it, and see how my neighbors live. How many families occupy the same house, whether they have partitions for sleeping rooms, whether they have children, if they attend school, and whether they have given their hearts to God and are doing their duty? We attend to some of the cultivation of the earth, and have a yard of pretty trees (after six years) and shrubbery, where there was not a green thing when we came, I am trying to have a garden for vegetables but the natives have little taste for it, they think it is enough to put the seed in the ground and water it well, and when I insist upon having an alley thro' the middle, and the ground on each side laid out in beds, according to our American custom, and have a border of pine apples and sugar cane, planted in a straight line, they laugh at my particularity, and think it unnecessary.

Along with their duties in the schoolroom, missionary women were sometimes called upon to cook for fifty people, three times a day. Lucy Thurston described her dining table, which could accommodate twenty-five guests, seated on benches:

It stood in a long open piazza which connected three cottages by the gable ends. Rushes were spread for the feet. A colored cloth was the table's accustomed covering, while salt beef, sea-bread, taro, coffee, tea, a small portion of goat's milk, and two molasses bottles well replenished, were seldom known to fail. On gala days, the somber covering of the table was exchanged for white damask. Molasses bottles, too, might give place to the more refined sweets of brown sugar.

F. A. Olmsted describes Lucy at Kailua, when her hard work and kindness had won the trust and respect of her neighbors:

The poor natives followed her in crowds wherever she went, displaying the strongest affection for her, and the most sincere grief at her removal from them . . . They eagerly assisted in conveying her effects down to the shore [when she traveled to Honolulu], and when she was lifted into the boat to go on board the brig, many of them waded into the water . . . and a wail of sorrow followed the boat.

It was not until 1824, however, having lived in the Islands for almost five years, that Lucy felt safe enough to walk alone through the village of Kona:

During the first few years of missionary life, the ladies were limited to the free use of their own houses and yards. To go beyond domestic premises, like prisoners or like queens, they must have an escort, and proceed with limited freedom . . . It was after a residence of four and a half years, that for the first time I walked alone through the village and thus soliloquized: Whence this freedom? Where am I? I can identify the scenery. The trees and the mountains are the same, but the people,—how different!

Not different at all, of course. It was Lucy who had changed.

Like others of her fellow missionaries—those travelers and journalists who were not in Hawai'i to save the souls of the heathen were quicker to succumb to the beauty of the Islands and their numerous charms—Lucy seems gradually to have fallen under the spell of the place, even if she was unaware of her seduction. Now and then in her journals and letters, she cannot help herself, and words of praise and admiration, even love, slip into her descriptions of the Hawaiians. In the end, Lucy was unable to resist altogether the affection and magnanimity of the people. Writing fifty years after the death of Queen Kamāmalu in London, Lucy still suffered from grief:

> There is no figure of speech in saying that [the queen] . . . found a daughter of America, a stranger in a strange land, under peculiar trials—she, being possessed of ample dimensions, cradled the afflicted one in her arms, pillowed her head upon her bosom, and wept over her tears of sympathy . . . A review of those early friendships, formed with those children of nature . . . stirs within me the deepest emotions of my soul.

When the missionary Sarah Lyman arrived in Hilo in 1830, ten years after Lucy Thurston, she wrote:

> Poor creatures how I pity them as I see them almost entirely destitute of clothing, all the sympathies of my soul are awakened for them. I earnestly desire to have it in my power to do them good . . . I had not correct ideas of their condition. The majority of them are more filthy than the swine. Their houses are wretched hovels, and the abode of vermin, and the inhabitants covered with sores from head to foot.

Returning heartbroken to Hilo after the death of her first child in Lahaina, Sarah was met at the dock by her Hawaiian neighbors, who brought chairs and sat on the landing with the Lymans and wept together, before carrying Sarah up the hill to her house. At the end of her life (she died in Hilo in 1885), Sarah did not remember her initial revulsion: "The people were numerous and had a healthy look; they were docile and very friendly. Nearly all were clad in their native costume . . . those were halcyon days . . . and they are now remembered with unfeigned pleasure."

Sybil Bingham, stationed in Honolulu, named her fifth child after Ka'ahumanu. Her husband Hiram wrote that she had so won the love of the queen, that she had bound a silken cord about Ka'ahumanu's heart, "from which I think she never broke loose while she lived."

In his memoir, *Reminiscences of Old Hawaii* (1916), Sereno Bishop, a second-generation missionary and son of Reverend Artemas Bishop, described his childhood in Kailua:

> A locality much frequented by us was a rocky cove at the shore where we often bathed, wearing flannel gowns. After the bath we stepped a little inland to a house where the native women would empty over us, to wash out the salt, calabashes of brackish water from a little pool or well four or five feet down, a sort of cave in the lava. There was a variety of animal life in the small pools of the cove, and an occasional live shell.

In 1840, after a six-month journey around the Horn from Lahaina to Rhode Island to attend school at Amherst, Bishop eagerly bought four apples when he arrived, only to throw them away in distaste. "I longed for sugar cane, bananas, and melons." It was nine months before he could bear the taste of an apple (this longing for the Islands was limited to *haole* pleasures, it would seem, as Bishop later gave thanks at a Thanksgiving service in Honolulu in 1886 that he was born a white man, as the native population was woefully "low in mental culture").

In *Incidents of a Whaling Voyage*, F. A. Olmsted wrote that life in Honolulu had great charm, particularly in the persons of Hawaiian women:

> The native women are dressed in long gowns like the loose morning dresses of the ladies of our country . . . With a bright yellow shawl around her waist, a wreath of brilliant feathers or flowers encircling her brow, and a huge comb towering up with masses of dark hair coiled around it, a Hawaiian lady is dressed a la mode . . . The principle [sic] vehicles are little four wheeled wagons, about the size of those . . . [in] a nursery at home, in which, drawn by one or two kanaka, a lady is seen riding in style through the streets, in going to church or making a fashionable call . . . The natives [on horseback] always gallop off at a . . . pace without any regard to life or limb, either of themselves or of the poor animals they are goading to death. The women ride in the same style, though with a perfect indifference to side saddles.

Charles Stewart, who was not insensible to the vivacity and beauty of Hawaiian women, described the queens of Liholiho on a visit to Ka'ahumanu

Riders in *pāʻū*, bare feet thrust through their skirts into stirrups. Illustration by Émile Bayard, from Charles de Varigny's *Fourteen Years in the Sandwich Islands, 1855–1868*

at her Mānoa retreat. The women, who were on horseback, wore silk and velvet *pāʻū*, and were covered in flowers and wreaths. Their long black hair hung loose down their backs, and their bare feet, wrapped in the trailing hems of their skirts, were thrust through the stirrups. They rode astride, and their mounts were spirited and fresh, unlike many of the horses in Honolulu. They appeared to the delighted Stewart to ride only at a canter.

Both Mark Twain and Robert Louis Stevenson frequently describe the skin of the irresistible Hawaiian women as resembling chocolate or leather:

> I saw long-haired, saddle-colored Sandwich Island maidens sitting on the ground in the shade of corner houses, gazing indolently at whatever or whoever happened along . . . I met dusky native women sweeping by, free as the wind, on fleet horses and astraddle, with gaudy riding-sashes streaming like banners behind them . . . I breathed the balmy fragrance of Jessamine, oleander and the Pride of India . . . I moved in the midst of a Summer calm as tranquil as dawn in the Garden of Eden . . . At night they feast and the girls dance the lascivious hula hula—a dance that is said to exhibit the very perfection of edu-

cated motion of limb and arm, hand, head and body . . . performed by a circle of girls with no raiment on them to speak of.

Later that year, Twain was unable to contain himself at the sight of girls swimming in the ocean (Jacques Arago thought the Hawaiians and the Carolinians the best swimmers in the world):

> At noon I observed a bevy of nude native young ladies bathing in the sea, and went down to look at them . . . When they rose to the surface, they only just poked their heads out and showed no disposition to proceed any further in the same direction. I was naturally irritated by such conduct, and therefore I piled their clothes up on a boulder in the edge of the sea and sat down on them and kept the wenches in the water until they were pretty well used up.

In 1870, Isabella Bird, an Englishwoman advised by her doctor to travel abroad when she suffered complaints of hysteria, arrived in Hawai'i from Australia. Bird, who would write *Six Months in the Sandwich Islands* (1875), as well as numerous books describing her adventures in the Rocky Mountains, Kurdistan, Nepal, and Manchuria, among other places, described the women's enticing walk:

> A majestic wahine with small, bare feet, a grand, swinging, deliberate gait, hibiscus blossoms in her flowing hair, and a lei of yellow flowers falling over her holoku [fitted long dress with train], marching through these streets, has a tragic grandeur of appearance . . . There were hundreds of native horsemen and horsewomen . . . The women seemed perfectly at home in their gay, brass-bossed, high peaked saddles, flying along astride, bare-footed, with their orange and scarlet riding dresses streaming on each side beyond their horses' tails, a bright kaleidoscopic flash of bright eyes, white teeth, shining hair, garlands of flowers and many coloured dresses.

George Vancouver had been captivated by the *hula* (the only objection he ever made was to the lively *hula ma'i*, a dance in honor of the genitals), sometimes performed by six hundred men and women at a time. "Such perfect unison of voice and actions, that it were impossible, even to the bend of a finger,

Wynee, lithograph after a sketch by a member of the crew on board the *Imperial Eagle*. Wynee was the servant of the wife of the ship's captain, Charles Barkley. She was left in Canton, and died on her voyage home to Hawai'i in 1788.

to have discovered the least variation." When the dancers collapsed into a heap on the ground in front of Vancouver and covered their heads with their *kapa*, "the idea of a boisterous ocean . . . [was] tranquillized by an instant calm." Archibald Menzies, the English botanist on board the *Discovery* with Vancouver, was also entranced, if not aroused by the dancers. "Every joint of [the dancer's] limbs, every finger of her hand, every muscle of her body, partook unitedly of the varied sympathetic impulses . . . The motion of her eyes transferring their transient glances and the harmony of her features were beyond description."

The bewitchment was not limited to the heterosexual. Charles Warren Stoddard, in his 1905 book of travel essays, *The Island of Tranquil Delights*, took the brave and somewhat reckless step of writing about a boy whose Hawaiian name, Kāne'aloha, translates as Man of Love.

> Kane-Aloha had been shedding garments by the way all the blessed afternoon. It was evident that presently there would not be a solitary stitch left for propriety's sake. Nobody seemed to care in the least . . . Is there anything more soothing, more cleansing, more ennobling and refining than the caress of the pure, cool air when it comes in immediate contact with the human body as God created it? . . . We slept the sleep of the just made perfect by the realization of our wildest dreams; meanwhile at the Mission House . . . [they were] joining in the prayer of the Family Circle, that we, the unregenerated, might be delivered from evil.

If the missionary men were disturbed by the sight of naked Hawaiians, what can the missionary women have made of them? One would think, reading their letters and journals, that they did not, could not, at least at first, see them at all, although the newly arrived Lucy Thurston, upon finding barely clothed chiefs stretched on mats on the deck of the *Thaddeus*, admitted to feeling "the climax of queer sensations."

It was not only the Hawaiians who were seductive but also the place itself. Lucy and Asa's daughter, also named Lucy, was not so confined behind the stone walls of her family's compound that she did not succumb to the beauty of the landscape. In 1839, the Thurstons made a long and difficult trip on foot and by canoe so that Thurston could preach, and marry the numerous Hawaiian converts, circling the Big Island in twelve days with their children, the younger ones in cribs slung from poles carried by Hawaiian bearers. The young Lucy wrote in her journal that the sight of Mauna Kea was "enchanting... the heights... beautifully sprinkled with clumps of trees... the blue peaks of Mauna Loa in the distance . . . [giving her] emotions of sublimity."

William Ellis, while disgusted by the sexual habits of Polynesians, could not help but admire the Islands themselves. The mysterious beauty of the cave on the Thurstons' land in Kona, with its freshwater spring, moved him as close to rapture as he would ever find himself, at least on Earth:

> More than thirty natives, most of them carrying torches, accompanied them in their descent; and on arriving at the water, simultaneously plunged in, extending their torches with one hand, and swimming about with the other. The partially illuminated heads of the natives, splashing about in this subterranean lake; the reflection of the torch-light on its agitated surface; the frowning sides and lofty arch of the black vault, hung with lava that had cooled in every imaginable shape; the deep gloom of the cavern beyond the water; the hollow sound of their footsteps; and the varied reverberations of their voices, produced a singular effect.

Unlike other colonialists—the British in India, for example, some of whom grew to admire the architecture and culture which they threatened by their very presence—foreigners in the Sandwich Islands succumbed for the most part only to Nature. It is thanks to their growing fascination with the flora and fauna, and the geology and volcanology of the Islands that the missionaries began to make cabinets of curiosity, many of the collections eventually going to museums and institutions in the United States and Europe. They collected everything—lava, snails, plants, lizards, birds, seeds, fish, and stones. Isabella Bird wrote, "Many of the residents possess valuable libraries, and these, with cabinets of minerals, volcanic specimens, shells, and coral, with weapons, calabashes, ornaments, and cloth of native manufacture, almost furnish a room in themselves. Some of the volcanic specimens and the coral are of almost inestimable value, as well as of exquisite beauty."

Sarah Lyman kept a diary of the occurrence of earthquakes in Hilo between 1833 and 1845 that later provided important data to scientists. Titus Coan studied volcanoes. Edward Bailey compiled the first list of native ferns.

Dr. Gerrit Judd studied fossil coral reefs. Lucy Thurston wrote of their large collection of shells: "We have each a drawer of shells, a pair of as many kinds as we have been able to collect . . . We gathered nearly a quart of Stewart shells . . . There are two species. One is named Oahuensis because they were first found in Oahu, the other Stewartii, as Mr. Stewart was the first who ever carried them to America."

This passion of the missionaries was intensified in their children, who wrote papers, painted flowers and birds, kept journals, made important discoveries, and founded libraries. John Gulick was fascinated by land shells, and while still at Punahou, where the study of natural history was one of the few diversions available, wrote a paper on the origin of Hawaiian land shells, published in 1905 (*Evolution, Racial and Habitudinal*). Sereno Bishop studied climatology, volcanoes, and ocean currents; Curtis Lyons became a meteorologist; Sanford B. Dole, the first territorial governor, who studied at Punahou and Williams College, published in 1869 the first list of native birds; Jeremiah Chamberlain was an authority on native seaweed; and A. B. Lyons studied the chemistry of Hawaiian soil.

Isabella Bird was admiring of the small community of second- and third-generation missionary families who lived in Hilo, where much had changed since the time of their hardworking and pious parents and grandparents. In Bird's description, they sound like the gentry of a small country town in a novel by Jane Austen:

> People are very kind to each other. Horses, dresses, patterns, books, and articles of domestic use, are lent and borrowed continually. The smallness of the society and the close proximity are too much like a ship. People know everything about the details of each other's daily life, income, and expenditure, and the day's doings of each member of the little circles are matters for conversation . . . I never saw people living with such easy, pleasant lives. They have such good health . . . They have abounding leisure for reading, music, choir practicing, drawing, fern-printing, fancy work, picnics, riding parties, and enjoy sociability thoroughly. They usually ride in dainty bloomer costumes even when they don't ride astride . . . One novel fashion is to decorate the walls with festoons of the beautiful Microlepia tenuifolia [a lace-like fern], which are renewed as soon as they fade, and every room is adorned with a profusion of bouquets.

A Light to My Path

When Kaumuali'i, grieving for his lost kingdom of Kaua'i and his lost wife Kapule, died in 1824, Ka'ahumanu covered the doors and windows to keep the crowds from peering inside the house. She wrapped his body in yellow satin, draped his feather war cloak around him, leaving his chest and head bare as was the tradition, and placed a feather *lei* across his forehead to hide his eyes. Kaumuali'i had asked to be buried in Lahaina in the same grave as Keōpūolani, Kamehameha's sacred wife, who had been baptized in 1823 as she lay dying, so that they might "rise together in the morning of the resurrection."

Soon after the funeral, Ka'ahumanu herself fell ill and sailed to Lahaina. Her relative, the high chiefess Kapi'olani, who had once been discovered by Asa Thurston "basking in the noonday tropical sun, like a seal . . . with her two husbands, all nearly nude, and in a state of beastly intoxication," had become a fervent convert. She told Ka'ahumanu that she was the great chief, but she was also an old chief, and she feared that Ka'ahumanu had come to Lahaina to die before she had done all the good that was required of her.

Ka'ahumanu admitted that she indeed feared that she would soon die, and promised Kapi'olani that she would try to do better. Soon after, she called her followers together in the largest gathering ever seen in Lahaina, and issued a number of decrees based on Christian teaching. Her first law was, simply enough, against murder and, in particular, infanticide. Other laws forbade drunkenness, fighting (boxing), and theft. More severely, the drinking of *'awa* or any other liquor was prohibited, the *hula* was banned, and people were commanded to observe the Sabbath and to go to school. Her chiefs sent criers throughout the Islands to announce the new laws, and the Lahaina missionary William Richards wrote in admiration, "She prefers to

Ali'i mourning the death of Keōpūolani. The young king, Kauikeaouli, and his sister, Nāhiʻenaʻena, are on the shoulders of their attendants. Engraving after a sketch by William Ellis, from the missionary William Richards's *Memoir of Keopuolani*, 1823

go before, rather than follow others, and consequently, whenever she acts, she acts in such a manner to distinguish herself from others."

The missionaries, quietly eager to baptize Kaʻahumanu, determined that the only way to convert her was to teach her to read. Whenever they called on her, however, they found her lounging on a mat, playing cards or stringing *leis* with other female chiefs, while her enormous pet hog, also named Kaʻahumanu, rooted about her rooms. The pig, treated with great respect, occasionally escaped from its attendant during a church service to wander among the worshippers, none of whom dared stop it, and who fled rather than risk offending both the queen and the pig.

Bingham complained that the queen confused him. At one moment, she listened to "vile songs" and "foolish stories," and the next moment asked perceptive and provocative questions. On one of his visits to her, he brought along a primer of the alphabet, waiting patiently while she and her women finished their card game before giving her his gift, with the suggestion that it could be made to speak to her. Three times he enunciated the vowels, asking her to repeat them after him, and three times she imitated him. Bingham praised her. "Her countenance brightened," he wrote. "She looked at her companions and said, 'Ua loaaiau! I have got it!'"

Kaʻahumanu taught herself to read in three days, and called for more books and nearly a thousand primers to give to her followers. A young Hawaiian man living with the Binghams was sent to her twice a day to continue her lessons. At a school examination in Honolulu, she asked that a message she had written on a slate be read before the five hundred students—"I am making myself strong. I declare in the presence of God, I repent of my sin, and believe God to be our Father"—as the students shouted, "*Hoorea ia Jehovah.*" "Hooray for Jesus."

On the Big Island, where the distances between villages was greater than on other islands, there were fewer schools and less teaching. The high chiefess Kapiʻolani, who lived with her husband Naihe in Kaʻawaloa, south of Kona, determined to put an end to the reverence in which the goddess Pele continued to be held by climbing the southwest slope of Kīlauea crater to confront Pele in her lair. Accompanied by the Hilo missionary Joseph Goodrich (Samuel Ruggles wished to go, too, but had no shoes), she was followed along the rough path by hundreds of people who pleaded with her to return to Kona, knowing that it was they, not the *haoles* or the *aliʻi*, who would suffer the revenge of the goddess. At the edge of the crater, Kapiʻolani defiantly ate a handful of the *ʻōhelo* berries sacred to Pele, and threw stones into the volcano, singing numerous hymns and praying with Goodrich in order to give Pele sufficient time to display her fury. When the goddess was silent, Kapiʻolani triumphantly turned her back on her and walked home, leaving the frightened Hawaiians to follow in astonishment.

There had been rumors among the foreigners for some time that the relationship between Kauikeaouli and his sister Nāhiʻenaʻena was incestuous. The chiefs knew that the missionaries were aghast at the idea, and that even a consideration of marriage between the two would be viewed as a deliberate refutation of their beliefs, but the *aliʻi* had begun to grow weary of the many strictures imposed on them, and bored by mandatory church services once their initial curiosity and interest had waned. A feast held in Lahaina to honor the prince and princess signaled the growing restlessness of the chiefs. The celebration was attended by the high chiefs of Maui, and Kīnaʻu, one of Liholiho's queens, who watched as twelve men carried Nāhiʻenaʻena on a litter covered with one hundred layers of *kapa*. In the weeks following the feast, the chiefs were seen to return to gambling, *hula* performances, boxing matches, and drinking, causing alarm to the missionaries. Kaʻahumanu sent criers throughout the kingdom to remind people of the laws forbidding drunkenness, theft, adultery, and murder, but her warning did not keep the chiefs from their pleasures.

In 1824, Ka'ahumanu's religious instruction was interrupted by the shocking news that in July, Liholiho had died of measles in the Caledonia Hotel in London, Queen Kamāmalu having died a few days before him. The party of Hawaiians had attracted much attention in England, especially the handsome Boki and Liliha, who exemplified a European fantasy of Polynesian nobility. The Hawaiians had been taken to the theater, to the ascension of a balloon, to the Royal Military Asylum, and to the races at Epsom. At a Whitsunday service in Westminster Abbey, the king remained standing to stare in admiration at the roof, causing the London press to note that his pea-green gloves were not long enough to cover his "sooty wrists." Kamāmalu, startled by the first sounds of the organ, was said to have leapt from her pew in fright, and was only prevented from bolting by an attentive Englishwoman in her entourage. The Hawaiians were painted by Sir John Hayter, a fashionable London portraitist (the paintings, and a pastel of Boki and Liliha in native dress, may be seen at the Bishop Museum in Honolulu). Although the crowds appeared enchanted by the guileless Hawaiians, the press made fun of them, gleefully reporting that the chiefesses smoked cigars and played whist with dirty cards.

During the two months that Liholiho and Kamāmalu were in London, they did not set eyes on the king of England, meeting only briefly with Foreign Secretary George Canning and his wife, and with Richard Charlton, the new British Consul to the Sandwich Islands, at a reception given for two hundred guests, including the Duke of Wellington and Prince Leopold of Belgium. At Kamāmalu's sudden death, the *Times* of London wrote of Liholiho, "He has four wives yet left to cheer the solitude of his widowed arms."

Liholiho insisted on keeping Kamāmalu's body on a small bed next to his own, sleeping alone with her corpse, which Liliha had wrapped in the traditional way in a *pā'ū*, with her legs and feet bare. Her feather cloak and a yellow coronet of feathers were placed atop her body, and her *kāhili* stood at her head with two candles. Five days later, Liholiho himself lay mortally ill. He spoke in Hawaiian to the doctor sent to attend him by the king, warning him that he was dying. He whispered goodbye to Boki and Liliha, and told them that he was already dead, and that he was happy.

A week of funeral ceremonies followed the deaths. The money that Liholiho had deposited in the Bank of England for his expenses was returned to

High chief Boki and his wife, the chiefess Liliha. Lithograph by Hull-
mandel, after a watercolor by John Hayter, 1824

the Hawaiians, and Boki was at last given an audience with King George at
Windsor. Never unmindful of an opportunity to advance the position of
Great Britain, Secretary Canning wrote to King George that his offer of a
warship to carry home the bodies comprised "an Attention perhaps the more
advisable as the Governments both of Russia and the United States of America
are known to have their Eyes upon those Islands: which may ere long become a very important Station in the trade between the N. W. Coast of
America and the China Seas."

In May 1825, the forty-six-gun frigate HMS *Blonde*, under Captain
George Byron, arrived in the Islands with the bodies of Liholiho and
Kamāmalu, stopping first at Hilo, where Boki's sister was brought to the ship

Satiric cartoon of Sandwich Island nobility dressing for an outing in London. Hand-colored etching, 1824

Queen Kamāmalu (on the left) in London. Watercolor and graphite by Julia Swinburne, 1824, Yale Center for British Art

by canoe. She presented her head *lei* to Captain Byron with a kiss, and disappeared below deck with Liliha (now called Mrs. Boki, according to Charles Stewart), reappearing later in a silk gown bought for her in London. The ship then sailed to Lahaina. William Richards waited on the beach with thousands of others, among them Princess Nāhiʻenaʻena, who held tight to his arm. He wrote that Liliha's father, Hoapili, threw back his head with a roar when Liliha and Boki stepped ashore: "In an instant all the chiefs present except the one which leaned on my side [Nāhiʻenaʻena] and all the thousands around set up a screaming which drowned the roaring of the ocean... The princess [Nāhiʻenaʻena], in utter neglect of all their ancient forms, sprang forward and... threw herself into the arms of Kuini [Liliha]; and the latter dropped into the sand, while the tears of the little girl were falling on her breast."

> When Governor Boki's barge came near enough for the parties to recognize each other, the queens "lifted up their voices" and wept aloud... perhaps to the more powerful effect of the attitude and expression of Boki and his wife... wringing their hands in agony, and exhibiting the strongest marks of an overwhelming emotion of mingled grief and joy. The parties stood thus for some minutes, without approaching each other, while the whole air was filled with lamentation, and the ground shaken with the thunderings of the minute-guns... They then rushed into each other's embrace, passing from the arms of one to another in a continued paroxysm of weeping, for an hour, while some of the more humble friends of those who had returned, embraced and kissed their feet.

Captain Byron gave to Kaʻahumanu a silver teapot engraved with her name and the English king's coat of arms, and to Kauikeaouli, now Kamehameha III, a soldier's uniform with a handsome sword and hat. The boy "instantly put it on, and strutted about the whole morning in ecstasy." After learning that an artist, Robert Dampier, was on board the *Blonde*, Kaʻahumanu ordered him to paint her portrait, insisting on precedence over the young king (she demanded a full-length portrait, even though Dampier explained that he had only half-size canvases). "This Old Dame," wrote Dampier, "is the most proud, unbending Lady in the whole island... To submit to my will for an hour or two, was a severe trial to her pride, and her lowering brow plainly indicated how derogatory to her dignity were my continual restrictions." Dampier had no trouble with his two other royal sitters, Kauikeaouli and Nāhi'ena'ena, whom he painted first, despite the queen's fury:

> The natives are extremely delighted . . . but are apt to be very impatient at the slowness of the work, especially when one eye in a portrait happens to be done while the other is not touched . . . The great queen Kahumanu, whose temper is violent, although she is a person of keen shrewd understanding, is very indignant that the little king and princess should be painted before her, and is not very well pleased at the frown she sees reflected from her own portrait.

When Dampier asked Ka'ahumanu to wear native dress, ignoring her demand that he paint her in black silk (she wished to give the portrait to George IV), she rolled out of her chair onto the floor, and refused to sit for him any longer.

Ka'ahumanu, Byron, Governor Kalanimoku, and the new British consul Richard Charlton met in Honolulu with Boki and other high chiefs to formalize the accession of the twelve-year-old Kauikeaouli. Ka'ahumanu was to remain as regent, and the boy would be under the guardianship of Kalanimoku. Hiram Bingham, who would continue as the boy's teacher, reassured the Englishmen that the missionaries, acting under the auspices of the American Board of Commissioners for Foreign Missions, had come to the Sandwich Islands only for the purpose of propagating the Gospel. They had not come to make laws, or to abrogate the authority and privileges of the chiefs, or to engage in commercial speculation. Their hope was simply to enlighten the nation through the doctrines and duties of Christianity. Bingham said it a second time in Hawaiian.

Of course, the missionaries did give laws to the nation, and did interfere with the authority of the chiefs, although they left commercial speculation and the accumulation and consolidation of wealth and power to their descendants. The irony of Bingham's claim did not escape Byron or Andrew Bloxam, whose brother, Richard Bloxam, later published Byron's account of the journey. They found Bingham sincere in his zealotry, but disingenuous, as it was apparent to everyone that the missionaries had already thrust themselves into the affairs of the kingdom.

On that same visit, Byron took Ka'ahumanu to the Big Island on the

Kamehameha III
(Kauikeaouli). Oil on canvas
by Robert Dampier, 1825,
Honolulu Museum of Art

Princess Nāhiʻenaʻena, sister
of Kamehameha III and
daughter of Kamehameha I
and his highest-ranking wife,
Keōpūolani. Oil on canvas
by Robert Dampier, 1825,
Honolulu Museum of Art

Blonde so that she might gather taxes that were owed her. The officers on board were astonished to see the reverence with which she was treated. The following is a description written by the missionary Charles Stewart of a similar collection of tributes on Maui:

> The procession consisted of one hundred and fifty persons led by the headman . . . They were all neatly dressed in new tapa, and walked in single file, the first twenty men bearing each a baked pig or dog, ornamented with green leaves. These were followed by fifty others, bearing thirty immense calabashes of poe, twenty of which were suspended, each on a long pole, and carried by two men, and ten others on the shoulders of the same number of men. Then came females to the number of seventy or eighty, each bearing on her shoulder a large package of tapa, or native cloth. The whole was deposited in front of the royal tent, and the company, with hundreds who followed them, seated themselves in a circle at a respectful distance.

It was during Kaʻahumanu's stay in Hilo that people first began to see a change in her, causing her to be given the nickname Kaʻahumanu *hou*, or the new Kaʻahumanu. The historian John Papa ʻĪʻī was not convinced, however, that she was in any way new, complaining that privilege had made her so proud that she did not consider the ways in which her actions affected other people. She was devoted to her own family, he wrote, rushing to tend them if they were ill or in trouble, and grieving profoundly when one of them died, but she did not take much notice of other people. She was certainly intolerant of the Catholic priests who had begun to arrive in the Islands, and of their few converts. H. Willis Baxley wrote in his account of a journey to Hawaiʻi in 1860:

> The arbitrary will of Kaahumanu, directed by the missionaries, who availed in all things relating to their interests, of the Kamehamehan policy of supreme control and unquestioned domination, was not to be resisted; and accordingly, Government *imposed fine and imprisonment* upon converts to Catholicism. The history of that period shows that such converts "were confined and set to work making stone walls, repairing roads, and fabricating mats . . . They were punished for their idolatry, and they who repeated the offence five times, either by wor-

shipping at the chapel or indulging in the old rites, were *obliged to remove the filth of the fort with their hands.*"

After the departure of the *Blonde*, Boki and the chiefs met with Ka'ahu-manu and Kalanimoku to write new laws for the kingdom. Boki's trip to England and his reception there had increased his confidence, and certainly his knowledge of the world (he had been so impressed with St. Paul's and other London churches that he'd had himself baptized by the chaplain of the *Blonde*). He was by nature more conservative than Ka'ahumanu, and although he was in name a Christian, he was not sympathetic to the missionaries. Among other things, Boki and Ka'ahumanu quarreled over the marriage of the king. Boki wished Kauikeaouli to follow his heart's desire by marrying Nāhi'ena'ena, but Ka'ahumanu, influenced by Bingham, believed such a marriage to be sinful. The young princess, caught between the traditions of her Polynesian heritage and the strict piety of her Christian teachers, wrote in a letter to a missionary wife, "One day my thoughts are fixed on God; another day I am ensnared; and thus it is continually." Her growing interest in the Christian god worried her chiefs, and they urged her to hold to the beliefs of her ancestors. A young Tahitian convert named Toteta was sent by Bingham to Lahaina to live with her, in the hope that he would encourage her conversion, and he kept a diary in which he noted the girl's ambivalence and confusion ("The chief gets no rest," he wrote). Her court was alarmed when she suddenly announced that those who did not read hymns and study the *palapala* (teachings of the missionaries) would no longer be allowed to enter her house. William Richards was surprised one midnight by the arrival of the agitated princess who asked for the loan of a lamp, in order to chase some wicked people from a nearby church. When Richards later wondered who had been in the church, and how the princess had known about them, he was told that it was her habit to visit the church late at night to pray alone.

Boki had the support of the traders and merchants, the English and American consuls, and more important, Kauikeaouli and Nāhi'ena'ena. Caught between Ka'ahumanu and Boki was Kalanimoku, Boki's older brother, who was politically more inclined to the views of the dowager queen, as were most of the chiefs and commoners, who continued to revere her as the favorite wife of Kamehameha I. Both factions, however, agreed on the need for laws to control the rowdy and licentious behavior of seamen in the ports of Honolulu and Lahaina, and a *kapu* on the seizure of Hawaiian women by foreign men was passed unanimously. Kaʻahumanu hoped to issue a set of Ten Commandments, but Boki, with the support of the foreign colony, vehemently opposed her, arguing that such laws showed the influence of the missionaries, who had no right to interfere in the governing of the kingdom. When Boki asked the young king what he thought of Kaʻahumanu's proposed laws, Kauikeaouli declared that no changes could be made without the consent of the people, thus avoiding any decision.

Pressed by the foreign merchants to pay his debts, Boki opened a liquor store in Honolulu, infuriating Kaʻahumanu, who had been pressing Kauikeaouli to ban the use of alcohol. She insisted that Boki close his store, and she canceled some of the leases on fields that Boki had awarded to traders and friends in order to grow the cane needed to distill rum. Kaʻahumanu then awarded large pieces of land to missionaries, commanding that houses be built for them at all of the mission stations across the Islands. She gave to Hiram Bingham some of the sacred images that she had taken from Hōnaunau on the Big Island, with the suggestion that he make collection boxes out of them. When an angry Boki summoned those chiefs loyal to him to Waikīkī, Kaʻahumanu sent the high chief Kekuanaoa, once her lover and a friend of Boki's, to tell the chiefs that she was aware of Boki's desire to kill her, and would remain at home with her grandchildren, without armed guards or attendants, where he would find her waiting for him. The chiefs were so ashamed by her gesture that all talk of murder was abandoned.

In the spring of 1825, Captain William Buckle of the British merchant ship *Daniel IV* bought a young mission girl named Leoiki from her *kahu*, a chiefess named Wahinepio, for ten gold doubloons (then approximately $160) to keep him company on a voyage to the South Pacific. When the frightened girl sent to William Richards for help, Wahinepio justified her action by claiming that the captain had promised to return the girl at the completion of his tour. Richards could not persuade the captain to release the girl, or Wahinepio to return her doubloons, but he began to work with some of the Lahaina chiefs to place a *kapu* on the taking of Hawaiian women on board foreign ships.

Hiram Bingham believed that *aliʻi* were obliged to behave with more virtue than ordinary men, striving under the guidance of a strict Christian god to be wise and just rulers. As he would not consider Kaʻahumanu a candidate for conversion as long as she was the wife of Kealiʻiahonui, the son of her late husband, she obediently separated from the prince (she knew, too, that he was living with a pretty girl from Maui), claiming that in the future her new husband would be her love for the word of God. With the approval of Bingham, she at last began to prepare for baptism. The missionaries had learned to keep a sharp eye on the chiefs (Charles Stewart believed that Kaʻahumanu was jealous of the missionaries' influence on the people), and a trial period was set to ascertain the sincerity of her wish for conversion.

In 1826, Kaʻahumanu and Kauikeaouli negotiated a treaty with the United States in which the kingdom assumed responsibility for $150,000 worth of debts owed by the people of Hawaiʻi to the traders and merchants, which was to be paid in sandalwood, winning Kaʻahumanu the deeper allegiance of the many chiefs who were in debt. The treaty also ensured American citizens the right to enter all ports of Hawaiʻi, the right to sue in Hawaiian courts, and the protection of Hawaiian laws, which some historians mark as a formal beginning to the end of Hawaiian sovereignty.

Mercy Whitney, the young wife of the missionary Samuel Whitney, wrote of Kaʻahumanu that her "haughty, assuming, disdainful air, which once appeared on her brow and looked so very forbidding, is now changed into a mild, tractable, childlike spirit . . . She wishes us to tell her how she should conduct herself, at home, and at church, in the house and by the way, when eating or drinking, when lying down or rising up." When Whitney gently scolded Kaʻahumanu for sitting with her back to the pulpit in church, the queen explained that no one had ever told her otherwise.

Returning from a tour of Kauaʻi, Kaʻahumanu again fell ill. She was attended by two Russian physicians from a ship then in port, and Sybil and Hiram Bingham visited her every day, and prayed for her. It was said that Bingham's comforting manner, which might have surprised his fellow missionaries, was particularly calming to her. Sybil wrote in her journal:

> She [Kaʻahumanu] is a little better, but not out of danger. Mr. Bingham said to her, after the usual salutations, in which she appeared to be more than usually cordial, "I hope you think seriously of the Great God and our Saviour." She replied, "I think more and more about him, since I have been sick." "Is it your desire that I should engage in prayer to God for you?" . . . Dr. Kavaleff gave also his permission, and

Mr. Bingham kneeled down by her couch, and commended her case to the great Physician of the soul and body . . . At the close, she subjoined, "*miti* [good]."

In the summer of 1828, Kauikeaouli and Boki, accompanied by the king's dissolute band of followers known as the Hulumanu, or Bird Feathers, sailed to Lahaina to visit Nāhiʻenaʻena. Kauikeaouli had long wished to make the trip to the volcano Kīlauea, which he had never seen, and desired that his sister accompany him. It was a difficult trip. Departing from Hilo, the party covered miles of open land before reaching a dense rain forest with a floor of jagged lava rock. The thirty-mile trip took two days, with outriders traveling ahead to prepare each day's camp with bowers of ferns and branches. When they returned to Lahaina, the king, noticing that the newly arrived Mrs. Judd wore a dress of plain red and brown, had his attendants make her a *lei* of flame-colored flowers. Laura wrote primly that she "felt obliged to wear it at dinner, although it was not to my taste, for I had given away all my muslins, ribbons, and embroideries when I became a missionary."

Boki, increasingly in debt to the merchants, left Honolulu that December in search of an island said to be covered in valuable sandalwood, which may have been Erromango (in present-day Vanuatu). Boki's ship disappeared, perhaps catching fire in the South Pacific, and he was never again seen in the Islands. With his absence, Kaʻahumanu imposed further restrictions on the people, forbidding the performance of *oli* (chants) and *mele* (songs) in public. At a council of chiefs, it was agreed that the Binghams be allowed to establish a boarding school for the children of the *aliʻi*. The site of an old barracks was provided by Kauikeaouli, and Dr. Judd helped to select teachers. Seven boys and seven girls were chosen as the first students, among them Emma Rooke, a granddaughter of John Young, who had been adopted as a child by her aunt, Grace Kamaikui, and her husband, the English physician Thomas Rooke; David Kalākaua; Princess Bernice Pauahi, a great-granddaughter of Kamehameha I; Princess Victoria Kamāmalu; Prince Lot Kamehameha; Prince William Lunalilo; and Prince Alexander Liholiho, heir presumptive to the kingdom (Alexander Liholiho arrived with thirty *kahu* who were quickly sent home, leaving the boy without attendants for the first time in his life). In the beginning, the mission had worried that the teaching of English to Hawaiians would create a separate class of natives who would leave behind those who only spoke Hawaiian, but the tuition at the new Chiefs' Children's

School was in English, and the syllabus determined by the headmaster, Amos Starr Cooke, and his wife, Juliette. (By 1849, the school was in decline as many of its students had died or married, and several female students had been expelled for illegitimate pregnancies, leading to the belief that the princes, including the childless Kamehameha V, have descendants still living in the Islands. *Haoles* were admitted in 1851.)

In 1831, Ka'ahumanu appointed Kauikeaouli's older half sister, Kīna'u, co-regent, but the king, who was then eighteen years old, showed uncustomary strength, announcing that he no longer saw the need for divided rule. He alone was ruler, although he asked that Kīna'u remain in his government as second in the kingdom. Despite this unusual assertion of independence, the day-to-day ruling of the Islands soon fell to Kīna'u, a responsibility that she held until her death eight years later.

It was observed by Sybil Bingham, among others, that Ka'ahumanu had dropped her customary aloofness and begun to listen to their religious teaching with interest. She was particularly fond of those chapters in the Epistles in which Paul addresses his disciples by name, delighted that the saint had so many friends. She asked that one of the missionary wives come to live with her, to make dresses for her, and to instruct her attendants in domestic care, as she wanted to live like the *haole* women, but they dissuaded her of her plan. Laura Judd wrote in a letter:

> As we were seated at our sewing, Kaahumanu very kindly inquired what we thought of wearing at the dedication of the new church. Without waiting for an answer, she added: "It is my wish that we dress alike; I have made a selection that pleases me, and it only awaits your approval." She ordered the woman in waiting to bring in the material; it was heavy satin, striped in pink, white and blue. She fixed her scrutinizing eyes upon us as we examined and commented upon it in our own language. As we hesitated in the approval, "What fault has it?" she hastily inquired. I replied, "No fault; it is very beautiful for you who are a queen; but we are missionaries, supported by the churches and the earnings of the poor, and such expensive material is not suitable for us." "*I* give it to you," she replied, "not the church, nor the poor." "Foreigners will be present," we said, "who will perhaps make ill-natured remarks." "Foreigners!" said she, "do you mean those in town who tear off calico? (meaning the salesmen in the shops). What

do you care for their opinions? It does not concern them; you should not heed what they say." We declined still further the acceptance, as we should not ourselves feel comfortable in such unaccustomed attire. She looked disappointed and displeased, and ordered the women to put it out of sight, adding, "If it is not proper for good people to wear good things, I do not know what they are made for." We were sorry to oppose her wishes, and she was taciturn all the afternoon. As we were about to take leave at evening, she resumed her cheerful manner, and asked what we would like to wear on the forthcoming occasion. We thanked her, and said we would like to make something very handsome for her, but we should prefer black silk to anything else for ourselves. She made no reply, but bade us an affectionate good night. The next morning we received two rolls of black silk, with an order to make her dress exactly like ours.

Bingham remained hesitant to baptize Ka'ahumanu, declaring that she had not yet proved that she was born "from above by the power of the spirit of God." During one of Charles Stewart's weekly sermons, she was seen to weep at the verse "Thy word is a lamp unto my feet, and a light to my path." When asked why she cried, she said, "We were all in thick darkness. We wandered HERE, and we wandered THERE, and we stumbled on this SIDE and on THAT SIDE and were hastening to the dreadful precipice down which our fathers have fallen!" Her very countenance had changed, wrote Stewart, and he found her dressing, behaving, and speaking "more like a Christian." When an insurrection on Kaua'i by Prince Humehume (the young convert known as Tamoree, who had sailed with the First Company on the *Thaddeus*) was quickly suppressed, Ka'ahumanu and her chiefs were encouraged to believe that the Christian god had given them their rapid victory. She asked for a day of prayer, and instructed the chiefs to build yet more schoolhouses.

Ka'ahumanu was at last baptized in early December 1825, along with several other chiefs, choosing Elisabeta as her new name. In a speech given to her followers that month, she declared that her wish was to give her heart to God, who was her trust and delight:

> The axe is at the trunk of my tree, and I do not know when the Lord will take away my soul. Let us therefore be steadfast in our efforts to keep the beautiful word of our Lord before the coming of the great

day of judgment. We, chiefs and rulers of these islands, set up in times past altars to sin, but these have been cast aside and we now have salvation from God.

Some historians believe that Ka'ahumanu's conversion to Christianity so soon after the death of Liholiho enabled her to retain her tremendous influence through her new alliance with the missionaries, who were increasingly abrogating power to themselves. Ka'ahumanu's subsequent tour of the Islands in a counterclockwise direction (like the returning god Lono at the Makahiki festival) to give orders to build churches and schools, could also be seen as a reenactment of the traditional procession once required of a new *ali'i nui* to perform the rites of human sacrifice.

The following year, Captain Buckle returned a pregnant Leoiki to Maui, as he had promised, only to discover that thanks to the efforts of William Richards, an order forbidding women to board foreign ships had been issued (reminiscent of earlier attempts by Captain Cook to keep women from becoming infected with venereal disease, and the later attempts by ship captains to keep their men from infection by Hawaiian women). Captain Buckle's infuriated crew attacked Richards's house, but local Hawaiians protected the missionary and his family, and the restriction stayed in place. In Honolulu, twenty sailors angrily confronted Bingham, who sent them to Ka'ahumanu. They told her that if they found women on shore, they would drag them to the ships, even if they would be arrested and put into prison (the most desired Hawaiian women were those whom the missionaries had themselves trained and educated in mission schools). Two women who were subsequently caught boarding ships in Waikīkī had their heads shaved as punishment, irritating the governor of O'ahu, who collected a dollar in tax from each Hawaiian woman who visited a foreign ship. It meant nothing to the sailors that the women would once have been strangled for violating such a *kapu*.

Their [whaling] voyages are three to four years' in duration, and their cruizes [*sic*] extend to six, and even twelve months, without dropping anchor. The men, consequently, on arriving in port are, generally, in debilitated health, from having been so long cooped up in the crowded and filthy forecastles, and fed on salt provisions. Free air and exercise are necessary for their renovation; but if they are found on shore after eight o'clock in the evening, they are dragged to the prison, by bands

The Reverend William Richards of Massachusetts, graduate of Williams College and Andover Theological Seminary,
and missionary of the Second Company. He was the devoted
friend of Princess Nāhiʻenaʻena, and later the kingdom's
ambassador to England. Photograph ca. 1845, from Samuel
Kamakau's *Ruling Chiefs of Hawaii*

The Reverend Charles S. Stewart
of New Jersey attended the
College of New Jersey (later
Princeton University) and
Princeton Theological Seminary.
Arriving with the Second
Company of missionaries, he
was stationed in Lahaina, and
kept an intriguingly perceptive
journal that was published in
1828. Photograph ca. 1863, from
*Portraits of American Protestant
Missionaries to Hawaii* (1901)

of spies always prowling about for their share of the plunder, placed in irons for the night, and next morning forced to pay a fine of two dollars . . . Should they . . . wish to live a regular and domestic life, they are prohibited from marrying a native until they have resided two years in the group, taking the oath of allegiance . . . and procured the written permission of the governor.

The following January, John Percival, captain of the American schooner *Dolphin*, arrived in Honolulu to detain a group of mutineers, and to ascertain on behalf of commercial interests in the United States the ability of the chiefs to pay their debts. In a meeting with Ka'ahumanu, Percival spoke to her of the many seamen who objected to the banning of Hawaiian women from foreign ships. Don Francisco de Marín recorded their meeting in his journal: "Today Captain Percival went to visit the Queen Ka'ahumanu, apprehensive of a tumult of the white people on account of the missionaries for they are always the ruin of the world. First he asked who was the King and she pointed him out—and who governs the King—I she says—& on this they had some conversation." According to Bingham, who was also present, the meeting was long and acrimonious. Percival threatened the queen and used rough language. In February, Percival again asked Ka'ahumanu to end the restrictions and to show clemency to the women who had been arrested and made to do hard labor (according to Marín, each woman was made to carry "10 stones for the Church"), but Ka'ahumanu refused to change her mind.

The missionaries had little hope of converting Kauikeaouli. The king was amiable to them, but like his late brother, Liholiho, he was thought to be undependable, and too fond of the traders, merchants, and whaling men, who disliked and mistrusted the missionaries, especially as they beseeched the Hawaiians not to throw away their money on cheap trinkets and alcohol. The missionaries also knew that in 1820 the traders had counseled Liholiho against them during the fortnight they waited on board the *Thaddeus* for permission to land, warning the king that the missionaries would ruin the Islands with their preaching. Over time, there had arrived in the Islands more respectable professional men who lessened the effect of the freethinking beachcombers and errant sailors who for so long had been representative of the white residents of Honolulu, Hilo, and Lahaina. The new entrepreneurs brought with them, however, a shrewd sense of business that was to be disastrous for the Hawaiians, depriving them of what little remained to them.

After much talk, the missionary women succeeded in persuading Ka‘ahumanu to condemn polygamy, prostitution, and adultery, and she dutifully issued new laws. There was at the time no word in Hawaiian for adultery. "The woman who sat sideways" is an old Hawaiian expression for a woman who takes another husband. Sexual license was not prevalent among commoners. *"He ‘uha leo ‘ole,"* "a thigh over which no word is spoken," was said disparagingly of a woman thought to be promiscuous, and a child whose paternal lineage was unknown was said to have been conceived by the wayside, a *"keiki a ka pueo,"* or "child of an owl." Before the coming of the missionaries, there had been no binding formal marital relationship between Hawaiians. If a man and a woman remained together through the night, it was tantamount to a declaration of marriage. When a man took a new wife to his house, it was left to her to decide whether any of his other wives might remain. Should a wife choose to leave her husband, her children remained with their father. If a person was abducted by a chief, his (or her) companion could go to the chief with an offering of a dog in hope of an exchange.

> If an insolent courtier were to see that a country clown had a beautiful woman for a wife he would say to her, "You come along with me," and the country clown would be too spiritless to make any resistance. Or one of the women about court, meeting a handsome young countryman whom she fancied, would turn his head with flattery and try to win him to herself, saying, "Why does such a fine fellow as you condescend to live with such a fright of a creature as that wife of yours? You'd better come along with me." . . . Men and chiefs acted strangely in those days.

It was shocking to Hawaiians when Ka‘ahumanu established prisons for violators of her law forbidding adultery. Male offenders were sent to the desolate island of Kaho‘olawe, while women were held at a camp on Lāna‘i, where many died of starvation, and others drowned themselves. As the number of prisoners grew, a group of men on Kaho‘olawe swam six miles across the channel to Maui, stole a canoe and food, and paddled to Lāna‘i. The men found the women who had once been their companions and returned to Maui, where, with the help of local people, they hid in caves in the mountains. Their escape became notorious, and Ka'ahumanu was forced to change the punishment for adultery from banishment to hard labor, which was harsh enough. "If a man was caught," wrote Samuel Kamakau, "... he might be sentenced to stone breaking until he died."

A seeming unanimity among the chiefs, guided by the indefatigable Ka'ahumanu, concealed much of the growing discontent in the kingdom. The initial curiosity and even fascination felt by the Hawaiians for the new teaching had somewhat dissipated with the strict rules that came with *palapala*, and many of them longed for the old pleasure-filled days of rum, music, and sport. Ka'ahumanu herself seems not to have given herself entirely to a life of sanctity. She attended church with a number of attendants, one of whom carried a branch on which sat three large green parrots, and stretched across a pew to nap throughout the service. When she was sixty-one years old, she took a young English captain as her lover, and bought a carriage to use in Honolulu, pulled by ten strong men. Her former husband, Keali'iahonui, rode on the footman's stand, while she sat alone in the coachman's seat.

John Papa 'I'i described a trip she made by sea to distant Waipi'o Valley on Hawai'i Island:

> Ka'ahumanu's circuits of the land were always by canoe, for she had learned all about canoeing and surfing from Kamehameha, her cousin, lord, and husband . . . She boarded a canoe and sailed to Waipio, while the king and chiefs traveled over land. When the canoes arrived . . . the waves were very rough, and there was no place to land. Therefore, Ka'ahumanu ordered the paddlers to go out and come in a second time. This time they were close to the back of a wave that rose up directly in front of them, and she encouraged her paddlers to head for it. The canoe came up very close to it and as the wave rose up to a peak and spread out, the craft rode in with the foam to where the prows could be caught by the men on shore. Those on shore remarked to each other how cleverly they were saved, and this became a great topic of conversation.

Charles Stewart called on her one morning in Lahaina and found her "quite fractious" in a loose satin morning robe, sitting before a large gilt mirror as her hair was brushed. When he returned later on a more formal call,

Ka'ahumanu at age
fifty. Pen, ink wash,
and watercolor by
Louis Choris, 1816,
Bernice Pauahi
Bishop Museum,
Honolulu

she was dressed in heavy black silk, with a black crepe shawl, white collar, and
fine lace cap. "With her portly figure and commanding face . . . we felt as if
before a respectable matron of our own nation." Her house in Lahaina was
said to be like an old *haole* woman's house, with chintz upholstery, porcelain
knickknacks, carpets, and comfortable armchairs. Two young *ali'i*, a boy
and a girl, attended her, both dressed in European clothes. According to Kamakau, Ka'ahumanu was less haughty in her old age than she once had been,
going so far as to visit people whom she would have previously disdained:

> She made favorites of toothless women and the old loose-jawed men
> and would pray with them. She made them her brothers and ate with
> them, and they shared her secret counsels and her activities in the
> church. Her interest in good works grew less political and more chari-
> table. She forbade the chiefs to levy taxes on the poor or to make them

travel long distances to work. On Oʻahu, she lifted the kapu that had for centuries reserved certain fish for the use of the chiefs. She outlawed the worship of idols, and more significantly, the practice of anana [praying people to death], and, unfortunately, dancing of all kinds.

As she neared the end of her life, she dressed simply in long white dresses and lived in a quiet manner. She was often ill and her doctor, Gerrit Judd, believed that the intestinal trouble from which she periodically suffered would soon cause her death. In the late spring of 1832, she summoned the king and her chiefs to hear her last instructions, as was traditional. She asked her brother, Governor Kuakini, about the heavy taxes he was said to be levying on Maui, reminding him that she had recently ordered the people relieved of any excessive burden of taxation. When he answered angrily that he could do as he liked on his own land, she began to cry, and covered her head with her blanket. Later that night, she was carried on a litter decorated with hibiscus, *maile*, and *ʻilima*, with a canopy of woven palm fronds, across the valley to her little house with shutters in Mānoa, named Pukaʻōmaʻo, or Green Opening. The procession, chanting old *mele inoa* (name songs in honor of a chief) and Christian hymns, stopped on their way at Ka Punahou, at the foot of the valley, where there was a spring thought to be restorative to the sick.

Her house had been built with a view of the mountains. A stream ran through a nearby grove of *ʻōhiʻa*, and at the edge of the wood there was a small cottage for the use of the missionaries when they came to visit. Her attendants made a bed of *maile* and ginger, and covered it with a velvet cloth. Kaheiheimālie, once the cause of such jealousy, sat by her side, as did Kamehameha's children Kaukieaouli, Nāhiʻenaʻena, and Kīnaʻu, and her favorite chiefs. As they heard the news, people began to walk across the island to be near her, gathering through the night to stand weeping in front of her house.

The missionary Lorenzo Lyons, whose station was Waimea on the Big Island, wrote in his diary: "A cloud is gathering over us and over the church and over the nation. Kaʻahumanu—must I say it? . . . As the meeting closed, many hastened to the mission house to learn the state of the Queen. They were informed that she was just going and that the young king was much affected. 'We hope he will become o ke kanaka maikai—a good man.'"

Kaʻahumanu lived for another week and a half. She treated her attendants with great care and kindness: "Do sit down; you are very tired. I make you

A view of Mānoa Valley from Waikīkī. Oil on canvas by Enoch Wood Perry, Jr., 1865, Bernice Pauahi Bishop Museum, Honolulu

weary." Bingham quickly arranged to print one of the first Hawaiian translations of the Bible, bound in red morocco with her name embossed in gilt on the cover. It had taken the missionaries seventeen years to translate the Bible into Hawaiian, working from the original Hebrew of the Old Testament, and the Greek of the New Testament, in part because they believed that there was so much else to be done. The queen wrapped the Bible in her handkerchief, and held it to her chest with two hands. Now and then she uttered a few words. Bingham read the verse "In my Father's house are many mansions. I go to prepare a place for you, that where I am there ye may be also."

When Laura Judd asked her if she was prepared to die, she answered, "If it is the will of God . . . I had it in my heart to do something more." Bingham said, "Lean on the Beloved through the waters of Jordan," and the queen whispered, "Yes, I shall go to Him and be comforted." The night before her death, at the wish of Kauikeaouli, she was asked if she had a dying thought for him. Unable to raise her head, she said, "O, my friends, have great patience. Stand firm on the side of the good way." Dr. Judd felt her abdomen, which was distended, and she told him that she was in pain and asked for medicine, repeating two lines of the native hymn taken from Psalm 52:

Eia no au, e Iesu,
E nānā oluʻolu mai.

Here I am, O Jesus,
O, look this way in compassion.

She died just before sunrise on June 5, 1832.

Reverend Lyon's wife, Betsy, wrote that Kauikeaouli was inconsolable:

> Since the death of Kaahumanu, it is in vain that any of his friends try to
> persuade the King to eat anything except what Mrs. B. [Mrs. Bingham]
> sent him. Though when Kaahumanu was in health he did not regard
> her instructions as he ought to yet, during her illness, he laid aside
> all other employment to watch at her bedside; and with his own hand
> administered to her wants. He seemed to feel that he could not give
> her up; and ever since her death, he has manifested an unfeigned
> sorrow.

With the death of Kaʻahumanu, the sense of ill ease that had been
growing in the kingdom grew stronger as people attempted to hold to the
fast-disappearing ways of the past. Kauikeaouli soon joined those of his
chiefs who disputed the word of their Christian teachers. He encouraged
the revival of ancient dance and chants, as well as such innocent games as the
pitching of round stones (*ʻulu maika*) and the throwing of darts. His irrever-
ence was sometimes extreme. When his pet baboon died, the animal was
placed in a coffin and buried in a mock Christian ceremony. He repealed the
laws that Kaʻahumanu had enacted, except for those forbidding theft and
murder, and sent criers through the streets of Honolulu demanding that
prostitutes pay homage to his favorite mistress. Now and again, he attempted
to assume a more responsible role as king, moving for a time to Maui where
his association with foreigners would be limited. His determination to
marry his sister had not lessened, and her indecision was a torment to him.
Nāhiʻenaʻena, fatally caught between the new religion and the old pagan
gods (the translation of her name is "the Fires that Rage") was the only
female *aliʻi* known to have possessed a feather *pāʻū*, but she refused to wear
it, as it left her breasts bare. The feather cloak, once a symbol of the gods,
and considered so valuable that it had been the finest object a Hawaiian king

could offer in tribute to white foreigners, had become a distasteful reminder of the past.

> This article, nine yards long and one yard wide, was made at great expense of time and labour . . . and designed to be worn by the princess as a pau . . . It was the desire of the chiefs that she should wear it, with the wreaths for the head and neck, necessary to form the complete ancient costume of a princess . . . but as it was necessary . . . that she should be naked to the waist, nothing could induce her to consent. To escape importunity, she fled to the Mission House early in the morning. She wept so as scarcely to be pacified by us, and returned to the chiefs only in time to take her seat, and have it thrown carelessly about her over her European dress, with one end cast across the arm of the sofa.

Suddenly, in late July 1836, Nāhiʻenaʻena and Kauikeaouli were married. As was traditional, they consummated their union (there were many who believed that they had been sleeping together since they were seven and eight years old) in the presence of her guardian Hoapili, his wife, and other high chiefs. A stunned William Richards sent a message to Nāhiʻenaʻena when he received the news, reminding her of the wishes of her late mother, and of her request that her daughter be a good Christian. Although his letter, delivered to the princess while she sat drinking and eating with her attendants, caused her much distress, she wrote to Richards that she wished never to see him again. She admitted that she had behaved in a shameless manner and had destroyed her soul, but she refused to repent. Richards threatened to excommunicate her, and she later met with him in Lahaina, where she vowed to return to Christian ways. His threat of excommunication, which had alarmed her, was dropped, and she felt hopeful in her remorse. The wary missionaries decided that she should formally marry as soon as possible the fourteen-year-old Kona chief Leleiōhoku, and she agreed, despite her recent ceremony with the king. In seeming betrayal, she was excommunicated after all, and married to the boy in a Christian ceremony performed by Richards.

The following year Kauikeaouli visited Nāhiʻenaʻena in Lahaina, where the two were frequently seen drunk. She gave birth to the king's child that September, but the infant lived only a few hours. She herself fell gravely ill (it was thought by the *haole* doctors who treated her that she had imprudently taken a cold bath shortly after giving birth), and died three months later. Mrs. Judd, who was with her when she died, wrote that she showed a deep agony over her past behavior. "Can there be hope for one who has sinned as I have?" (As there are no other written accounts of her death, it is not possible to know if Mrs. Judd is telling the truth. The same may be said of Judd's recording of Ka'ahumanu's last words.)

After her death, Kauikeaouli built a large stone house in Lahaina, the top floor of which he made into a mausoleum in honor of his mother, Keōpūolani, and his sister and their child. Nāhi'ena'ena's coffin, covered in a cloth of red velvet, rested on a large bed in the center of the room, surrounded by her hereditary *kāhili*. Along one wall, behind glass, were her clothes—silk and taffeta gowns, satin slippers, a black lace shawl, and a white silk cape, although not her feather *pā'ū*. The king frequently took guests and visitors to see her coffin and the little display of her belongings.

In 1841, land that Ka'ahumanu had ordered Boki's wife, Liliha, to give to the Binghams ten years earlier became the site of a school for the children of missionaries. Named after its famous spring, Ka Punahou, the school had fifteen students. Daniel Dole of the Ninth Company was made headmaster. Henry Lyman described arriving at Punahou as a boy from the rural isolation of Hilo, where he was "thrust into a class of big boys who were reading Caesar . . . Salt tears of mortification sterilized my blushes during those early recitations; but one of my schoolmates, who was remarkable as a linguist, and subsequently was salutatorian at Yale, cheered me on, and lent a helping hand . . . and there was no more trouble." (The private school now has nearly four thousand students, kindergarten through grade twelve, its most famous graduate being Barack Obama.)

That same year, the national legislature introduced the right of commoners to own land, and foreigners were encouraged to lease land for as long as fifty years. In 1846, the newly appointed Board of Land Commissioners allowed people two years in which to register land claims and to settle disputes, leading in 1848 to the division and appropriation of land known as the Great Mahele. The crown claimed one third of the land, with the remaining divided equally between the chiefs and the people (in the end, commoners received less than 1 percent). Foreigners profited greatly from the legislation, buying or claiming for themselves large tracts of land (one man bought 2,500 acres in Niu Valley in east Oʻahu; another claimed 7,000 acres west of Honolulu). Chiefs applied for fee-simple titles to land they had once held in fief, and commoners were permitted to buy small pieces of land, or *kuleana*, in fee-simple. Others claimed ownership of land that had been farmed by their families for generations. Traditionally, land belonged to the man who worked it; if he left only to return some day, he was treated generously, but he had lost all rights to the land. Hawaiians were not fully aware of the advantages of ownership, whether of land or goods, and did not understand the meaning of a fee-simple title. Their claims were often lost in disputes, counterclaims, and misunderstandings, many of which continue to this day. Even the process of surveying the land, not sufficiently explained to them, caused confusion and mistrust.

> The surveyors' native helpers were enthusiastic but muddled. The poles and flags reminded them of the makahiki [the four-month-long yearly festival], and the folded tripod of the measuring instruments looked to them like the bundled bones of their ancestors. They thought the chain being dragged along the ground marked the boundary, and the compass was a mystery to them. A systematic government survey did not begin until 1870, and it took a generation after that to reduce confusion about boundaries to a minimum.

The old landscape of *kalo* patches, fish ponds, stone house platforms, enclosures, *heiau* and other *kapu* areas began to disappear. Epidemics of cholera and smallpox resulted in so many deaths that numerous landholdings and farms were abandoned. No longer did the king's *konohiki* (overseer) collect taxes and manage the royal lands. Each possessor of a *kuleana* was allowed to decide his property's use for himself. With the right to buy land came the right to sell it, and much of the land won by commoners was sold or leased to foreigners. Fifty years after the Great Mahele, descendants of the missionaries, traders, and merchants who had settled in the Islands, and large American companies doing business in the Islands, owned four acres of land to every one acre owned by a Hawaiian.

Crucified to the World

In the fall of 1855, having been in the Islands for thirty-five years, Lucy Thurston discovered a tumor in her breast, indicated by a dark spot that was rapidly changing in shape. Her doctors determined that her breast should be removed, and Asa sailed with her to Honolulu for the surgery. As she had earlier suffered from frequent pneumonia and paralysis, the doctors advised against the use of chloroform, and she wrote in her journal that she was relieved that she would be allowed the use of her senses.

The operation was held in the grass cottage of her daughter Persis, which was arranged to afford Lucy the most comfort, with two sofas, one with mosquito netting; a reclining Chinese chair; a table for surgical instruments; a washstand with bowls, sponges, and pails of water; two dozen towels; a table for stimulants and restoratives; and "one more table with the Bible and hymn book." There are few early descriptions of a mastectomy other than that of the English writer Fanny Burney, in 1811, that match Lucy Thurston's telling.

That night I spent in the house alone for the first time. The family had all retired for the night. In the still hour of darkness, I long walked back and forth in the capacious door-yard. Depraved, diseased, helpless, I yielded myself up entirely to the will, the wisdom and the strength of the Holy One. At peace with myself, with earth, and with heaven, I calmly laid my head upon my pillow and slept refreshingly. Dr. Judd arrived early in the morning, bringing with him Dr. Hoffman of Honolulu, and Dr. Brayton of an American naval ship then in port. The instruments were then laid out upon the table. Strings were prepared for tying arteries. Needles threaded for sewing up the wound. Adhesive plasters were cut into strips, bandages produced, and the

Chinese chair placed by them in the front double door . . . Persis and I stepped behind a curtain. I threw off my cap and dressing gown, and appeared with a white flowing skirt, with the white bordered shawl purchased in 1818, thrown over my shoulders.

I took my seat in the chair. Persis and Asa stood at my right side; Persis to hand me restoratives; Asa to use his strength, if self-control were wanting. Dr. Judd stood at my left elbow for the same reason; my shawl was thrown off, exhibiting my left arm, breast and side, perfectly bare . . . Dr. Ford looked me full in the face, and with great firmness asked: "Have you made up your mind to have it cut out?" "Yes, sir; but let me know when you begin, that I may be able to bear it. Have you your knife in your hand now?" He opened his hand that I might see it, saying "I am going to begin now." Then came a gash long and deep, first on one side of my breast, and then on the other. Deep sickness seized me, and deprived me of my breakfast. This was followed by extreme faintness. My sufferings were no longer local. There was a general feeling of agony through the whole system. I felt, every inch of me, as though flesh was failing . . . Persis and Asa were devotedly employed in sustaining me with the use of cordials, ammonia, bathing my temples . . . It was nearly an hour and a half that I was beneath [Dr. Ford's] hand, in cutting out the entire breast, in cutting out the glands beneath the arm, in tying the arteries, in absorbing the blood, in sewing up the wound, in putting on the adhesive plaster, and in applying the bandage.

The views and feelings of that hour are now vivid to my recollection. It was during the cutting process that I began to talk. The feeling that I had reached a different point from those by whom I was surrounded, inspired me with freedom . . . The doctor, after removing the entire breast, said to me, "I want to cut yet more, round under your arm." . . . The wound had the appearance of being more than a foot long. Eleven arteries were taken up.

Lucy's memory of events after the surgery was less clear. She told Persis that it must have been the paregoric that caused her to forget, but Persis reminded her that no sedative of any kind had been given her. "For weeks my debility was so great, that I was fed with a teaspoon, like an infant. Many dangers were apprehended. During one day, I was a duplicate of every person and every thing that my eye beheld." Six weeks later, Lucy wrote in a letter to her daughter, "And here again is your mother, engaged in life's duties, and life's warfare."

When Dr. Holman precipitously resigned from the mission in 1820, seven months after his arrival with the First Company, Asa Thurston had written to the Board in Boston to ask for more helpers, feeling himself to be lost in darkness. "We want men and women who have souls; who are crucified to the world, and the world to them; who have their eyes and their hearts fixed on the glory of God in the salvation of the heathen; who will be willing to sacrifice every interest but Christ's; who will cheerfully and constantly labor to promote His cause; in a word, those who are pilgrims and strangers." Thurston might have been describing himself and his wife. There cannot have been much gaiety in their lives, and they would not have expected any, but there was pride in their work and in their children and native students, and contentment, despite Lucy's unceasing fear that she was not sufficiently selfless and devoted. When the Thurstons' seventeen-year-old daughter Lucy sailed to America to attend school, she wrote in her shipboard journal:

> I am ashamed of myself many times a day for giving way to so much laughter, but there are so many witty remarks made, that it is almost impossible to refrain from it. I have heard more jokes, more hyperbolical expressions and comical remarks on board, than I did during seventeen years of my residence at the Sandwich Islands . . . I feel that I have parted far from God and my duty since being on board.

On reading this, one can only be happy for her. Shortly after landing in New York, she fell ill with fever and died a few days later.

Before undertaking her own journey to the United States for medical treatment (she was to make five such trips of 18,000 miles each), Lucy Thurston wrote a farewell note to her husband.

> I address a line to the companion of my youth, my protector, my counselor, the father of my children, my husband. Now I go to be repaired like a worn shoe, that in active life I may hold on by your side. But I am borne up by your sanction, advice, and wishes, and by the approval of our fathers, great and good men. I go, and in so doing, strip your home of its remaining olive plants. I leave you in a house so

solitary, that in midnight silence you will hear no other sound than the ticking of the clock. As Lucy on her deathbed said: "Alone, all alone." Thus desolate, should sickness prostrate, and death do its work, farewell. The life to come. The life to come. For myself, I give up rest and the quiet pleasures of domestic life in the house of an affectionate indulgent husband. Without a shield, with woman's weakness and woman's infirmities, I go to take my chance, and become a wanderer on ocean and on land . . . You have, with unsurpassed kindness, opened our way before us . . . Often write to me across the continent. Tell me of your welfare, and how you prosper. Remind me of my duty. Thus I shall be ever made to feel your left hand beneath my head, and your right hand embracing me.

Each afternoon, Thurston worked on his translation of the Old Testament, sitting at a desk covered with books. His Hawaiian friends would stop to visit with him, and came again at night to join what Lucy described as the " 'fa, so, la' company, as it is here called." The high chief Kuakini, who lived in Kona, had grown fond of Thurston. The two studied English together, and Kuakini built Moku'aikaua Church for him, out of affection rather than Christian devotion. Thurston wisely never tried to convert Kuakini, praising

Asa and Lucy Thurston, published in Lucy Thurston's book, *Life and Times*, 1882

A drawing by Persis Thurston of Kaʻawaloa at Kealakekua Bay, 1835, Mission Houses Museum, Honolulu

him as a gentleman and at heart a Christian, despite his very public lack of piety. (Another of Thurston's students, a young woman sailing from Kailua to Honolulu, is said to be the source of the proverb "After Kalaʻau Point is passed, the virtues taught by Thurston end.")

As an old man, Thurston suffered from dementia, slipping into a pleasing but incoherent mixture of Hawaiian, English, and Latin. He died in 1868, after forty years of hard work devoted to the people of Hawaiʻi. The following is from a letter that Lucy wrote to her children and grandchildren:

> He died March 11, aged eighty years and five months. We had lived together forty-eight years and five months. His reason was at times dethroned during his illness of nine weeks. He forgot almost everything, even his own wife and children . . . The last two days of his life he did not speak . . . His laborious breathing, his convulsive movements, his clammy sweat told me that the last sands of his life were falling. That whole night I lay on the back side of the bed, unable to sit up from extreme prostration. Once he turned his head, fixed his eyes fully upon me, but could not utter a syllable . . . I took hold of his arm with one hand, and placed the other upon his forehead. His serene eyes were fixed upon mine . . . His convulsions had ceased. His

hard respirations had gradually ended. His breathings were shorter and shorter, softer and softer, till they became gentle . . . Then he calmly closed his eyes . . . It was eight o'clock. The strongest tie that bound me down to earth was then severed . . . I adore that power and love which formed and watched over our companionship for more than forty-eight years, and for the great privilege allowed me of smoothing his rough pathway through life, even down to the river's brink.

In 1876, Lucy, sick with heart disease, found consolation in the hope that she would soon meet her childhood friends and relatives in Paradise. She wrote of herself, "To have her early friends restored to her, in all the vigor of immortal youth, one more beautiful change in her alone is wanting,—going to sleep on earth, and waking up in heaven." After six months of suffering, she died in Honolulu on October 14, a few weeks before her eighty-first birthday. Queen Lili'uokalani, the last ruler of Hawai'i, admired Lucy (although not her grandson, Lorrin Thurston, who helped to depose her) and wrote somewhat equivocally that she was a woman of the "greatest determination and of extraordinary strength of character." At her memorial, one of Lucy's eulogists reminded the mourners that she had considered herself a missionary to the end. In his praise of her, she sounds much like her friend Ka'ahumanu: "She had strong desires. She was hopeful. She had a strong mind, and a strong self-will. As she said to me the day before her death, she had a great deal of human nature."

Falling Are the Heavens

The high chiefess Kīna'u, daughter of Kamehameha I and Kaheiheimālie, bore five children of divine rank, including Lot Kapuāiwa and Alexander Liholiho. With the death in 1854 of Kauikeaouli, who had adopted Alexander Liholiho and named him his heir, Liholiho became Kamehameha IV. His father was the high chief Mataio Kekūanāo'a, governor of O'ahu. Along with his wife, Emma Rooke, Liholiho had been a student of Amos and Juliette Cooke at the Chiefs' Children's School. The Cookes, while strict and austere, were known to be comparatively worldly in their views, and Liholiho dreamed of sending his son to Eton. As a young man, he had traveled through Europe and Asia with his older brother, Prince Lot, and Dr. Judd, and he and his wife were the leaders of a young Honolulu set which included *haoles* and *ali'i*. Although Emma, who was raised by her adoptive father, the Englishman Dr. Thomas Rooke, had been taught by missionaries, as well as an English governess, and was one of the founders of the Episcopal Church in Hawai'i, she was extremely proud of her Hawaiian blood. In a letter to her cousin, confined to a leper colony on Moloka'i, she wrote that she wished her people to "become acquainted with ancient songs, their origin, object, composers, effects . . . for that is the way our Island history has been preserved—entirely oral."

The once pervasive and often destructive influence of the missionaries from New England was coming to an end—even they cannot have missed the irony when the beautiful Emma appeared at a masked ball as the pagan goddess Cybele. In 1863, Dr. Rufus Anderson of the American Board of Commissioners for Foreign Missions (he who had once advised against the teaching of English to Hawaiians), realized that the work of the mission was finished. The number of men and women sent in twelve companies to seventeen

ABOVE: Kamehameha III in his uniform embroidered with the Hawaiian crown. Lithograph after a watercolor by Alfred T. Agate, ship's artist on board the *Vincennes*, 1841. RIGHT: A Hawaiian chief in 1870. Illustration from Charles Nordhoff's *Northern California, Oregon and the Sandwich Islands*, 1875

stations on five of the Hawaiian Islands between 1830 and 1863 was 178, almost half of whom had been teachers, doctors, agents, and lay members. The clergymen who had served in Hawai'i, many of whom were elderly, if not exhausted by their years of labor, were encouraged to put their pastorates in the hands of Hawaiian students trained by them or at schools in the United States.

> By the end of the sixties the retreat of the missionaries had turned into a rout. Their own children, confined to calisthenics ("Presbyterian dancing") at Punahou, were quick to take up real dancing once they left school . . . At the opening of a skating rink at Honolulu Queen Emma sat in the royal box and watched the lancers, the quadrille, and the grand march performed—all on skates . . . The elderly wife of the Reverend Lowell Smith . . . was seen swimming at Waikiki on a Sunday; and the children of missionaries were "dancing themselves silly" at weekend parties in the country.

Alexander Liholiho's reign as Kamehameha IV (1855–1863) was marred by scandal, including the king's shooting of his private secretary, whom he

Prince Albert, son of Queen Emma and Kamehameha IV, in the garden of the old 'Iolani Palace. The prince died in childhood. Oil on canvas by Enoch Wood Perry, ca. 1864, Bernice Pauahi Bishop Museum, Honolulu

wrongly suspected of dishonoring his wife. Dead by age twenty-nine, he was succeeded in 1863 by his brother Lot (Kamehameha V), the *hana'i* son of Nāhi'ena'ena. A fervent advocate of his people, Lot cared little what *haoles* thought of him. He encouraged the dancing of *hula*, chanting, and native healing, and repealed the laws that forbade what missionaries liked to call "kahunaism," which referred to anything hinting of paganism. He refused to sign a bill permitting the sale of alcohol to Hawaiians, however, as he saw drink as the cause of much death among them. He had been betrothed at birth to Princess Bernice Pauahi, but she married instead the American banker Charles Reed Bishop, and he did not speak to her for the rest of his life. A powerful female sorcerer, Kama'ipu'upa'a, said to be expert in healing and in prophecy, lived with him, and was believed by many to be his mistress. Like his brother and cousins, he suffered from ill health and from an addiction to drink, but despite his frequent melancholia, his concerns were always those of his people. Those who lined against him—American business interests, the church, and the educated, confident, acquisitive descendants of missionary families—had become too powerful to defeat. The Islands, valuable both economically and as a military outpost, were no longer a sleepy tropical backwater. During Lot's reign, the legislature fell into turmoil, with certain *haole* members refusing to speak Hawaiian, and Hawaiian senators refusing to speak English. In bad health for some time, he died without children on his fortieth birthday, marking the end of the Kamehameha line of kings.

Lot's cousin, William Charles Lunalilo, had been in love since childhood with Lot's sister, Princess Victoria Kamāmalu, who was a granddaughter of Kamehameha I, and heir to Kaʻahumanu's large estates. Lot, who had wished Kamāmalu to be the consort of David Kalākaua (who would himself become king), at last gave Lunalilo permission to marry her, despite her long intimacy with Marcus Monsarrat, a married *haole* auctioneer in Honolulu. Lunalilo refused to marry her at the last moment, promising to arrive too drunk for any ceremony to be binding. He wrote the following poem, "The Prince's Words to the Princess":

I loved you once, I believed you.
Even I thought you were true.
You made me swear to be loyal and remember.
Remember your own oath and keep it true.
For this body, beloved, brims with my love.
At the thought of your mouth my heart leaps
with love remembered in a magic pool.
Now as we climb a winding way at Maʻemaʻe,
here where buds of Mauanaʻala shed the fragrance
we knew from childhood only too well,
what flower will burn from your body
if I, beloved, lie in your arms?

With Lot's death, Lunalilo, a descendant of a half brother of Kamehameha I, became the favorite of both Hawaiian and American interests to succeed him. David Kalākaua, the ambitious son of a high chief of Maui (whose father had been hanged for killing Kalākaua's mother), was also a candidate, but the legislature, which had been granted the right to choose a new king under the Constitution of 1862, settled on Lunalilo. Isabella Bird somewhat condescendingly described the king, who lived with his mistress, Eliza Meeks, the part-Hawaiian daughter of a harbor pilot:

The king is a very fine-looking man of thirty-eight, tall, well formed, broad-chested, with his head well set on his shoulders, and his feet and hands small. His appearance is decidedly commanding and aristocratic: he is certainly handsome even according to our notions. He has a fine open brow, significant at once of brains and straightforwardness, a straight, proportionate nose, and a good mouth. The slight tendency to Polynesian overfulness [*sic*] about his lips is concealed by a well-shaped moustache . . . His eyes are large, dark brown of course, and equally of course, he has a superb set of teeth . . . He is remarkably gentlemanly looking, and has the grace of movement which seems usual with Hawaiians.

Despite the shortness of his reign (1873–1874), Lunalilo succeeded in subverting and supplanting many of the prejudicial practices and beliefs that the missionaries had worked so hard to impose. He was an admirer of Shakespeare and would often ride through Honolulu on horseback "in a state of undue excitement," according to the English traveler Lady Franklin, gathering crowds to whom he would recite long passages from the plays. Charming, witty, and intelligent, he was given to excess in all things (he is said to have once made the Royal Hawaiian band play "God Save the King" seven times in a row, not notably a sign of decadence, but sufficient to set people talking). His ambivalence about the role of America, increasingly aggressive in its push for annexation of the Islands, caused him to neglect his responsibilities as king, and in 1873, the kingdom's standing army, the Royal Household Troops, mutinied, purportedly agitated by the possible cession of Pearl Harbor to the United States.

White men were not used to the threat of violence from Hawaiians. They were accustomed to thinking of the natives in crowds—the waterfront gapers of the early days, the hula dancers of the twenties, the chanting temperance marchers and revival converts of the thirties, the smallpox victims of the fifties, and the aimless drifters and lockstep voters of the sixties, even the agitated political crowds of the moment—but the thought of an armed Hawaiian mob was strange and frightening to them.

Lunalilo left Honolulu for Kailua, while the dowager queen Emma and David Kalākaua separately began to campaign quietly for the throne. When

Lunalilo died a year later, the thirty-eight-year-old Kalākaua, backed by armed troops from three American warships in Honolulu Harbor, was declared king amid rioting by Emma's supporters.

With the growth of the sugar industry in the second half of the nineteenth century, Hawaiians found work on the large plantations owned by the descendants of missionary families and early settlers, although the mill workers, boiler tenders, coopers, and carpenters were all *haoles* from Honolulu. Hawaiians were good at heavy labor, but they did not like the routine of daily fieldwork, and between 1852 and 1856, thousands of Chinese, most of them Cantonese men from the Pearl River delta near Macao, were brought to the Islands as indentured workers. Laborers from Japan began to arrive in 1868, hired by the plantations against the wishes of the Japanese government (by the end of the nineteenth century, 40 percent of the population of Hawai'i was Japanese). The plantation owners were disappointed in the workers conscripted from Asia—they ran away, quarreled with the Hawaiians, smoked opium, protested that the law mandating nine-hour workdays was too arduous, fell sick, and most irritating of all, died (plantation managers complained that many of the Chinese were already half-dead when they arrived). The Hawaiians began to find work more amenable to their temperament on the growing number of cattle ranches. Already fearless horsemen, they were taught by cowboys (*paniolo*) brought by ranchers from Mexican territory in the 1830s. Hawaiians, already adept at riding over lava, became known for their courage, stamina, and skill in running cattle, and by 1890, when sugar and pineapple were dominant, Hawaiians were no longer part of the plantation workforce.

The oral history of the Hawaiians and their music and dance were kept alive with the help of numerous Hawaiian-language newspapers, especially during the reign of King Kalākaua (1874–1891). Intent on preserving his people's history, Kalākaua encouraged the study of Hawaiian culture. The fire-burning *kapu* which had once allowed those *ali'i* who possessed it to light torches by day, had originated with a high chief whose daughter had been killed by one of his wives, causing him to roam across the island of Hawai'i with lighted torches. It was a prerogative long out of use, but Kalākaua, as one of the chief's descendants, insisted on restoring the practice (he did not, however, order that his subjects fall to the ground in his presence, as was also his right), and the torches in his court burned day and night. Despite his efforts at good governance, Kalākaua's reign was fraught with ineptitude, compromise, foreign interference, rebellion, and the increasing threat of annexation by the United States.

In 1885, Kamehameha School was founded for the education of Hawaiian children by Bernice Pauahi Bishop, who had inherited an estate that made her the largest private landowner in the kingdom, with 10 percent of all Hawaiian land. When it was founded, Kamehameha School mandated that all instruction be in English—a practice that continued until 1924 when the formal teaching of Hawaiian was allowed. The princess, married to the American businessman Charles Reed Bishop, also endowed the Bishop Museum in Honolulu, which collects and preserves the ethnographic and natural history of the Islands.

Kalākaua's poor health was aggravated by chronic drinking, and in 1891, he suffered a stroke at the Palace Hotel in San Francisco, dying a few weeks later. His sister, Liliʻuokalani, became queen, inheriting a kingdom whose chaotic and riven politics were beyond her capacities to control or to mend. One of the new queen's first acts was to request the making of a constitution in which the rights of native Hawaiians would be protected. Lorrin Thurston, a lawyer and state legislator and grandson of Asa and Lucy Thurston, held that the queen, by demanding the rewriting of the constitution, was guilty of an act of sedition. He formed a Committee of Safety with a group of friends, which aimed to end the monarchy and to establish a provisional government. The committee, six of whom were Hawaiian citizens by birth or naturalization, wrote to the United States Minister to Hawaiʻi, John L. Stevens, to ask for the protection and support of the American forces under his command. Marines from an American warship were posted throughout the town as Thurston and his fellow annexationists took possession of several government buildings.

Liliʻuokalani and her supporters surrendered, certain that once the United States learned the true nature of the revolt, she would be restored to power. The newly elected American president, Grover Cleveland, was at first willing to support Liliʻuokalani, provided she give amnesty to the revolutionaries, which she refused to do. Cleveland then asked Thurston if the provisional government would be willing to relinquish its authority and restore the monarchy, and Thurston answered that it would not. The queen eventually changed her mind, but Cleveland had by then grown tired of what he viewed

Queen Liliʻuokalani, by an unknown photographer, 1891, Hawaiʻi State Archives

Some Hawaiian *aliʻi* and their *haole* husbands. Seated from left are Laura Cleghorn, Princess Liliʻuokalani, Princess Likelike, and Keawepoʻoʻole; standing are Thomas Cleghorn, Liliʻuokalani's husband John Owen Dominis, and Archibald Scott Cleghorn, the husband of Likelike, ca. 1880, Bernice Pauahi Bishop Museum, Honolulu

as a regional fracas, and left it to Congress to resolve. When Sanford B. Dole was made president of the new Hawaiian republic in July 1894, Cleveland sent a letter of recognition. That year, the McKinley Act, which had raised protective rates 50 percent for most American-made products and goods, and had increased tariffs on imports while removing those on sugar, tea, molasses, and coffee, was repealed, restoring to grateful Island planters their favorable trading position and their profits.

A counterrevolution led by Robert Wilcox (not of the missionary family) came to nothing when contraband arms were discovered hidden at the foot of Diamond Head and in the garden of the queen's house in Honolulu. Liliʻuokalani was arrested and detained in ʻIolani Palace, where she signed a letter of abdication which she later claimed was forced. She was released the following year, and immediately traveled to Washington in an emotional attempt to save her kingdom, as did her heir, the young Princess Kaʻiulani, the daughter of Miriam Likelike and Archibald Cleghorn. Sereno Bishop, son of the missionary Artemas Bishop and the Hawaiʻi correspondent for

United Press, had spent the previous few years undermining the cause of the monarchists, writing, among other things, that Lili'uokalani was under the influence of black-magic sorcerers, and that she made sacrifices to the fire goddess. (He also helped to popularize the rumor that Kalākaua and Lili'uokalani were the children of a minor chiefess and a Negro bootblack named John Blossom.) Lorrin Thurston published a pamphlet in which he wrote that annexation by the United States would bring an end to the growing danger of a militaristic Japan, and incalculable benefits to commerce, agriculture, ranching, and shipping. In the spring of 1898, the United States, at war with Spain, sank a fleet of Spanish ships in Manila harbor, reminding Americans that the nation's global hegemony could only be enhanced by strengthening its position in the North Pacific. Three months later, on July 6, the Congress of the United States voted by joint resolution to annex the Hawaiian Islands. The kingdom of Hawai'i was no more.

The Voice of Land Shells

The artist Jacques Arago mournfully predicted that it would take a thousand years for the Hawaiians to be civilized, yet in 1820, six months after the arrival of the First Company of missionaries, an examination of forty scholars was conducted by Sybil Bingham in Honolulu, in which the students were tested on words of one syllable, and twenty lines translated from English into Hawaiian. The following year, most of the students were able to read the Bible. Five years later, according to Ephraim Eveleth, *nine chiefs* (his italics) had converted to Christianity; a dozen churches had been erected by natives who carried the building materials on their shoulders; more than twenty thousand were able to read; and fifty Hawaiian graduates of missions schools were employed as schoolteachers throughout the Islands. The Friday Meeting for women that Lucy Thurston began in 1827 grew from seventy women its first year to fifteen hundred by 1829, and nearly three thousand women in 1830. By 1833, twenty thousand Hawaiians were literate, having begun their lessons on banana leaves, wet sand, and stones. "No one reign of thirty years, in any country," wrote Captain George Byron, "had ever witnessed so great a change in the condition of the people as did that of Tamehameha in the Sandwich Islands."

In late-nineteenth-century journals and letters, however, both chiefs and commoners begin to be portrayed as lazy, greedy, and slovenly. Isabella Bird deplored the apparent lassitude of the people, writing that the more she came to know Hawaiians, the more she was "impressed . . . with their carelessness and love of pleasure, their lack of ambition and a sense of responsibility, and the time which they spend in doing nothing but talking and singing as they bask in the sun, though spasmodically and under excitement they are capable of tremendous exertions in canoeing, surf-riding, and lassoing cattle."

This supposed sloth and ineptitude had been nowhere in evidence at the time of Captain Cook's landing in the Islands. David Malo wrote that the Hawaiian people were not lazy, but hard-working:

> In the old days laziness brought lack. Here are those who did not work in the old days: favorite children, for whose indolence their parents were responsible; prostitutes, who were ceremonially unclean; the wandering class who had nothing to do; those who lived with the chief who acted as his attendants. All the others were workers. The chiefs had work to do as chiefs in looking after the interests of the land and of the people. The kahunas had work to do in worshipping one or another god. The craftsmen worked at one thing or another for their living. Men worked at farming, fishing, building houses and at any other work by which they gained a living. The women's work was beating tapa [*kapa*], making designs, weaving mats, and other things by which they made a living.

Cook, Vancouver, Menzies, and Shaler (who brought the first horse to the Islands in 1803), among others, all marked the kindness, intelligence, and most particularly, the industry of the Hawaiians. Archibald Campbell, who lived in Honolulu in 1810, thought that he had never seen a people who worked as hard:

> [The British] could not help but admiring the manner in which the little fields on both sides of us were laid out to the greatest advantage and the perseverance and great attention of the natives in adapting to every vegetable they cultivate . . . by which their fields are productive of good crops that far exceed in . . . perfection the produce of any civilized country within the tropics . . . Some [of the men were] felling of large timber for various purposes; others in hollowing out and forming canoes and planks in the rough, which, after laying some time in the sun to season, were dragged down . . . to the sea side to be finished by their canoe builders, who are distinct persons from those who thus form them in the rough. A third set seemed to have no other occupation than that of catching small birds for the sake of their feathers, especially those of a red, yellow or black colour.

With the arrival of foreign explorers, navigators, seamen, and merchants, the fixed world of the Hawaiians, governed by a hereditary *ali'i* and priest-hood with a distinctive system of *kapu*, suddenly became one of flux, if not chaos. The alienation and depression that Hawaiians began to suffer after the arrival of foreigners and their vulnerability to diseases from which they had no immunity were often mistaken for shiftlessness and even degeneracy. There was nothing in the missionaries' view of humankind that encompassed the idea of racial grief, and little in the experience of the majority of foreigners who settled in the Islands to provoke compassion. Incapable of imaginative sympathy, they could not begin to ameliorate the sorrow that was overtaking the Hawaiian people.

For centuries, Hawaiians had been able to find all that they needed in their own *ahupua'a* of land. The old system had given them a form of independence, despite their indenture to the chiefs and their tenuous possession of property, dependent as it was upon the will of the *ali'i*. Samuel Kamakau wrote, in *Ruling Chiefs of Hawaii*:

> From the summits of the purple mountains to the sea-girt beaches of the shore the people lived long lives, and natural, even to extreme old age. Now in many places the land goes uncultivated because there are none to need it; and in some places the ground is white with our bones . . . The old villages lie silent in a tangle of bushes and vines, haunted by ghosts and horn-owls. We are lost like one hidden away in a clump of grass.

The nineteenth-century historian Kepelino, who was born in 1830, was both romantic and bitter about the fate of the Hawaiian people, and alarmed by what he feared awaited them:

> This was a great people at the beginning. It filled the Hawaiian group. A people with clean body, plump, large-limbed and strong, a little less than the lion in strength, long-lived on the earth. A lovable people, amiable, kind-hearted, hospitable to strangers. A race easily led into sin by rude and shameless white people from America so that from the days of Lono until today epidemics have become common, shame-less deeds are done and innumerable other evils abound. A humble

race, not arrogant, pleasant-voiced like the chirpings of little chickens in the bush, of the petrels in their holes or of the doves in the rocky cliffs.

The travel writer Charles Stoddard was also alarmed, and did not hesitate to blame the missionaries:

One has only to glance at a comparative table of the census during the last three score years, or to take the dimensions of the numerous and now almost vacant Protestant churches scattered through the length and breadth of the land to draw a conclusion by no means flattering to any Board of Missions. Having spied the gentlest of savages out of the lonely sea for the purpose of teaching them how to die, the American Missionary calmly folds his hands over the grave of the nation and turns his attention to affairs more private and peculiar.

The illnesses caused by contagion, abetted by the emotional distress and cultural disruption experienced by the Hawaiians, resulted in the mid-nineteenth century in a fall in the birth rate, and an increase in mortality at all ages. Isabella Bird wrote that, with few exceptions, those chiefs who had survived were childless:

I came everywhere upon traces of a once numerous population, where the hill slopes are now only a wilderness of guava scrub, and upon churches and school-houses all too large, while in some hamlets the voices of young children were altogether wanting. This nation . . . has to me the mournful aspect of a shriveled and wizened old man dressed in clothing much too big, the garments of his once athletic and vigorous youth.

Charles Darwin was interested by the change in the life expectancy of Hawaiians, and the decline in fertility, but attributed it not to despair and disease, but to social habits and alcohol:

The islands were visited by Cook in 1779, Vancouver in 1794, and often subsequently by whalers. In 1819 missionaries arrived, and found that idolatry had been already abolished and other changes effected by the king. After this period there was a rapid change in almost all the habits of life of the natives, and they soon became "the most civilised of the Pacific Islands." One of my informants, Mr. Coan, who was born on the islands, remarks that the natives have undergone a greater change in their habits of life in the course of fifty years than Englishmen during a thousand years. From information received from Bishop Staley, it does not appear that the poorer classes have ever much changed their diet, although many new kinds of fruit have been introduced, and the sugar-cane is in universal use. Owing, however, to their passion for imitating Europeans, they altered their manner of dressing at an early period, and the use of alcoholic drinks became very general. Although these changes appear inconsiderable, I can well believe, from what is known with respect to animals, that they might suffice to lessen the fertility of the natives.

The teacher and missionary Sheldon Dibble, who arrived in Hawai'i in 1831 with the Fourth Company, was appalled by what foreigners had brought to the Islands:

Cheating, trade in arms and rum, physical violence, murder, arrogance, and general exploitation are the white man's contribution to Hawaiian civilization . . . Sin and death were the first commodities imported to the Sandwich Islands. As though their former ruin were not sufficient, Christian nations superadded a deadlier evil [venereal disease]. That evil is sweeping the population to the grave with amazing rapidity. And it is yet to be seen whether the influences of Christianity on the rising race shall stay that desolation.

William P. Alexander, stationed in Hanalei on the island of Kaua'i, echoed Dibble's fears when he wrote that if the missionaries were to be of any help, they would have to act quickly, as the Hawaiian people were "melting away." He believed that their continued existence would depend on their acceptance of foreign ways, but Hawaiians, bewildered and weakened, were already close to losing what little remained of their spiritual and physical fortitude. David Malo wrote, "Confused, abandoned by his gods, beset by foreigners and their diseases, the Hawaiian lost his resistance to death. The people dismissed freely their souls and died."

In 1824, William Richards in Lahaina noted that ten out of thirty high chiefs had died in the previous two years. Many Hawaiians, unaware of immunity and contagion, attributed this increase in mortality to the books and teachings that the missionaries had brought to the Islands. The high rate of death among natives was not solely due to books, however. Although Don Francisco de Marín, Archibald Campbell, and others do not report any serious illnesses other than venereal disease appearing before 1818, prior to 1803 Hawaiians were dying of such newly introduced illnesses as tuberculosis, gastroenteritis, and even the common cold. Thousands of people died in an epidemic of whooping cough and measles that lasted from 1824 to 1826. In 1832, there was another outbreak of whooping cough that killed thousands more. The first case of leprosy was discovered in 1830. In 1853, smallpox reached the Islands, most likely due to the Gold Rush in California:

> The dead were stacked up like a load of wood . . . some in coffins, but most of them just piled in, wrapped in cloth with heads and legs sticking out . . . Only when they saw the dead strewn like *Kukui* branches did terror fall upon them.

In 1866, a crude settlement for those infected with leprosy, almost all of them Hawaiian and all of them treated like criminals, was established on a remote peninsula on the island of Moloka'i. Those thought to be sick were rounded up and forced aboard ships (*The Folding Cliffs*, by William Merwin, is the story of a Kaua'i cowboy who hides in the mountains with his wife and child rather than be sent to Moloka'i, and who resists the company of Hawaiian soldiers sent to arrest him). In 1873, a Belgian Catholic priest, Father Damien, who was later to die of leprosy, was sent to Moloka'i to administer the lawless colony, whose inhabitants were dying of hunger and neglect as well as the disease. Before the arrival of Father Damien, many of the sick were drowned or killed by sharks when sailors, afraid to touch them or to ferry them ashore, simply shoved them overboard. The following is a song written by the chanter Ka'ehu of Kaua'i, who was among those sent forcibly to Moloka'i:

> Never again would we look upon this land of ours,
> this lovely harbor town.
> Quickly the sails were hoisted.
> Ropes dangled from the foremast,

tails of wild animals writhing,
whipping in the channel breeze.
The *John Bull* drew anchor.
In the stern the rudder turned.
So sailed we forth to dim Moloka'i Island,
enshrouded in fog.

The Hilo missionary Sarah Lyman wrote that when the Islands were first visited by Captain Cook, the population was estimated between 250,000 and 800,000 people. (The sociologist David Swanson estimates that the 1778 population was around 683,000 people.) In 1821, the population of the Big Island dropped to an alarming 80,000 people, and seven years later, the number declined to 50,000 (if it occurs to Sarah Lyman that she and her fellow missionaries are responsible for some of this decimation, she does not note it). In the last decades of the nineteenth century, the *kanaka maoli*, or native population, fell to 40,000 people, the first time that native Hawaiians were a minority in their own country. The missionary George Kenway, stationed in Waimea on the island of Hawai'i, wrote:

> The hill sides and the banks of watercourses show for miles the ruins of the "olden time"—Stone walls half sunk in the ground, broken down and covered with grass.—large broken squares of trees and imperfect embankments.—remains of old taro patches and water runs now dried up and useless, and many other such tokens that . . . impress one with a melancholy curiosity about a people that cannot now be found.

Although profound disruption and loss had not been the intention of the missionaries, they achieved in many instances what they had come to do, that is, to make the Hawaiians accept the social, religious, political, and legal institutions of the West. (Mark Twain described the missionaries as "pious; hard-working; hard-praying; self-sacrificing; hospitable; devoted to the well-being of this people and the interests of Protestantism; bigoted; puritanical; slow; [and] ignorant of all white human nature and natural ways of men.") David Malo is said to have prophesied in the nineteenth century: "These people [the missionaries] are going to rebel; not they themselves, but their children and grandchildren. The ruler at that time will be stripped of power, and the government established then will be the permanent government of Hawai'i." Out of 4,000 court convictions in 1874 (presumably most of them native Hawaiians), 10 were for performing the *hula*; 348 for the violation of the marriage tie; 67 for desertion; 61 for violating the Sabbath; 674 for drunkenness; 197 for "furious riding"; 37 for cruelty to animals; and 13 for murder. Apart from murder, all of these convictions are for acts that would not have been considered criminal were it not for the missionaries.

The lives and thoughts of the missionaries are accessible to us through their journals and letters, which are suffused with piety and instruction. Now and again, a hint of confusion and estrangement appears, along with an occasional note of frustration—a moment's revelation, followed by remorse and guilt, but nothing more. A few of them would be enthralled by island life and the Hawaiian people, and stay long after they had fulfilled their mission; others left as soon as they could, and some even before their time of service was complete. Their descendants, however, prospered in ways unimaginable to their forebears. Hiram Bingham's great-grandson, Hiram Bingham III, married the granddaughter of Charles L. Tiffany, the founder of Tiffany & Co. in New York, and later discovered Machu Picchu. The lawyer Lorrin A. Thurston, a member of the legislature instrumental in the overthrow of the monarchy, and grandson of Asa and Lucy Thurston, attended Punahou School and law school at Columbia University (Thurston referred to himself and his friends as the "mission boys"). Sanford B. Dole, the son of Daniel Dole of the Ninth Company, and whose cousin James started the Hawaiian Pineapple Company, became the first president of the Republic of Hawai'i. Other descendants of missionary families were the founders, owners, and presidents of Hawai'i's sugar plantations, cattle ranches, mercantile concerns, banks, shipping lines, railroads, gas and electric companies, and communications and rapid transit companies, among many other interests—men named Castle, Alexander, Cooke, Baldwin, Smith, Judd, Hall, Bishop, Chamberlain, Spaulding, Rowell, Emerson, Kinney, Alexander, Dillingham, Damon, Rice, Shipman, Thurston, and Wilcox.

The task of understanding the past is never-ending. It is impossible not to feel at times ambivalent, and to resist the ease of disapproval, if not condemnation of foreign interference when reading Hawaiian history. It will be the obvious view of most readers that the Hawaiians should have been left to work out their own history. Although it has become useful for scholars and writers to blame the influence of foreigners, particularly the missionaries, for the near annihilation of the Hawaiian race, it is impossible to exempt the *aliʻi* from hastening its decline. Putting aside the inexorability of historical determinism, it is too easy to fault foreigners for the dissolution and eventual collapse of the Hawaiian monarchy, too simplistic to decry the acquisitive traders and shopkeepers who followed the ships, or the native chiefs who lost their kingdom through negligence and misrule. "The gods did not die: slowly they withdrew from the people, who no longer honored them."

The reworking of oral, that is, mythological history is often used as a means to justify and support contemporary political positions. An example of the tendency in the writing of contemporary historians to revise the past so as to exempt Hawaiians from any responsibility may be found in Malcolm Chun's book of Hawaiian beliefs and practices, *No Na Mamo* (2011). Chun uses a version of the legend of Kamehameha and the Law of the Splintered Paddle, written by the Hilo minister Stephen Desha in *Kamehameha and His Warriors*, to illustrate the way in which Hawaiian history is distorted by writers who revere without qualification the memory of Kamehameha I. In Desha's telling, Kamehameha chances upon the fishermen, rather than hunting them to use as sacrifices. Desha writes from Kamehameha's point of view: "We entered there because we saw some fisher-folk mending their nets. However, the remarkable thing was that when they saw us they ran away. I attempted to call to them, but they would not listen and only increased their speed." Chun points out, as another example, that it is seldom mentioned that the *kapu* placed by Kamehameha on the cattle given him by Vancouver was to blame for much of the destruction of native flora. Nor is it commonly conceded that the rapacity of the chiefs for the profits from the sale of sandalwood resulted not only in the loss of forests but also in the psychological and physical decline, if not the death, of native Hawaiians.

When the cabinet minister William N. Armstrong, who accompanied David Kalākaua on a trip around the world in 1881, warned him that the future of the Hawaiian people was in danger, Kalākaua insisted that his people were happy enough—there was food, their small *kuleana* (homesteads) supported them, and no one robbed them. "If they are [dying out], I've read lots of times that great races died out, and new ones took their places; my people are like the rest. I think the best thing is to let us be." They were not left to themselves, as both the king and Armstrong must have foreseen, and they did begin to disappear. There is no little irony in recognizing that the speed with which this occurred—a short 120 years from the arrival of Captain

Cook in 1777 to the annexation of the Islands in 1898 by the United States—serves as testimony to the generosity of spirit, patience, and adaptability of the Hawaiians themselves. In their grace lay their defeat.

The mythic navigator, Ka'uluakalana, is said to have composed this chant, only a fragment of which has been preserved, when he first landed in the Islands in the eleventh century A.D.:

> Falling are the heavens, rushing through the heavens
> Falls the dismal rain, rushing through the heavens
> Falls the heavy rain, rushing through the heavens
> Falls the gentle rain, rushing through the heavens
> Soars the dragonfly, rushing through the heavens,
> Passed away has this one to Moanawaikaioo.
> The strong current, the rolling current, whirl away,
> It will be overcome by you,—
> Passing perhaps, remaining perhaps.

The history of Hawai'i may be seen as a story of arrivals—from the first hardy seeds and insects that found their way to the Islands and the confused birds blown from their customary migratory routes, to the early Polynesian adventurers who sailed across the Pacific in double canoes and the Spanish galleons en route to the Philippines and the navigators in search of a Northwest Passage, followed by pious missionaries, whalers from New England, shipwrecked sailors, and rowdy Irish poachers escaped from Botany Bay—all wanderers washed ashore, sometimes by accident. This is true of many cultures, but in Hawai'i, no one seems to have left, although flora and fauna have become extinct (and continue to do so with alarming regularity), and the Hawaiian people, thanks to the introduction of diseases to which they had no immunity, and an encompassing melancholia that overtook them with the loss of their culture, came close to disappearing as a race. Today, native Hawaiians are a minority of the population, and intermarriage has resulted in a high percentage of people of mixed heritage (some sociologists attribute the continuation of the race to this), but they have survived. In 2014, the population of the state of Hawai'i was estimated to be 1,419,561; the nationwide population of native Hawaiians in 2013 was 89,704.

A closed and isolated culture, bound by superstition and religious ritual, with no understanding of individual freedom or private property, Hawai'i was transformed in little more than one hundred years into a society of thriving capitalism, Protestant values, and democratic institutions. Captain Cook first sighted the island of Kaua'i in 1777; the last human sacrifice was held at Papa'ena'ena *heiau* in 1819, on the side of Diamond Head, a few steps from what are now Kapi'olani Park and the hotels of Waikīkī Beach; the missionaries from New England arrived in 1820; a written language was introduced in 1822; the last king in the Kamehameha dynasty of high chiefs died in 1872; and the United States annexed the Islands in 1898, with little resistance from the Hawaiians, and little effort by the acquisitive Americans who had for years tirelessly sought such a treaty.

Pālea, a Hawaiian chanter from Ka'ū who was born in 1852, composed this chant after he and his wife came upon a mirror for the first time. It is called "Piano Ahiahi," or "Piano at Evening" (the native land shell is now an endangered species):

O Piano I heard at evening,
where are you?
Your music haunts me far into the night
like the voice of land shells
trilling sweetly
near the break of day.
I remember when my dear and I
visited aboard the *Nautilus*
and saw our first looking glass.
I remember the upland of Ma'eli'eli
where the mists creeping in and out
threaded their way between the old
houses of thatch.
Again I chant my refrain
of long ago and a piano singing
far into the night.

Notes

This Realm of Chaos and Old Night

4 "Indeed it is hypothesized . . .": Sohmer and Gustafson, *Plants and Flowers of Hawaii*, p. 21.

4 "Born was the earth . . .": Pukui and Korn, *The Echo of Our Song*, p. 20.

7 "Only the sea was treacherous . . .": Bushnell, *The Gifts of Civilization*, p. 9.

12 "Those first Hawaiians . . .": Ibid., p. 9.

13 " 'The forty thousand little gods' . . .": Ibid., p. 8.

22 "My royal guest . . .": Boelen, *A Merchant's Perspective*, p. 52.

Awe of the Night Approaching

31 "The . . . tabu were strictly enforced": Ellis, *Journal of William Ellis*, p. 293.

34 "Fear falls upon me on the mountain top . . .": Beckwith, *The Kumulipo*, p. 92.

39 "If any one did, they killed him": Malo, *Hawaiian Antiquities*, p. 186.

40 "What is my great offence . . .": Handy, *Polynesian Religion*, p. 242.

43 "When I was a little girl . . .": Pukui, *Nānā I Ke Kumu*, vol. 1, p. 28.

44 "This is a death I inflict . . .": Kamakau, *Ka Po'e Kahiko*, p. 125.

44 "What is the food it is calling for?": Ibid., pp. 125–26.

45 "Choke and live . . .": Ibid., p. 128.

46 "There were in old days . . .": Kamakau, *Ruling Chiefs of Hawaii*, p. 214.

46 "You are a hawk, I am a hawk . . .": Pukui, *'Ōlelo No'eau*, p. 72.

The Source of the Darkness That Made Darkness

50 "with accuracy the Situation . . .": "Secret Instructions for Lieutenant James Cook Appointed to Command His Majesty's Bark the Endeavour 30 July, 1768" (Sydney: National Library of Australia), NLA: MS 2.

54 "Above, below; seaward, inland . . .": Pukui, *'Ōlelo No'eau*, p. 273.

55 "Three things made them our fast friends . . .": James Cook, *The Three Voyages of Captain James Cook around the World*, vol. 3, p. 335.

57 " 'The god enters, man cannot enter in' . . .": Bushnell, *The Gifts of Civilization*, p. 133.

59 "Nip off the bud of the poison gourd": Pukui, *'Ōlelo No'eau*, p. 32.

59 "A numerous guard had been set . . .": Kamakau, *Ruling Chiefs of Hawaii*, p. 67.

61 "Thus beautiful physiques . . .": 'Ī'ī, *Fragments of Hawaiian History*, p. 7.

62 "Though they seem . . .": Handy, *Ancient Hawaiian Civilization*, p. 75.

76 "You are a white-finned shark . . .": Pukui and Korn, *The Echo of Our Song*, p. 3.

79 "When you go from here . . .": Pukui, *'Ōlelo No'eau*, p. 81.

80 "The whole land belongs to the chief . . .": Fornander, *Fornander Collection of Hawaiian Antiquities*, p. 375.

The Cloak of Bird Feathers

89 "the head-covering over the land, my beloved": Pukui, *'Ōlelo No'eau*, p. 286.

102 "We are sorry for . . .": 'Ī'ī, *Fragments of Hawaiian History*, p. 18.

103 "The chiefess gave birth . . .": Pukui and Korn, *The Echo of Our Song*, p. 20.

103 "The husband is the one beloved . . .": Kamakau, *Ruling Chiefs of Hawaii*, p. 316.

104 "She swam out to sea . . .": Pukui, *'Ōlelo No'eau*, p. 218.

110 "It was a very virulent pestilence": Kamakau, *Ruling Chiefs of Hawaii*, p. 189.

110 "Like a peal of thunder is your tread . . .": Ibid., p. 316.

111 "Six of Kamehameha's islands . . .": Pukui, *'Ōlelo No'eau*, p. 81.

112 "My mother in the house well-peopled . . .": Kamakau, *Ruling Chiefs of Hawaii*, p. 317.

119 " 'We are all here, your younger brothers . . .": Pukui, *'Ōlelo No'eau*, p. 43.

119 "This body is not ours . . .": Kamakau, *Ruling Chiefs of Hawaii*, p. 212.

120 "Here is the food offered . . .": Ibid., p. 213.

123 "Your grandfather . . .": Ibid., p. 224.

125 "Place a shield of ti leaves . . .": Pukui, *'Ōlelo No'eau*, p. 45.

127–128 "Because of that loss . . .": Bushnell, *The Gifts of Civilization*, p. 242.

130 "Now as he comes along . . .": Zwiep, *Pilgrim Path*, p. 59.

131 "a victim of the 'Hoodoo' . . .": Wetmore, *Sounds from Home*, p. 106.

One Great Caravanserai

137 "The Sandwich Islands became one great caravanserai . . .": Bushnell, *The Gifts of Civilization*, p. 160.

139 "At noon a single proa . . .": Arago, *Narrative of a Voyage*, p. 59.

A Pilgrim and a Stranger

149 "5:00 private devotion and sewing . . .": Hiram Bingham, Asa Thurston, Elisha Loomis, et al., "*Thaddeus* Journal, Journal of the Sandwich Islands Mission, 1819–1825," holograph and typescript (Honolulu: Hawaiian Mission Children's Society, November 19, 1819), in Zwiep, *Pilgrim Path*, pp. 49–50.

152 "The appearance of destitution ...": Bingham, *A Residence of Twenty-One Years in the Sandwich Islands*, p. 81.

152 "Crowds gathered ...": Kamakau, *Ruling Chiefs of Hawaii*, p. 247.

157 "Head of the Church Triumphant ...": Bingham, *Twenty-One Years*, p. 82.

162 "Before I was aware ...": Thurston, *Life and Times*, p. 50.

163 "Four hundred and seventy-five souls ...": Ibid., p. 30.

164 "An improvement of window frames ...": Ibid., p. 55.

165 "It looks neither like myself nor any other man": Ibid., p. 36.

166 "The consummate profligacy of attempting to dance ...": Steegmuller, *James Jackson Jarves*, p. 19.

174 "In the presence of them and their wives ...": Thurston, *Life and Times*, p. 216.

176 Before the funeral ...: Kamakau, *Ruling Chiefs of Hawaii*, p. 254.

182 "His guards assembled ...": *Missionary Herald*, p. 183.

182 "Spontaneous was your love ...": *Missionary Herald*, p. 317.

183 "I am going to a distant land ...": Ellis, *Journal of William Ellis*, p. 342.

183 "They have long despised us": Zwiep, *Pilgrim Path*, p. 213.

183 "the posse of Longnecks ...": Judd, *Honolulu*, p. 31.

185 "After dinner ...": Ibid., p. 6.

186 "During the night ...": Thurston, *Life and Times*, p. 75.

187 "Our old people tell us ...": Ibid., p. 83.

188 "There is no entrance to the yard ...": Ibid., p. 102.

190 "No one of us had conceived ...": Ibid., p. 209.

198 "Poor creatures ...": Sarah Lyman, *Her Own Story*, pp. 28, 45.

199 "low in mental culture": Daws, *Shoal of Time*, p. 241.

203 "the climax of queer sensations": Mellen, *The Magnificent Matriarch*, p. 53.

A Light to My Path

207 "rise together ...": Stewart, *Journal of a Residence*, p. 216.

207 "basking in the noonday tropical sun ...": *Memoirs of the Bernice Pauahi Bishop Museum*, vol. 7, no. 1, p. 50.

207–208 "She prefers to go before ...": Silverman, *Ka'ahumanu*, p. 92.

209 "I am making myself strong ...": Bingham, *Twenty-One Years*, p. 214.

213 "instantly put it on ...": Byron, *Voyage of H.M.S. Blonde*, p. 117.

216 "The procession consisted ...": Stewart, *Journal of a Residence*, p. 146.

216 "The arbitrary will of Kaahumanu ...": Baxley, *What I Saw*, p. 569.

217 "One day my thoughts ...": Marjorie Sinclair, *Nāhi'ena'ena*, p. 122.

219 "haughty, assuming ...": Ibid., p. 96.

221 "As we were seated at our sewing ...": Judd, *Honolulu*, p. 40.

222 "We were all in thick darkness ...": Silverman, *Ka'ahumanu*, p. 91.

222 "The axe is at the trunk ...": Kamakau, *Ruling Chiefs*, p. 322.

223 "Their [whaling] voyages ...": Simpson, *The Sandwich Islands*, p. 42.

226 "If an insolent courtier . . .": Malo, *Hawaiian Antiquities*, p. 84.

229 "Do sit down; you are very tired . . .": Judd, *Honolulu*, p. 71.

230 "O, my friends, have great patience . . .": Silverman, *Ka'ahumanu*, p. 145.

232 "This article, nine yards long . . .": Stewart, *Journal of a Residence*, p. 343.

234 "The surveyors' native helpers . . .": Daws, *Shoal of Time*, p. 127.

Crucified to the World

239 "After Kala'au Point is passed . . .": Pukui, *'Ōlelo No'eau*, p. 13.

Falling Are the Heavens

242 "By the end of the sixties . . .": Daws, *Shoal of Time*, p. 163.

244 "I loved you once . . .": Pukui and Korn, *The Echo of Our Song*, p. 94.

245 "White men were not used . . .": Daws, *Shoal of Time*, p. 193.

The Voice of Land Shells

256 "The dead were stacked up . . .": Kamakau, *Ruling Chiefs of Hawaii*, pp. 416–17.

256 "Never again would we look . . .": Pukui and Korn, *The Echo of Our Song*, p. 125.

257 "The hill sides . . .": Daws, *Shoal of Time*, pp. 168–69.

259 "The gods did not die . . .": Bushnell, *The Gifts of Civilization*, p. 153.

259 "If they are [dying out] . . .": Armstrong, *Around the World with a King*, p. 276.

260 "Falling are the heavens . . .": Fornander, *An Account of the Polynesian Race*, p. 15.

261 "O Piano I heard at evening . . .": Pukui and Korn, *The Echo of Our Song*, p. 106.

Glossary

The first known glossary of Hawaiian words is found in Captain James Cook's *A Voyage to the Pacific Ocean*, vol. 3, written in 1778. Two hundred and fifty words are listed, using an English orthography—*oo* for *u*, *ai* for *y*. There have been numerous other lists—one assembled by Archibald Menzies in 1792 and another by Jacques Arago in 1819—but it was not until 1829 that the missionaries decided by vote to codify a Hawaiian alphabet containing six vowels and seven consonants (*h*, *k*, *l*, *m*, *n*, *p*, and *w*), although there are five vowels and eight consonants in modern usage.

There are two diacritical markings: the *'okina*, which represents a glottal stop, and the *kahako*, a macron which lengthens and adds stress to a vowel, but both are of modern use, and do not appear in early spellings.

In words of two syllables, the accent is on the first syllable (there are exceptions, of course, as in the words *makai* and *kapu*). The accent is on all vowels marked with macrons, or on the next-to-last syllable, or alternating preceding syllables. In general, the stress is on the second-to-last syllable. After the letters *i* and *e*, *w* is pronounced like *v*; after *a*, like *v* or *w*.

An *'okina* is used to indicate a separation in the pronunciation of vowels, with a sound like the English *oh-oh*.

Diacritical markings serve to indicate not just pronunciation but also the meaning of the word: *ala* means road or path; *'ala* means fragrant; *'alā* means basaltic rock. Words often have various meanings, many of them metaphoric. For example, the word *'a'ā* may mean rough lava, or the verb to burn. Mary Kawena Pukui's spelling of Hawaiian words is used throughout the book.

I have used the word "marriage" to describe the conjugal relationships of Hawaiians living before the advent of Christianity, although the word is clearly anachronistic in this context, and does not describe the actual nature of their domestic or sexual arrangements.

'a'ā (ah-ah): rough, jagged lava

ahupua'a (ah-hoo-poo-ah-ah): a pie-shaped division of land, usually from the uplands to the ocean; thus named because the boundary was indicated by a pile (*ahu*) of stones onto which tribute of a pig (*pua'a*) was placed as a levy paid to the landowner *aikāne* (eye-ka-nay): friend, to become a friend; *moe aīkāne* is to commit sodomy; lit., friend mating

'aina (eye-na): land, earth

'ai noa (eye-no-ah): to eat without the restriction of *kapu*; men and women eating together; lit., free eating

akua (ah-koo-ah): god or goddess; spirit or ghost; devil

ali'i (ah-lee-ee): royal, noble; a chief or chiefess

ali'i nui (ah-lee-ee new-ee): king or supreme chief

'anā 'anā (ah-na-ah-na): evil sorcery, black magic through prayer and incantation; the practice of sorcery

'anu'u (ah-noo-oo): wooden oracle tower built on a *heiau* and covered in *kapa* or feathers from which the king or priests made pronouncements in the name of the gods

'aumakua (ow-ma-koo-a): family or personal god; revered spirit guide and protector

'awa (ah-va): *Piper methysticum*, shrub native to the Pacific, the root of which is the source of a mild narcotic drink

'Āwini (ah-vee-nee): remote valley where Kamehameha I was hidden as a child

'ehu (ay-hoo): red-haired Polynesian; said to be the mark of a guardian (*kahu*) of Pele

hala (ha-la): *Pandanus odoratissimus*; its leaves were used to weave mats and sails

haole (how-lee): white person; foreigner

hapa (ha-pa): portion or fragment; half

heiau (hay-ow): pre-Christian temple or place of worship; often a rectangle or parallelogram with constructed stone platforms and terraces; images of the gods and bones of dead chiefs were kept in thatched structures on the *heiau*

Hikiau (he-kee-ow): *heiau* sacred to the god Kū at Kealakekua Bay where human sacrifice was performed; visited by Cook and his officers

hōlua (ho-loo-a): wooden sled used by chiefs for racing downhill

Hualālai (hoo-ah-la-lye): shield (built over time by successive flows of lava) volcano of 8,271 feet in North Kona, last erupted in 1801

Kahiki (ka-hee-kee): an unspecified foreign land in Polynesia

kāhili (ka-hee-lee): feather staff which was a symbol of royalty

Kaho'olawe (ka-ho-oh-la-vay): "Carrying Away by Currents"; presently uninhabited island of 45 square miles, 11 miles long, 6 miles wide; 7 miles southwest of Maui; traditionally known as the home of the god Kanaloa; used by the U.S. Navy for target practice from 1920 to 1990

kahu (ka-hoo): honored attendant, guardian, nurse, keeper; pastor of a church

kahuna (ka-hoo-na): priest, sorcerer, magician

kalo (ka-low): also taro, *Colocasia esculenta*, a tuber spread widely through Polynesia; *poi* is made from the root

kama'āina (ka-ma-eye-na): native-born; acquainted, familiar

kāne (ka-nay): male; husband; brother-in-law

kaona (ka-own-a): hidden meaning; veiled language; concealed reference, often sexual

kapa (ka-pa): also *tapa*, cloth made from *wauke* or *māmaki* bark and used for mats and clothing, and in sacred ritual *kapu* (ka-poo): taboo, forbidden, sacred; privilege; exemption

Kawaihae (ka-why-high): "the Water of Wrath"; harbor and village on the dry Kohala coast; home to John Young and the royal compound named Pelekane; site of Puʻukoholā, war *heiau* of Kamehameha I

kī (key): also *ti, Cordyline terminalis*, upright evergreen shrub used for thatching, food wrappers, *hula* skirts, sandals; alcohol is distilled from the roots

kihei (key-hay): a short cape, sometimes made of feathers, reaching the middle of the breast

Kīlauea (kill-oh-ay-a): "Much Spewing"; active shield volcano of 4,190 feet, in eruption since 1983; home of the fire goddess Pele

koa (ko-a): *Acacia koa*, large hardwood forest tree used for making canoes, surfboards, paddles, calabashes, furniture, and roof posts

kōnane (ko-na-nay): ancient game resembling checkers, played with pebbles placed in even lines on a stone or wooden board

kukui (koo-koo-ee): *Aleurites moluccana*, candlenut tree; the oily kernels were used for illumination, the nuts were eaten in a relish, the wood was used to make canoes, the gum to stain *kapa*; now the source for the polished black nuts worn as *leis*

kuleana (koo-lee-ah-na): right, title; property; responsibility; jurisdiction; authority

kumulipo (koo-moo-lee-po): source of life, name of the Hawaiian creation chant

Lānaʻi (la-nah-ee): "Day Conquest"; island of 140 square miles; 13 miles long; 13 miles wide; formerly used in growing pineapple; 98 percent of island bought in 2013 by Larry Ellison

Laniākea (la-nee-ah-kay-ah): "Wide Sky"; large cave on property of Asa and Lucy Thurston in Kailua which gave its name to their compound

lapaʻau (la-pa-ow): medical practice; healing

lau hala (lao-ha-la): pandanus leaf used to make mats, fans, and sails

lele (lay-lay): to fly; jump; leap

luakini (loo-a-key-nee): war *heiau* of a ruling chief where human sacrifice was practiced

lūʻau (loo-ow): top leaves of young *kalo*; feast

luna (loo-na): high, above, over, up; an overseer

mahiole (ma-hee-oh-lay): helmet of wickerwork, often overlaid with bird feathers, fitting the head closely; its shape not unlike the helmets of ancient Greece; worn by chiefs during religious ceremonies and in battle, its colors (red, yellow, and black) indicating rank and allegiance

maikaʻi (my-ka-ee): good, well, fine; righteousness; morality

maile (my-lee): *Alyxia oliviformis*, fragrant native vine of the periwinkle family used for making long *leis*, usually open at one end

makai (ma-kai): toward the ocean

malo (ma-lo): loincloth, often made of *kapa*

mana (ma-na): supernatural or divine power; psychic influence of a person, place, or object

manō (ma-no): shark; fig., a passionate lover

mauka (mao-ka): inland; toward the mountains

Mauna Loa (mao-na loa): "Long Mountain"; active shield volcano of 13,677 feet on the island of Hawaiʻi; ancient site of adze quarries and the trees from which poison gods were made; famous for its *hōlua* slides; has erupted 33 times since 1843, most recently in 1984

Mauna Kea (mao-na kay-a): "White Mountain"; dormant volcano of 13,976 feet on the island of Hawai'i which last erupted in 2460 B.C., and is now the site of the world's largest observatory for the study of optical, infrared, and submillimeter astronomy

maunu (mao-new): bait used in fishing; objects such as spittle, excreta, clothing, nail parings, hair, and food scraps necessary for black magic

Menehune (men-ay-hoo-nay): mythical race of tiny people who worked at night to build *heiau* and fish ponds; thought by anthropologists to be original sixth-century settlers, later overrun by Tahitian settlers of the eleventh century

mō'ī (mo-ee): king or queen; supreme ruler

Moloka'i (mo-lo-ka-ee): island of 261 square miles; 38 miles long and 10 miles wide; noted for sorcery; home to the leper colony of Kalaupapa

naha (na-ha): bent, curved, arched; also *pi'o*

nī'aupi'o (nee-ow-pee-oh): offspring of a brother and sister, first cousins, or half brother and half sister; lit., of the same stalk

niho palaoa (nee-ho pa-la-oa): whale tooth pendant suspended from necklace of braided hair; sign of high rank

Ni'ihau (nee-ee-how): island of 73 square miles; 18 miles long and 6 miles wide; 17 miles west of Kaua'i; privately owned by the Robinson family, who bought it for $10,000 from Kamehameha V in 1864; there is no airport on the island, and no electricity or telephone service; only Hawaiian is spoken

'ōahi (oh-ah-hee): the hurling of wood firebrands from a mountain or cliff into the ocean, especially practiced on Kaua'i

'ōhi'a lehua (oh-hee-a lay-who-a): *Metrosideros collina*, plant of many forms from shrub to tree with red, pink, yellow, or white flowers; the flower of Hawai'i Island

oli (oh-lee): chant that is not danced

'ōlohe (oh-low-hee): bare; naked; hairless, as a dog

ono (oh-no): *Acanthocybium solandri*, large mackerel-like fish; wahoo

pāhoehoe (pa-hoy-hoy): smooth, unbroken lava

pahupū (pa-hoo-poo): severed; cut short; chopped off

palapala (pa-la-pa-la): characters used in stamping *kapa*, or in the making of petroglyphs, hence writing; document of any kind; formerly Scripture or Bible learning

pali (pa-lee): precipice; cliff in Nu'uanu Valley on O'ahu where Kamehameha I won decisive battle to unify the Islands

pā'ū (pa-ooh): woman's skirt

Pō (po): night; darkness; obscurity; the realm of the gods; hell

pololū (po-lo-loo): long spear used by elite warriors of Kamehameha I; war canoe

Puna (poo-na): district on Hawai'i Island, east of Kona and north of K'aū

pu'u (poo-oo): hill

pu'uhonua (poo-oo-ho-new-a): designated place of refuge or sanctuary for criminals and the defeated in war and their families

Pu'ukoholā (poo-oo-ko-ho-la): "Whale Hill"; Kamehameha's large *heiau* at Kawaihae, built for the war god Kūkā'ilimoku

ulua (oo-loo-a): species of crevalle, jack fish, or pompano *'ume* (oo-may): a sexual game for commoners (counterpart of *kilu*, the chiefs' version of game)

wahine (wa-hee-nay): woman; wife; sister-in-law; female of species

wiliwili (will-ee-will-ee): *Erythrina sandwicensis*, leguminous tree found on dry coral plains or lava flows, used to make chiefs' surfboards, canoe outriggers, and net floats

wohi (woe-he): high chief exempt from the prostration *kapu*; he followed the king on public occasions to ensure that others prostrated themselves

Gods and Personages

Alapaʻinui (ah-la-pa-ee-new-ee), (c. 1708–1754), ruling chief of Hawaiʻi Island, in whose court Kamehameha was raised as a boy; said to have poisoned Kamehameha's father, Keōua.

Bingham, Hiram (1789–1869), born in Bennington, Vermont; educated at Middlebury College and Andover Theological Seminary; Congregationalist minister and leader of the First Company of missionaries of the American Board of Commissioners for Foreign Missions (1820); stationed in Honolulu; teacher to Kaʻahumanu; married to Sybil Moseley; seven children born in Hawaiʻi.

Bingham, Sybil Moseley (1792–1848), born in Westfield, Massachusetts; married Hiram Bingham only months before sailing with the First Company to the Sandwich Islands; a favorite of Queen Kaʻahumanu; her journal (1819–1823) is in the Hawaiian Mission Children's Society Library in Honolulu.

Bishop, Artemas (1795–1872), born in Pompey, New York; educated at Union College and Princeton Theological Seminary; clergyman in the Second Company (1823); married to Elizabeth Edwards.

Boki (bo-kee) (c. 1785–1830), "Boat" or "Boss"; high chief and younger brother of Kalanimoku; governor of Oʻahu 1819–1829; sailed with Liholiho to England; disappeared in 1829 in the South Pacific while searching for sandalwood; married to the high chiefess Liliha.

Chamberlain, Daniel (d. 1881), born in Brookfield, Massachusetts; farmer with the First Company (1820), accompanied by five children and his wife, Jerusha Burnap; stationed in Honolulu and in Waimea, Kauaʻi.

Coan, Titus (1801–1881), born in Killingworth, Connecticut; educated at Auburn Theological Seminary, New York; arrived with the Seventh Company (1835); known for his powerful sermons and the number of converts made during the great religious revival of

1838; stationed at Hilo, where he was the first pastor of Haili Congregational Church; married to Lydia Bingham.

Ellis, William (1794–1872), English missionary of the London Missionary Society, served in Tahiti for eight years before arriving in Hawai'i in 1824.

Ellis, William (1751–1785), graduate of Cambridge University, surgeon's mate on the HMS *Discovery* on Cook's third voyage to the Pacific; under the influence of ship's artist John Webber, made sketches of the Islands that were published under the name W. W. Ellis; died in Belgium after falling from a mast.

Emerson, Nathaniel Bright (1839–1915), son of the Reverend John Emerson of the Fifth Company (1832); studied at Punahou, Williams College, Harvard Medical School, and Columbia's College of Physicians and Surgeons; practiced medicine at Bellevue Hospital in New York before returning to Hawai'i in 1878; translator and ethnographer.

Holman, Thomas (1791–1826), born in Cooperstown, New York; physician with the First Company; left the Islands in bitterness a year after his arrival; married to Lucia Ruggles; accepted free passage home in a whaling ship via China and Cape of Good Hope; Lucia became first American woman to circumnavigate the globe.

'I'i, John Papa (ee-ee) (1800–1870), historian; young attendant to Kamehameha II; author of *Fragments of Hawaiian History.*

Judd, Dr. Gerrit P. (1803–1873), born in Paris, New York; physician in the Third Company (1828); doctor to Ka'ahumanu; served in the government as minister of finance and adviser to King Kamehameha IV; accompanied Prince Alexander Liholiho and Prince Lot to France, England, and the United States; married to Laura Fish (1803–1871), whose journal was published as *Honolulu: Sketches and Times* (1880); nine children born in the Islands.

Ka'ahumanu (ka-ah-who-ma-new) (c. 1768–1832), "The Cloak of Bird Feathers"; oldest daughter of Kona high chief Ke'eaumoku and Namahana, high chiefess of Maui; favorite wife of Kamehameha I; prime minister and regent of the kingdom of Hawai'i from 1820 to her death.

Kaheiheimālie (ka-hey-ee-hey-ee-ma-lee-ay), (c. 1778–1842), also known as Kalaku; younger sister of Ka'ahumanu and one of the twenty-two wives of Kamehameha I; mother of his three surviving children, two of whom became queens to Kamehameha's son, Liholiho (Kamāmalu and Kīna'u).

Kahekili (ka-hay-kee-lee), "God of Thunder"; tattooed from head to heel on one half of his body; said to be the natural father of Kamehameha I; *ali'i nui* of Maui.

Ka'iana (ka-ee-ana), handsome chief said to be Ka'ahumanu's lover; caused a sensation in China when he visited with Captain Meares in 1788; killed in battle of Nu'uanu in 1795.

Kalākaua, David (cal-a-cow-a) (1836–1891), "The Day of Battle"; elected king in 1874 to succeed Lunalilo; married to the high chiefess Kapi'olani.

Kalanimoku (ka-la-nee-mo-koo) (1768–1827), "Island Carver"; also called Kalaimoku (head counselor); named Billy Pitt after the English statesman William Pitt; adviser to Kamehameha I; cousin to Ka'ahumanu.

Kalaniōpu'u (ka-la-nee-o-poo-oo) (c. 1729–1782), "Chief of the Whale Tooth Pendant"; *ali'i nui* of Hawai'i Island at the time of Captain Cook's arrival; father of Kiwala'ō and Keoua; uncle of Kamehameha I.

Kamakau, Samuel M. (ka-ma-cow) (1815–1876), historian and journalist; author of newspaper articles later collected in *Ruling Chiefs of Hawaii* and the three-volume ethnography *Ka Po'e Kahiko: The People of Old*.

Kamāmalu (ka-ma-ma-loo) (1802–1824), "Shade of the Lonely One"; favorite wife of Liholiho; daughter of Kamehameha I and Kaheiheimālie; niece of Ka'ahumanu; died of measles in London.

Kamehameha I (ka-may-ha-may-ha) (c. 1758–1819), "The Lonely One"; said by the historian Ralph Kuykendall to be one of the "great men of the world."

Kanaloa (ka-na-low-a); god of the sea and of healing; known as the Hot-Striking Octopus, the Enemy, or the Prince of Darkness.

Kāne (ka-nay), god of sunlight, fresh water, and forests; the Lord of Creation; brought to the Islands in the second migration of the eleventh century.

Kanihonui (ka-nee-ho-noo-ee), "Big Teeth"; young lover of Ka'ahumanu, put to death in 1819 for adultery by his uncle, Kamehameha I.

Kapi'olani (ka-pee-oh-la-nee) (c. 1780–1831), "Heavenly Arch"; high chiefess of Hawai'i Island; defied Pele at Kīlauea crater after her conversion to Christianity.

Kapuāiwa (Ka-poo-a-eva), Lot (1830–1872), Kamehameha V; became king in 1863; the last direct descendant of Kamehameha I.

Kapule (ka-poo-lay) (c. 1798–1853), "The Prayer"; beloved wife of King Kaumuali'i of Kaua'i, known for her beauty; left on Kaua'i when Kaumuali'i was kidnapped by Liholiho and forced to marry Ka'ahumanu; also named Deborah.

Kauikeaouli (cow-ee-kay-ah-oh-oo-lee) (1813–1854), Kamehameha III; second son of Kamehameha I and the royal chiefess Keōpūolani; became king in 1824 with the death of his brother in London; in love with his sister, Princess Nāhiʻenaʻena.

Kaumualiʻi (cow-moo-a-lee-ee) (1778–1824), undefeated king of Kauaʻi; kidnapped by Kamehameha II in 1822; husband of Kapule.

Kealiʻiahonui (kay-ah-lee-ee-ah-ho-noo-ee), "Chief Whose Strength Is Found Through Patience"; son and heir of Kaumualiʻi of Kauaʻi; forced to marry Kaʻahumanu along with his father in 1821; repudiated by Kaʻahumanu at the insistence of Hiram Bingham when she converted to Christianity.

Keʻeaumoku (kay-ay-oh-mo-ku) (1736–1804), "Island-Climbing Swimmer"; high chief of Kona and father of Kaʻahumanu; an early supporter and trusted adviser of Kamehameha.

Kekāuluohi (kay-ka-ulu-oh-hee), daughter of Kaheiheimālie and Kamehameha's half brother, who became wife to Kamehameha in 1809; she was later married to his son, who gave her to one of his chiefs.

Kekuaokalani (kay-koo-a-oh-ka-la-nee), high chief and cousin of Liholiho; rebelled against the abolition of *kapu*; killed in battle by Kaʻahumanu's forces in 1819.

Kekuʻiapoiwa II (kay-koo-ee-a-po-eva), daughter of the Kohala high chief Haae, niece of Kalaniōpuʻu, wife of her cousin Keōua Nui, and mother to Kamehameha.

Keōpūolani (kay-oh-poo-oh-la-nee) (c. 1778–1823), "Gathering of the Clouds of Heaven"; born on Maui; the highest-ranking chiefess in the kingdom and sacred wife of Kamehameha I; mother of Liholiho, Kauikeaouli, and Nāhiʻenaʻena; baptized a Christian on her deathbed.

Keōua Nui (kay-oh-oo-a noo-ee), "Rain Cloud"; high chief of Hawaiʻi Island; father of Kamehameha I; husband to Kekuʻiapoiwa II; half brother of Kalaniōpuʻu.

Keoua (kay-oh-oo-ah) (c. 1762–1791), "Rain Cloud of the Red Cloak"; high chief of Kaʻū; half brother of Kiwalaʻō; son of Kalaniōpuʻu; cousin of Kamehameha; murdered by Keʻeaumoku at Puʻukoholā *heiau*.

Kīnaʻu (key-nah-oo) (1805–1839), daughter of Kamehameha I and Kaheiheimālie; half sister and wife of Liholiho; mother of Victoria Kamāmalu, Kamehameha IV, and Kamehameha V; became *kuhina nui* or prime minister at death of Kaʻahumanu in 1832.

Kiwalaʻō (key-va-la-o) (c. 1760–1782), son of King Kalaniōpuʻu; cousin of Kamehameha I; killed in battle by Keʻeaumoku.

Kuakini (koo-ah-kee-nee), younger brother of Kaʻahumanu; known as John Adams; governor of Oʻahu 1820–1845; known for his charm and extravagance.

Kūkāʻilimoku (koo-ka-ee-lee-mo-koo), war god given to Kamehameha I by his uncle, Kalaniōpuʻu.

Liholiho (lee-ho-lee-ho) (1791–1824), Kamehameha II, "Great Chief with the Burning Back Taboo," as *kapu* dictated that he could not be approached from behind; son of Kamehameha I and Keōpūolani; broke the ancient system of *kapu* by eating with his mother and Kaʻahumanu in 1819; died of measles in London.

Liholiho, Alexander (1834–1863), Kamehameha IV; grandson of Kamehameha I; son of Kīnaʻu and high chief Mataio Kekūanāoʻa; husband of Emma Rooke.

Liliha (lee-lee-ha), daughter of high chief Hoapili, governor of Maui; wife of high chief Boki.

Liliʻuokalani (lee-lee-oo-oh-ka-la-nee) (1838–1917), "Smarting of the High-Born One"; last queen of Hawaiʻi; deposed in 1893.

Loomis, Elisha (1799–1836), born in Middlesex, New York; printer in the First Company; married to Maria Sartwell; printed gospels in Hawaiian; two children born in Hawaiʻi.

Lunalilo (loo-na-lee-lo), William Charles (1835–1874), "So High as to Be Lost to Sight"; succeeded Kamehameha V; grandson of a half brother of Kamehameha I; made king in 1873; died childless.

Lyman, Sarah Joiner (1806–1885), born in Royalton, Vermont; wife of Reverend David Lyman of the Fifth Company (1832); stationed in Hilo where they established the Hilo Boys' Boarding School; eight children born in Hawaiʻi.

Malo, David (ma-lo) (1793–1853), historian; contributor to Hawaiian-language newspapers; author of *Ka Moʻolelo Hawaii* (*Hawaiian Antiquities*).

Naeole (na-ay-o-lay), "Without Gasping"; chief of Kohala who saved the newborn Kamehameha from death at the hands of rival chiefs, hiding with him in the gulches of North Kohala until the boy was five years old.

Nāhiʻenaʻena (na-hee-en-ah-en-ah) (1815–1836), "Raging Fires"; daughter of Kamehameha I and Keōpūolani; sister of Liholiho and Kauikeaouli; married Kauikeaouli in 1834 and bore him a stillborn son; said to have died of a broken heart.

Namahana (na-ma-ha-na) (c. 1787–1809), high chiefess of Maui; wife of Keʻeaumoku; mother of Kaʻahumanu.

Opukaha'ia (o-poo-ka-hai-a) (1792–1818), born in Ka'ū; orphaned when his parents were killed in battle; ran away to sea at fifteen; abandoned in New Haven where he came to the attention of students and teachers at Yale and was baptized a Christian; died of typhus in Cornwall, Connecticut, while training to be a missionary to the Sandwich Islands.

Pā'ao (pa-ow), priest in the second migration of the eleventh century, said to be from Tahiti or Samoa; built Mo'okini *heiau* in North Kohala; believed to have introduced human sacrifice to the Islands.

Pele (pay-lay), tempestuous volcano goddess who lives in Kīlauea crater on Hawai'i Island.

Richards, Reverend William (1793–1847), born in Plainfield, Massachusetts; educated at Williams College and Andover Theological Seminary; member of the Second Company; stationed in Lahaina, where he was the friend and adviser of Princess Nāhi'ena'ena; married to Clarissa Lyman; translated seventeen books of the Bible into Hawaiian; left the mission in 1838 to serve as ambassador to Britain, and later as minister of public instruction; eight children born in Hawai'i.

Rooke, Emma (1838–1885), descended from a younger brother of Kamehameha I; granddaughter of John Young; adopted daughter of English businessman Thomas Rooke; made queen in 1856 with her marriage to Alexander Liholiho; widowed in 1863; campaigned unsuccessfully for the throne in 1873, losing to David Kalākaua.

Stewart, Charles S. (1798–1870), born in Flemington, New Jersey; educated at the College of New Jersey (now Princeton University) and Princeton Theological Seminary; missionary with the Second Company; stationed in Lahaina, Maui; married to Harriet Bradford Tiffany.

Stockton, Betsy (1798–1865), teacher with the Second Company; born into slavery in Princeton, New Jersey; served in Lahaina with her friends Reverend and Mrs. Charles Stewart.

Thurston, Asa (1787–1868), born in Fitchburg, Massachusetts; educated at Yale and Andover Theological Seminary; member of the First Company; married to Lucy Goodale; stationed in Kailua; five children born in Hawai'i; admired for his mellifluous pronunciation of Hawaiian.

Thurston, Lucy Goodale (1795–1868), born in Marlborough, Massachusetts; wife of Asa Thurston; stationed in Kailua; author of informative journal *Life and Times*; five children born in Hawai'i.

Bibliography

Alexander, James M. *Mission Life in Hawaii: Memoir of Rev. William P. Alexander*. Oakland, 1888.

Alexander, Mary C., William R. Castle, and C. P. Dodge. *Punahou 1841–1941*. Berkeley: University of California Press, 1941.

Alexander, W. D. *A Brief History of the Hawaiian People*. New York, 1891.

Anderson, Dr. Rufus. *The Hawaiian Islands: Their Progress and Conditions under Missionary Labors*. Boston, 1864.

Arago, Jacques. *Narrative of a Voyage Round the World*. New York: Da Capo Press, 1971.

Armstrong, Clarissa. "Letter to Reuben Chapman, April 1836." Honolulu: Hawai'i State Archives.

Armstrong, William. *Around the World with a King*. New York, 1904.

Atkinson, A. T. "Early Voyagers of the Pacific Ocean." Paper no. 4. Hawaiian Historical Society, Honolulu, 1893.

Baldwin, Dwight D. *Catalogue of Land and Freshwater Shells of the Hawaiian Islands*. Honolulu, 1893.

Ballou, Howard M., and George R. Carter. "The History of the Hawaiian Mission Press." Honolulu: Hawaiian Historical Society, 1908.

Barrere, Dorothy B. *Kamehameha in Kona: Two Documentary Studies*. Honolulu: Bishop Museum Press, 1979.

Bates, George Washington (A. Haole, pseud.). *Sandwich Island Notes*. New York, 1854.

Baxley, H. Willis. *What I Saw on the West Coast of South and North America, and at the Hawaiian Islands*. New York, 1865.

Beaglehole, John Cawte. *The Exploration of the Pacific*. Palo Alto: Stanford University Press, 1966.

Beckwith, Martha. *The Kumulipo: A Hawaiian Creation Chant*. Translation by Martha Beckwith. Chicago: University of Chicago Press, 1951.

Belcher, E. *Narrative of a Voyage Round the World*. London, 1843.

Bennett, F. D. *Narrative of a Whaling Voyage Round the Globe, 1833 to 1836*. London, 1840.

Bingham, Hiram. *A Residence of Twenty-One Years in the Sandwich Islands; of the Civil, Religious, and Political History of Those Islands*. Hartford, 1848.

Bingham, Sybil. "Journal 1792–1842." American Board of Commissioners for Foreign Missions Journals and Letters. Honolulu: Hawaiian Mission Children's Society Library.

Bird, Isabella. *Six Months in the Sandwich Islands*. Honolulu: Mutual Publishing Co., 1998.

Bishop, Sereno Edwards. *Reminiscences of Old Hawaii*. Honolulu, 1916.

Bishop Museum. *Memoirs of the Bernice Pauahi Bishop Museum of Ethnology and Natural History*, vol. 7. Honolulu, 1918.

Boelen, Jacobus. *A Merchant's Perspective: Captain Jacobus Boelen's Narrative of His Visit to Hawaii in 1828*. Translated and edited by Frank J. A. Broeze. Honolulu: Hawaiian Historical Society, 1990.

Bushnell, O. A. *The Gifts of Civilization: Germs and Genocide in Hawai'i*. Honolulu: University of Hawaii Press, 1993.

Byron, George Anson, and Richard Rowland Bloxam. *Voyage of H.M.S. Blonde to the Sandwich Islands, in the Years 1824–1825*. London, 1826.

Cahill, Emmett. *The Life and Times of John Young*. Honolulu: Island Heritage Publishing, 1999.

Campbell, Archibald. *A Voyage Round the World from 1806 to 1812*. Honolulu: University of Hawaii Press, 1967.

Chamberlain, Levi. "Journal 1822–1849." American Board of Commissioners for Foreign Missions Journals and Letters. Honolulu: Hawaiian Mission Children's Society Library.

Chan, Gaye, and Andrea Feeser. *Waikiki: A History of Forgetting and Remembering*. Honolulu: University of Hawaii Press, 2006.

Charlot, Jean. *Choris and Kamehameha*. Honolulu: Bishop Museum Press, 1958.

Cheever, The Rev. Henry T. *Life in the Sandwich Islands*. New York, 1851.

Chillingworth, William S. *'Io Lani: The Hawaiian Hawk*. Hong Kong: W. S. Chillingworth, 2014.

Chun, Malcolm. *No Na Mamo: Traditional and Contemporary Hawaiian Beliefs and Practices*. Honolulu: University of Hawaii Press, 2011.

Coan, Titus. *Life in Hawaii*. New York, 1882.

Colnett, James. "The Journal of Captain James Colnett Aboard the *Prince of Wales* & *Princess Royal* from 16 October 1786 to 7 November 1788," vol. 1. Typewritten manuscript in Hamilton Library, University of Hawai'i.

Cook, James. *The Journals of Captain Cook*. Abridged edition. Edited by John Cawte Beaglehole. London: Penguin Classics, 2000.

Corley, J. Susan. "The British Press Greets the King of the Sandwich Islands: Kamehameha II, in London, 1824." *Hawaiian Journal of History* 42, 2008.

Corney, Peter. *Voyages in the Northern Pacific*. Honolulu, 1896.

Creighton, Margaret S. *Rites and Passages: The Experience of American Whaling, 1830–1870*. Cambridge: Cambridge University Press, 1995.

Damon, Ethel. *Father Bond of Kohala*. Honolulu: The Friend, 1927.

Dana, J. D. *United States Exploring Expedition during the Years 1838, 1839, 1840*. New York, 1849.

Darwin, Charles. *More Letters of Charles Darwin: A Record of His Work in a Series of Hitherto Unpublished Letters*, vol. 1. London, 1903.

Daws, Gavan. *Shoal of Time*. Honolulu: University of Hawaii Press, 1974.

Diamond, Jared. *Collapse*. New York: Penguin, 2005.

Dibble, Sheldon. *History of the Sandwich Islands*. Honolulu, 1909.

Duhaut-Cilly, Auguste Bernard. *Voyage autour du Monde, principalement à la Californie et aux Îles Sandwich, pendant les années 1826, 1827, 1828, et 1829*. 2 vols. Paris: 1833–35. Translated by Alfons L. Korns, *Hawaiian Journal of History* 17, 1983.

Elbert, Samuel H., and Noelani Mahoe. *Nā Mele o Hawai'i Nei: 101 Hawaiian Songs*. Honolulu: University of Hawaii Press, 1970.

Eliade, Mircea. *Myth and Reality*. New York: Harper Torchbooks, 1963.

Ellis, William. *Journal of William Ellis*. Honolulu: The Honolulu Advertiser, 1963.

Emerson, Nathaniel B. *Unwritten Literature of Hawaii: The Sacred Songs of the Hula*. Project Gutenberg edition, January 6, 2007.

———. "The Long Voyages of the Ancient Hawaiians." Paper no. 5. Hawaiian Historical Society, Honolulu, 1893.

Eveleth, Ephraim. *History of the Sandwich Islands, with an Account of the American Mission Established There in 1820*. Philadelphia, 1831.

Fawcett, Derby. *Secrets of Diamond Head: A History and Trail Guide*. Honolulu: University of Hawaii Press, 2014.

Forbes, David W. *Encounters with Paradise: Views of Hawaii and Its People, 1778–1941*. Honolulu: Honolulu Academy of Art, 1992.

Fornander, Abraham. Translations and annotations by Thomas G. Thrum. *Fornander Collection of Hawaiian Antiquities and Folk-lore*. 3 vols. Honolulu: Bishop Museum Press, 1999.

———. *An Account of the Polynesian Race*. Berkeley, 1890.

Frear, Walter F. *Anti-Missionary Criticism*. Honolulu: Advertiser Publishing Co., 1935.

Freycinet, Louis Claude de Saulces de. *Hawaii in 1819: A Narrative Account*. Translated by Ella L. Wiswell. Edited by Marion Kelly. Honolulu: Bishop Museum Press, 1978.

Freycinet, Rose Marie Pinon. *A Woman of Courage: The Journal of Rose de Freycinet on Her Voyage Around the World, 1817–1820*. Translated by Marc Serge Rivière. Sydney: National Library of Australia, 2003.

Gast, Ross H. *Don Francisco de Paula Marin*. Edited by Agnes C. Conrad. Honolulu: Hawaiian Historical Society, 1973.

Gavalek, Fern. "Uncle Billy Paris Talks Story," *Ke Ola*, July–August 2013.

Golovnin, V. M. *Around the World on the Kamchatka, 1817–1819*. Translated by Ella Lury Wiswell. Honolulu: Hawaiian Historical Society and University of Hawaii Press, 1979.

Grimshaw, Patricia. *Paths of Duty: American Missionary Wives in Nineteenth-Century Hawaii*. Honolulu: University of Hawaii Press, 1989.

Gulick, Orramel Hinckley, and Ann Eliza Gulick. *The Pilgrims of Hawaii: Their Own Story of Their Pilgrimage from New England and Life Work in the Sandwich Islands, Now Known as Hawaii*. New York: 1918.

Handy, E. S. Craighill. "Polynesian Religions." Bishop Museum, Bulletin 34, no. 12. Honolulu, 1927.

Handy, E. S. Craighill, Elizabeth Handy, and Mary Kawena Pukui. *Native Planters in Old Hawaii: Their Life, Lore, and Environment*. Honolulu: Bishop Museum Press, 1972.

Handy, E. S. Craighill, and Mary Kawena Pukui. *The Polynesian Family System in Kaʻu, Hawaii*. Vermont: Charles E. Tuttle Co., 1972.

Handy, E. S. Craighill, and others. *Ancient Hawaiian Civilization*. Edited by Helen Pratt. Honolulu: Kamehameha School Press, 1933.

Hillebrand, William. *Flora of the Hawaiian Islands*. London, 1888.

Hiroa, Te Rangi (Peter H. Buck). *Arts and Crafts of Hawaii: Clothing*, vol. 5. Honolulu: Bishop Museum Press, 1964.

———. (as Sir Peter Buck). *Vikings of the Sunrise*. New York: Frederick A. Stokes Co., 1938.

Hitchcock, C. H. *Hawaii and Its Volcanoes*. Honolulu, 1911.

Holman, Lucia Ruggles. "A Journal of the Wife of the First Medical Missionary to Hawaii, 1819–1821." Honolulu: Bishop Museum Special Publication XVII, 1931.

Holt, John Dominis. *Monarchy in Hawaii*. Honolulu: Ku Paʻa Publishing, 1995.

Hommon, Robert J. *The Ancient Hawaiian State: Origins of a Political Society*. London: Oxford University Press, 2013.

Hopkins, Manley. *Hawaii: The Past, Present and Future of Its Island-Kingdom*. New York, 1869.

Howarth, F. G., and W. P. Mull. *Hawaiian Insects and Their Kin*. Honolulu: University of Hawaii Press, 1992.

ʻĪʻī, John Papa. *Fragments of Hawaiian History*. Translated by Mary Kawena Pukui. Honolulu: Bishop Museum Press, 1959.

Instructions of the Prudential Committee of the American Board of Commissioners for Foreign Missions to the Sandwich Islands Mission (Lahainaluna, 1838). New York: Ulan Press edition, 2012.

Jarves, James J. *Scenes and Scenery in the Sandwich Islands*. Boston, 1844.

Johnson, Rubellite Kawena, and John Kapio Mahelona. *Nā Inoa Hōkū: A Catalogue of Hawaiian and Pacific Star Names*. Honolulu: Topgallant Publishing Co., 1975.

Jones, Stella M. "Economic Adjustment of Hawaiians to European Culture." *Pacific Affairs* 4, no. 11, 1931.

Judd, Laura Fish. *Honolulu: Sketches of Life in the Hawaiian Islands*. Honolulu: Star Bulletin Press, 1928.

Kamakau, Samuel Manaiakalani. *Ka Poʻe Kahiko: The People of Old*. Edited by Dorothy B. Barrere. Translated by Mary Kawena Pukui. Honolulu: Bishop Museum Press, 1991.

———. *Ruling Chiefs of Hawaii*. Translated by Mary Kawena Pukui et al. Honolulu: Kamehameha Schools Press, 1992.

Kepelino. *Kepelino's Traditions of Hawaii*. Edited by Martha Warren Beckwith. Honolulu: Bishop Museum Press, 1932.

King, James. *A Voyage to the Pacific Ocean*, vol. 3. London, 1785.

Kirch, Patrick Vinton. *Feathered Gods and Fishhooks: An Introduction to Hawaiian Archaeology and Prehistory*. Honolulu: Kamehameha Schools Press, 1985.

Kirch, Patrick Vinton, and Marshall Sahlins. "Anahulu: The Anthropology of History in the Kingdom of Hawaii." *Historical Ethnography*, vol. 1. Chicago: University of Chicago Press, 1992.

Kono, Hideto, and Kazuko Sinoto. "Observations of the First Japanese to Land in Hawaii." *Hawaiian Journal of History* 34, 2000.

Kotzebue, Otto von. *Voyage of Discovery*, vol. 2. London, 1830.

Kuykendall, Ralph S. *The Hawaiian Kingdom, Vol. 1. 1778–1854: Foundation and Transformation.* Honolulu: University of Hawaii Press, 1968.

Langsdorff, G. H. von. *Voyages and Travels in Various Parts of the World, During the Years 1803–1807.* London, 1814.

Ledyard, John. *Journal of Captain Cook's Last Voyage.* Edited by James Kenneth Mumford. Corvallis: Oregon State University Press, 1963.

Liholiho, Alexander. *The Journal of Prince Alexander Liholiho.* Honolulu: Hawaiian Historical Society, 1967.

Lili'uokalani. *Hawaii's Story by Hawaii's Queen.* Vermont: Charles E. Tuttle Co., 1964.

Linnekin, Jocelyn. *Sacred Queens and Women of Consequence: Rank, Gender and Colonialism in the Hawaiian Islands.* Ann Arbor: University of Michigan Press, 1990.

Loomis, Albertine. *Grapes of Canaan: Hawaii 1820.* Honolulu: Hawaiian Mission Children's Society, 1972.

Luomala, Katharine. *Voices on the Wind: Polynesian Myths and Chants.* Honolulu: Bishop Museum Press, 1951.

Lydgate, J. M. "The Endemic Character of the Hawaiian Flora." *Thrum's Hawaiian Annual*, Honolulu, 1910.

Lyman, Henry M. *Hawaiian Yesterdays: Chapters from a Boy's Life in the Islands in the Early Days.* Chicago, 1906.

Lyman, Sarah Joiner. *Her Own Story.* Hilo: Lyman House Memorial Museum, 1970.

Lyons, Curtis J., W. D. Alexander, J. F. Brown, et al. *History of Hawaiian Government Survey.* Honolulu, 1902.

Macdonald, G. A., A. T. Abbott, and F. L. Peterson. *Volcanoes in the Sea.* Honolulu: University of Hawaii Press, 1983.

Macrae, James. *With Lord Byron at the Sandwich Islands in 1825, Being Extracts from the Diary of James Macrae, Scottish Botanist.* Edited by W. F. Wilson. Hilo: The Petroglyph Press, 1972.

Malo, David. *Hawaiian Antiquities.* Translated by Nathaniel B. Emerson. Honolulu: Bishop Museum Press, 1987.

Manby, Thomas. "Journal of Vancouver's Voyage to the Pacific Ocean (1791–1793)." *Honolulu Mercury*, June–August 1929.

Martin, Margaret Greer. *The Lymans of Hilo.* Hilo: Lyman House Memorial Museum, 1979.

Mathison, Gilbert. *Narrative of a Visit to Brazil, Chile, Peru, and the Sandwich Islands.* London, 1904.

Mellen, Kathleen Dickenson. *The Magnificent Matriarch.* New York: Hastings House, 1952.

Menzies, Archibald. *Hawaii Nei 128 Years Ago.* Honolulu: The New Freedom Press, 1920.

Missionary Herald. The Missionary Herald for the Year 1823, vol. 19. Boston: Samuel T. Armstrong, 1823.

————. *The Missionary Herald for the Year 1828*, vol. 19. Boston: Crocker & Brewster, Printers, 1824.

Mortimer, George. *Observations and Remarks Made During a Voyage to Teneriffe, Amsterdam, Maria's Island near Van Diemen's Land*. New York: Da Capo Press, 1975.

Newman, T. Snell. "Man in the Prehistoric Hawaiian Ecosystem." In *A Natural History of the Hawaiian Islands*. Edited by E. Alison Kay. Honolulu: University of Hawaii Press, 1972.

Nordhoff, Charles. *Northern California, Oregon and the Sandwich Islands*. Berkeley: Ten Speed Press, 1974.

Obeyesekere, Gananath. *The Apotheosis of Captain Cook: European Mythmaking in the Pacific*. Princeton: Princeton University Press, 1997.

Obookiah, Henry. *Memoirs of Henry Obookiah, a Native of Owhywee, and a Member of the Foreign Mission School*. Honolulu: Woman's Board of Missions for the Pacific Islands, 1968.

Olmsted, Francis Allyn. *Incidents of a Whaling Voyage: To Which Are Added Observations on the Scenery, Manners and Customs, and Missionary Stations of the Sandwich and Society Islands*. New York: Bell Publishing Co., 1969.

Olson, S. L., and H. F. James. "The Role of Polynesians in the Extinction of the Avifauna of the Hawaiian Islands." Edited by P. S. Martin and R. G. Klein. In *Quaternary Extinctions: A Prehistoric Revolution*. Tucson: University of Arizona Press, 1984.

Paris, John Davis. *Fragments of a Real Missionary Life*. Honolulu: The Friend, 1926.

Pierce, R. A. *Russia's Hawaiian Adventure, 1815–1817*. Berkeley: University of California Press, 1965.

Piercey, LaRue W. *Hawaii's Missionary Saga*. Honolulu: Mutual Publishing Co., 1992.

Porter, K. W. "John Jacob Astor and the Sandalwood Trade of the Hawaiian Islands, 1816–1828." *Journal of Economic and Business History* 2. May 1930.

Portlock, Nathaniel. *Voyage Round the World; But More Particularly to the Northwest Coast of America: Performed in 1785, 1786, 1787, and 1788, in the King George and Charlotte, Captains Portlock and Dixon*. London, 1789.

Pratt, Elizabeth K. *History of Keoua Kalanikupuapa-i-kalani-nui, Father of Hawaii Kings, and His Descendants, with Notes on Kamehameha I, First King of All Hawaii*. Honolulu: Ke Ali'i Publishing, 1920.

Pukui, Mary Kawena. *'Ōlelo No'eau: Hawaiian Proverbs & Poetical Sayings*. Honolulu: Bishop Museum Press, 1983.

Pukui, Mary Kawena, and Samuel H. Elbert. *Hawaiian Dictionary*. Honolulu: University of Hawaii Press, 1957.

————. *Place Names of Hawaii*. Honolulu: University of Hawaii Press, 1974.

Pukui, Mary Kawena, and Laura C. S. Green. *Folk Tales of Hawai'i*. Honolulu: Bishop Museum Press, 1995.

Pukui, Mary Kawena, E. W. Haertig, and Catherine A. Lee. *Nānā I Ke Kumu*, vols. 1 and 2. Honolulu: Hui Hānai, 1972.

Pukui, Mary Kawena, and Alfons L. Korn. *The Echo of Our Song*. Honolulu: University of Hawaii Press, 1973.

Religious Intelligencer. "Journal of Messrs. Richards and Stewart at Lahinah." *Religious Intelligencer*, 24 September 1825.

———. "Letter of the Reinforcement." *Religious Intelligencer*, vol. 9. New Haven, 1824.

Restarick, Henry Bond. *Hawaii, 1778–1920, from the Viewpoint of a Bishop*. Honolulu: Paradise of the Pacific Press, 1938.

Reynolds, J. S. *Voyage of the United States Frigate Potomac*. New York, 1835.

Rickman, John. *Journal of Captain Cook's Last Voyage to the Pacific Ocean*. Ann Arbor: University Microfilms, Inc., 1966.

Rotar, P. P. *Grasses of Hawaii*. Honolulu: University of Hawaii Press, 1968.

Sahlins, Marshall. *Historical Metaphors and Mythical Realities: Structure in the Early History of the Sandwich Islands Kingdom*. Ann Arbor: University of Michigan Press, 1981.

———. *How "Natives" Think: About Captain Cook, for Example*. Chicago: University of Chicago Press, 1995.

Salmond, Anne. *The Trial of the Cannibal Dog: The Remarkable Story of Captain Cook's Encounters in the South Seas*. New Haven: Yale University Press, 2003.

Samwell, David. *A Narrative of the Death of Captain James Cook*. Project Gutenberg, 2010.

Sartre, Jean Paul. *Existentialism Is a Humanism*. Translated by Carol Macomber. New Haven: Yale University Press, 1946.

Schweitzer, Sophia G. *Kohala ʻĀina*. Honolulu: Mutual Publishing, 2003.

Shaw, H. R., E. D. Jackson, and K. E. Bargar. "Volcanic Periodicity along the Hawaiian-Emperor Chain." *American Journal of Science* 280-A, 1980.

Silverman, Jane L. *Kaʻahumanu*. Honolulu: Friends of the Judiciary History Center of Hawaii, 1987.

Simpson, Alexander. *The Sandwich Islands: Progress of Events Since Their Discovery by Captain Cook*. London, 1843.

Sinclair, Marjorie. *Nāhiʻenaʻena: Sacred Daughter of Hawaiʻi*. Honolulu: Mutual Publishing, 1995.

Sinclar, Mrs. F., Jr. *Indigenous Flowers of the Hawaiian Islands*. London, 1885.

Smith, Bernard. *Imagining the Pacific*. New Haven: Yale University Press, 1992.

Smith, Bradford. *Yankees in Paradise*. New York: J. B. Lippincott Co., 1956.

Sohmer, S. H., and R. Gustafson. *Plants and Flowers of Hawaii*. Honolulu: University of Hawaii Press, 1987.

Stearns, H. T. *Geology of the State of Hawaii*. Palo Alto: Pacific Books, 1985.

Steegmuller, Francis. *The Two Lives of James Jackson Jarves*. New Haven: Yale University Press, 1951.

Stevenson, Robert Louis. *Dr. Jekyll and Mr. Hyde and Other Stories*. New York: Penguin Classics, 1979.

———. *Travels in Hawaii*. Honolulu: University of Hawaii Press, 1973.

Stewart, Charles S. *Journal of a Residence in the Sandwich Islands During the Years 1823, 1824, and 1825*. Charleston, SC: Nabu Press, 2010.

Stoddard, Charles Warren. *The Island of Tranquil Delights*. Boston, 1905.

Stokes, John F. G. "When Paao?" Paper no. 15. Honolulu: Hawaiian Historical Society, 1927.

———. "The Hawaiian King: Mo-i, Alii-Aimoku, Alii-Kapu." Paper no. 19. Honolulu: Hawaiian Historical Society, 1932.

Thomas, Nicholas. *The Extraordinary Voyages of Captain James Cook*. New York: Walker Publishing Company, 2003.

Thurston, Lucy. *Life and Times*. Honolulu, 1882.

Twain, Mark. *Letters from the Sandwich Islands Written for the Sacramento Union*. Palo Alto: Stanford University Press, 1938.

———. *Mark Twain in Hawaii: Roughing It in the Sandwich Islands, Hawaii in the 1860's*. Honolulu: Mutual Publishing, 1994.

Tyerman, Daniel, and George Bennett. *Journal of Voyages and Travels 1821–1829*. London, 1839.

Valeri, Valerio. *Kingship and Sacrifice*. Translated by Paul Wissing. Chicago: University of Chicago Press, 1985.

Varigny, Charles de. *Fourteen Years in the Sandwich Islands, 1855–1868*. Translated by Alfons L. Korn. Honolulu: Hawaiian Historical Society and University of Hawaii Press, 1981.

Wallace, A. R. *Island Life*. London, 1880.

Westervelt, William D. *Hawaiian Historical Legends*. New York: Fleming H. Revell Co., 1923.

Wetmore, Mary B. *Sounds from Home and Echoes of a Kingdom*. Cincinnati, 1898.

Whitman, John B. *An Account of the Sandwich Islands*. Salem: Peabody Museum, 1979.

Williams, Glyndwr. *Captain Cook: Explorations and Reassessments*. Rochester: Boydell Press, 2004.

Wright, Louis B., and Mary Isabel Fry. *Puritans in the South Seas*. New York: Henry Holt & Co., 1936.

Ziegler, Alan C. *Hawaiian Natural History: Ecology and Evolution*. Honolulu: University of Hawaii Press, 2002.

Zimmerman, E. C. *Insects of Hawaii*. Honolulu: University of Hawaii Press, 1948.

Zwiep, Mary. *Pilgrim Path: The First Company of Women Missionaries to Hawaii*. Madison: University of Wisconsin Press, 1991.

Index

Page numbers in *italics* refer to illustrations.